A Case of Confidence

About Highland Books
You can find out more about our publishing programme
from our website www.highlandbks.com. If you see any
mistakes, you can email us on errata@highlandbks.com.
There is also an error page on our website.

The book-specific web page is:
http://i1897913729.highlandbks.net
["i"+ISBN+"highlandbks.net"].

A Case of Confidence

**Sinai to Istanbul
Finding oases of Christian
spirituality in the Bible Lands**

Ian R. Smith

Highland

Godalming, Surrey

First published in 2005 by Highland Books,
Two High Pines, Knoll Road, Godalming,
Surrey, GU7 2EP.

ISBN: 1-897913-72-9

Cover design by Steve Carroll

Printed in England by Bookmarque Ltd

Contents

ACKNOWLEDGEMENTS

This book is dedicated to the Christian people I met on my journey. Their kindness and willingness to share what, in some cases, were personally harrowing memories is much appreciated.

I am deeply indebted to all the people who encouraged and welcomed me along the way. Space does not allow me to name them all, but I would mention Judy Goans and Joanne Cummings in El Maadi, Brian and Toni Whitehead in Cairo, Sister Agapie in Beni Suef, Naiim Ateek and Sevak Assayan in Jerusalem, Bishara Awad and his team at the Bethlehem Bible College, Brother Andrew of Open Doors, Matthew Hanning and Brother Andrew of HLID in Salt, Colin and Anne Chapman in Beirut, Stephen Griffith in Damascus, Jihad Tafas in Sadad, Archbishop Timotheos Aktas and Father Dale Johnson in Tur Abdin, Ian Sherwood in Istanbul and Donna Brewster in Scotland.

I am grateful to William Dalrymple for his book *From the Holy Mountain* that launched me on my journey and especially grateful to CMS, for whom I work, in allowing me the space to travel. Finally Carol, Luke and Colletta deserve exceptional thanks as they released me from family responsibilities to go, put up with my writing when I returned, and listened as we agonised during the period up to completion of the finished product.

What you now have in your hand is, I believe, a gift from the Christians of the Eastern Mediterranean allowing you to enter a little into the reality of everyday life, their feelings and their faith.

Ian R Smith, York

ON THE BEACH

The rhythmic heave and suck of the waves on the sand was hypnotic. Lying on that beach in Devon I might normally have been dozing, but the book I was reading was compelling. Carol and the children were enjoying the sea, but I seemed to be transported to the deserts and oases of the Eastern end of the Mediterranean – the Levant, or Near East, as it used to be called. I was in a different world. Before going on holiday, as an after-thought, I had packed William Dalrymple's *From the Holy Mountain*. This is an epic account of a modern day journey from Greece to Egypt in the footsteps of fifth century monks. It might not sound the most obvious topic for a gripping travelogue, but for me it was speaking directly to a deep yearning.

In the course of my work I have made a number of visits to 'interesting' places overseas, always within a tightly controlled programme. I had visited some of the countries of the Levant, but it was usually for short work-related business, with little opportunity for deep reflection. Brief contact with the people of the region over a decade led to a deep longing to experience what was happening to some of the ancient Christian communities in the Middle East and, if possible, to touch their spirituality. This they trace back to the early New Testament church.

The Christians of the Eastern Mediterranean claim a spiritual ancestry back to the time of Christ. For two thousand years they have survived onslaughts, from Islam, and from Western Christendom; they have been the victims of genocide, they have seen mass emigration, and found themselves in the centre of many wars. As a result they have tended to be very insular. Through all this they have survived as a people of deep faith and integrity. They have had good cause to be sceptical about the West. Many Western Christians dismiss them as exotic cousins in the faith. Dalrymple's book confirmed for me that they were great survivors with a real story of faith and strength.

It seemed to Dalrymple that the fifth century marked a high point in Christian confidence across that region, but that the seeds of decline were evident even then. He went on to wonder whether he might have been witnessing the final gasp of that decline. Instinctively, without any hard evidence, I wanted to disbelieve this idea. That was how the plot to go was hatched. I desperately wanted to experience the spiritual strengths of the people. In the face of numerical decline of fearful proportions, might any of them have any confidence today? Or were they living in an entrenched ghetto? I was sure that there would be both viewpoints, but which would be dominant? Was this a case of observing the death throes, or would I experience a case of confidence?

Eventually I was cajoled into the caressing swell of the sea and enjoyed the afternoon, but my mind had been hooked. For the rest of that holiday I was engrossed in the book, and on returning to York set to work to engineer the journey. It fell into place remarkably well and I experienced a deep sense of God as I was led from encounter to encounter.

CHAPTER ONE

FLIGHT TO EGYPT

As the cold winds swept across northern England, bringing a cruel end to the late summer warmth, my plans to visit the Levant were formulating. Thinking of the indigenous Christian communities brought conflicting ideas into my mind. Were they about to be extinguished by a rising tide of Islam, or would they have the ability to survive, come what may? The Coptic, Armenian, Syriac and Greek Orthodox were strangely vague in my consciousness. The Coptic Church is credited with the origins of the Christian monastic movement, even possibly having inspired aspects of the later Celtic Christianity of Northern Britain and Ireland. I had certainly been aware that the Orthodox Churches practised rituals that appeared confusing to Western eyes and even had an underlying apprehension about them. When I was a child I can remember seeing Archbishop Makarios of Cyprus on television. This imposing man in black was not a friend of Britain and was virtually portrayed as the devil incarnate. With its impressive clergy and confusingly ornate churches, I wanted to know why I had been conditioned into distrusting this branch of the Christian church. I had the impression that ruthless politicians dressed in clerical gear led it. A mental image of a wolf in sheep's clothing emerged, but was it true?

For some time I had been sensing a strong urge to cut loose from the security of my normal existence and to rely more on my wits in a strange place. Having turned fifty, maybe I was getting on the hippie trail a bit late in life. When my employers offered me the opportunity to spend an unstructured three months overseas I jumped at it, but a fine juggling act would be necessary to find the right space in my hectic diary. The spring of 2000 offered such a gap. They call it a 'window of opportunity' in manage-ment-speak; for me it was a gift to be used. And I knew exactly what I wanted to do.

To embark on a journey with only the air tickets as fixed and the rest negotiable was part of my personal challenge. Another was to listen. I'm the maddening sort of person who has twelve answers to anyone's problems but none for my own. I decided therefore that my contract with myself was to be that I would not offer anyone advice nor would I compare wherever I was with life back home.

I love travelling. I love the journey. I'm pleased to arrive. Even so, the thought of preparing for a journey across the countries of the Eastern Mediterranean, euphe-mistically called the Bible Lands, was almost enough to paralyse me. Call me an ostrich, but it was the final afternoon before I began to throw things into the largest suitcase that was ever made to run on wheels. In retro-spect, that suitcase was a mistake. It was gargantuan. With a journey that stretched out over the next three months, with not knowing whom I might meet or what sort of clothing would be appropriate, I was able to err on the side of caution. There was room for me to pack at least two of everything. Into the case went enough underwear and socks to keep me going for three weeks and the sort of T-shirts that really might be an embarrassment in the garden. I even included a Pakistani shalwar kameez in case it might be useful. I threw in several pairs of shoes, reams of paper, guidebooks, pens, photographic film, batteries, toiletries and towels. At last it was full. Then came the difficult job of zipping it up and trying to stand it upright on its wheels. It was then that I had to cajole it to move without doing major damage to the carpet. Slowly I urged it along the landing, coaxing it to the top of the stairs. It seemed to have a life of its own and was almost growling at me as I bumped it down each stair. It took several attempts and a few scratches along the skirting boards before I could leave it sulking near the front door ready for the morning departure.

The journey nearly got off to a bad start. Catching early trains is not one of my favourite activities and, not having got into bed until after midnight, I nearly slept through my five o'clock alarm. Breakfast was in silence. Outside it was still as dark as pitch. Carol, my wife, came downstairs yawning. She had offered to drive me to York station. With twenty minutes to the train's departure we opened the front door and had to take a sharp intake of breath. Overnight there had been a heavy frost and the car looked as if it had been stored in the deep freeze. This was the end of March. We were now into spring following one of the mildest winters on record. The de-icer had been stored in the garage so we had to scrape the ice off the windscreen. The truculent case had to be heaved into the boot, but the lock was frozen. Frantically blowing on it I managed to persuade it to release and allow access to the boot. Even driving along the deserted streets with the heater and fan on full, the view ahead kept freezing over. Every set of traffic lights seemed to go to red as we approached but we drew up outside the station with five minutes to spare. The train was scheduled to depart from the other side of the station so, whilst Carol went to park the car, I rolled my luggage to the lift and through the subway. I got on to the waiting train with a minute to spare and Carol came up breathless just as the doors were about to close.

So that was it. A final kiss and I was on my own. The airport train roared out of York station leaving me with an image of Carol, wrapped up against the cold, waving frantically from the platform. As the train raced towards the Pennines I tried to doze but it was impossible. The brightly lit carriage, the chattering of two men behind me, and my own sense of impending adventure all prevented it. I was now to make my own waves, make a lot of my own contacts, and try to make some sense out of what I might find.

I always enjoy airports and Manchester that morning was no exception. Bearing in mind the last minute nature of my preparations for the trip, those shops were going to be useful. Top of my list of items was a back-up disk for my palm top computer. I looked in vain. The assistant was a homely middle-aged Mancunian lady. 'Eh, love? Can you come back next week? We're bound to have some in by then,' she offered. Small help to me! Another purchase was the mighty dollar: travelling for no more than three weeks in any one country I certainly did not want wadges of local currency.

I flew via Paris to Cairo. It was as if I was in a culture warp. I might be going to a world of different values but the flight did all it could to reinforce Western values. The airline magazine, the food and drink, the duty-free goods on offer all shouted that Western values were best. The in-flight movie was *Rogue Trader*. It had been on screen for just about an hour when it blinked and was turned off. The steward made an apologetic announcement in French to the effect that they had been showing the wrong film and that we would now see the one advertised for this journey. *The World is not Enough*, the most recent James Bond offering, began. Of course both films were about Western obsessions with wealth and power. They both assumed a post-modern worldview that what we see is all there is. It was a totally different perspective to that which I hoped to explore by going to Egypt, and then travelling to Turkey over the following three months.

CHAPTER TWO

ARRIVAL

Night had descended along with the plane as we arrived in Cairo. Almost childlike in their eagerness, many passengers leapt to their feet and opened the overhead storage racks, sometimes spilling coats and other items over whoever was sitting underneath. A well-heeled Egyptian lady aggressively took up a place in the aisle by my seat, preventing me from standing to get my coat. She was clutching her fur coat as she stood steadfastly in the aisle, expecting to be released from the plane any moment. But she had to wait. Outside a succession of flashing orange lights seemed to swarm around the plane. Various noises denoted the arrival of the luggage trolleys and the connecting tube through which we would enter the terminal. But we were still incarcerated in the plane. Cairo was not ready for us! By now the Egyptian lady was snorting with impatience. Whenever she pivoted around to address her husband, her coat kept gently smacking my face. My travelling companion, a hitherto silent Frenchman, murmured something and I smiled. We seemed to be on the same wavelength.

Although it was evening, the temperature was still 25 degrees, all but bathing us in its warmth as we entered the labyrinth of stale aluminium tubes leading to the heart of the airport. Without the benefit of air conditioning the temperature soon began to have an effect. People were jostling one another as they stampeded towards Baggage Reclaim, where we found that it would be some time before our luggage would be available. All around me were Egyptians eager to greet their friends and relations. Loaded up with electrical goods that must defy all definitions of 'hand luggage' they all seemed to be in animated conversations. Whether it was the fact that I was alone, or just had nothing else to do, the noisy atmosphere struck me as being very different from the intense silence found at airports back home. Even the approach to luggage retrieval was different. In the Western world quite a lot of people perch near to the flap through which their luggage will emerge, and they stare intently so as to recognise it as soon as it bursts on to the scene. They want to grab their luggage and get on to the next thing in their life. There is a sense of shame if it is missed and goes round again. In stark contrast, a different game was unfolding here. The rule seemed to be that Egyptians would stand apart from the carousel, almost as if it were irrelevant. However once the luggage appeared there was a mad scramble as people almost climbed over one another to grab what belonged to them. Perhaps they needed to. Perhaps they were afraid of their possessions going missing. But when my black giant lunged on to the scene there was no danger of anyone making a quick dash and grab. I needed help to get it off the moving belt. Then, landing with a thump on the floor, it seemed to shake itself before standing up challenging me to take it on for the next stage of the journey.

Queuing to obtain Egyptian currency and then to clear Immigration all took time but I was in no hurry. Over the years my contact with Arabic-speaking countries has taught me the expression and attitude of 'Inshallah'. When something is delayed or difficult then this term is used. Literally it means 'as God wills' and underlines a basic acceptance of the human effort in the perspective of an eternal plan. It can be an excuse for laziness or corruption but it can also be used to remove the stress of a situation. There is nothing more we can do … for now. So I just queued. I know that I would not have shown such patience back home. But in Cairo the world could wait.

Whilst I might not have been in a rush, I still did not want to be fooled. Having waited for a long time in the queue for the currency exchange, the clerk never looked up but just gave me a fistful of notes and a computer receipt as I gave him my Sterling. Trying to decipher the Arabic information, printed on a computer just about devoid of ink, was confusing. My brain was addled after a long day. Was I being given the right amount? It slowly dawned on me why the queues had moved so slowly as I looked at each denomination of grubby bank note now in my hands. Each had a side with Arabic script and numerals and on the other side it was in English with what we mistakenly call European numbers. I tried to add up the thousands of Egyptian pounds in my head but it did not correlate to the printed total. The clerk shrugged his shoulders, throwing a few measly coins across the counter. I grabbed them, assuming that this now tallied with my receipt. It was as I sat down and reckoned up the transaction that I understood that my being short-changed had amounted to mere pence. I learned quickly that in Egypt, where small change is scarce, traders frequently approximate the change they offer. And always it is in their favour.

My arrival in Cairo had been arranged in advance. Apart from the ticket to Cairo, and one to get me back from Istanbul, this was the only part of my trip that had any certainty: I was to be met by Mr Aziz. He was the driver employed by the Anglican Bishop of Cairo and it was arranged that he would take me in the bishop's car to El Maadi. The local Anglican priest, Matthew Rhodes, had arranged for me to have initial accommodation with one of his congregation. Having cleared all the entry formalities, it was a great relief to see a smiling Egyptian holding up a card proclaiming my name. A tall man, probably in his late forties, he was wearing a crumpled lounge suit. His shiny brown shoes competed with a smile of welcome that beamed out from a careworn face. This man had known the hard side of life. Later he told me of his large family and that, as a member of the Coptic Orthodox Church, he sometimes suffered discrimination. He eyed my case with disbelief as it stood almost leering on the tiled floor. Then, having winced at its weight, he trailed it through an underpass and across a car park. It was then, as I noticed that my case was choosing to roll in a way that was alarming, it became clear that its tiny nylon gliders were totally inappropriate for a case of this size and bulk. Three months of lugging a dead weight across the Middle East flew at my mind like a swarm of manic bees.

There was only one car in this part of the car park. An old battered Lada. Sitting in the driver's seat was an overweight man, introduced to me as Mr Merrit. He quickly put out his cigarette and squeezed himself out in order to load my suitcase but it was too large for the boot! With difficulty it was forced into the back seat and I wedged myself alongside. The two men eased themselves into the front seats and the engine roared into life. Having progressed no more than the exit point from the car park, Mr Merrit was flagged down by the police. A few words were muttered through the car window but this did not seem to be sufficient. With a resigned heave the portly Mr Merrit climbed out of the car and waddled wearily across the road to the policeman who had just parked his motorbike. They seemed to be in deep animated conversation with arms flailing. Aziz turned round to me and grinned nervously. 'What's wrong?' I asked. He pretended not to understand but his eyes appeared to say, 'Ask no questions and you'll be told no lies.'

It seemed like an age and was probably a few minutes, but eventually Aziz got out and joined in the argument that had developed. By now voices were raised. It presented me with a dilemma. There I was, sitting alongside my upright suitcase, listening to the argument. Should I get out? Would the presence of a foreigner cause restraint or make it worse? Deciding that discretion is the better side of valour I sat tight. Mr Merrit was by now handing over some crumpled bank notes from his back pocket.

The two men returned rather sheepishly and climbed into the car. They spoke to one another in Arabic. So what had gone on? I felt that I understood all too well and was convinced that I had just seen an example of bribery and corruption. As we joined the main road away from the airport I was debating with myself whether I should ask what had happened. In the end I asked and Mr Merrit explained that he had intended to meet me in the bishop's car but, unfortunately, it was being repaired. At the last minute he had arranged with Mr Merrit to come in his taxi. They had not wanted me to know that this was a taxi but were stopped by the police. It transpired that Mr Merrit did not have a licence to operate from the airport. The policeman would not accept the explanation that this was not an ordinary fare but that it was a private arrangement. The money had been a spot fine and was legal.

With that explanation, Aziz turned back and we drove on in silence. Of course, I had imagined the worst and they probably knew it. It said something about my assumptions and I was feeling very sorry for having been the cause of such upset. The atmosphere was tense when suddenly Mr Merrit started to accuse Aziz. He got as good as he gave and I just sat looking out at the traffic. I learned a lesson that I was able to use later to understand one aspect of thinking in the Middle East. It is the sense of honour. These men had been humiliated. Worse – their humiliation had been unjust and in front of a foreigner. All across the region Arabs and Jews will argue but resolution can only come when both parties are seen to win. This put an interesting perspective to the Middle East Peace Process. If either side appeared to capitulate then their honour, their dignity and their credibility was lost. Until that could be resolved there would never be a solution.

On the plane I had read of an even older dispute affecting this area. This was the split between the Coptic Orthodox and the Greek Orthodox Churches. It had occurred in the fifth century over a very fine difference of theological interpretation resulting in centuries of isolation of one from the other. In recent years scholars on both sides have come to the conclusion that the split was caused by a mistranslation and that both groups believed the same things. Thus honour could be maintained and allow rapprochement. Nevertheless a decision was taken not to unite, as it was not possible to unpick one and a half millennia of tradition!

The journey took about three-quarters of an hour. Being Saturday night the streets were busy, the last night of the Egyptian weekend. I got the impression that most of Cairo's young population was in party mood on the streets. Packs of motorised youths were parading their bulled-up cars round the blocks just to be noticed. Others rode motorbikes and scooters, sometimes three on one machine, weaving in and out of the traffic with their hooters blaring. It was chaos and yet strangely alluring. At least it was unlikely that alcohol was a contributory factor in the merriment.

As we drove on, the volume of traffic impressed me. Of course, Cairo is a huge city and I might have anticipated this but I had imagined that the income of Egyptians might not sustain such apparent wealth. The shops and arcades displayed a continuous show of affluence as the journey progressed. This initial impression was correct. There is a sizeable number of people in Cairo who have plenty of disposable income. But unseen by me that night was the huge majority of people who live on or below the poverty level.

At last we pulled up in a leafy suburb and I was told that in the building was Matthew's apartment. As soon as they could do so with decency, my two humiliated friends departed and drove off into the night. They would lick their wounds and argue with one another for some time to come. Slowly, one step at a time, I pulled the suitcase up to Matthew's first floor flat. It was such a relief to be welcomed. Cathy, his wife, saw to it that I had a mug of English tea and I gradually began to unwind from the long journey. Meanwhile Matthew explained that Judy, a member of his church had agreed to put me up. No problem, I thought. My luggage has wheels! Bumping my case back down the stairs and then taking a quarter mile walk along very rough-surfaced streets, and crossing a railway track, it finally gave up. One of its wheels disintegrated and I ended up carrying this huge black beast to Judy's flat. Something would have to be done before I ventured forth with that case again!

I had planned to stay in Egypt for three weeks. Part of that time would be in Cairo where I felt it was important to acclimatise as well as to arrange my visas for the other countries I would visit later. This proved to be a mistake and added days of frustration as I hung around waiting for each visa to be processed. Whilst my passport was in one consulate I was effectively grounded in Cairo as it was a requirement for a passport to be available if I wanted to visit places beyond the metropolis. So gradually I got to know Cairo. Being the kind of person that likes to walk the streets rather than get a taxi my sense of direction and understanding of how the different parts of the city related was quickly developed. But everywhere there was a visible clash between the traditional Egyptian culture and the commercial and ideological ideals of the West. Nowhere was that seen more clearly than by experiencing the expatriate communities.

El Maadi is a fashionable suburb to the south east of the city. Tree lined avenues with pleasant gardens lead to impressive and sometimes opulent apartment blocks. Many of the expatriate workers live in areas like this. Of course it is usually the men who are out all day, often working long hours. Their wives and children have to live as 'normal' a life as possible. As a result the expatriates try to recreate a sort of mini-America or Europe. They have a hectic social whirl and tend to have very little contact with the 'real' Egypt all around them. Most have Egyptians helping with domestic duties but few would ever have seen the homes or families from which these servants came.

Judy, my host, was an American lawyer working on a project to try and bring patent and copyright laws into Egypt. She was a warm-hearted woman from Louisiana and it was wonderful to hear her articulate Arabic words in a deep Southern drawl. But she was there for a purpose and when her project finished she, like most expatriates, would return home as quickly as possible. And who could blame her? Whilst I was really looking for the true spirit of Coptic Christian spirituality there was no way that I could pretend that this little island of Western culture and hospitality was going to provide an adequate launch pad. However its comfort was reassuring and I found myself willingly drawn into the social whirl. Each evening, having explored a new part of this fascinating city, I would be offered coke and pizzas as well as videos. Of course the diet from Hollywood inevitably emphasised how America won the war, how it is always right, and how it is smarter than any other country. The contrast between the make-believe expatriate world and the 'real' Egypt, with the inevitable clash of cultures in my head, was difficult to reconcile. But I realised that I was coming at it from a position of cultural strength and confidence. As my trip unfolded, as I gradually laid down my own dependence on Western cultural values, I would begin to see all this from the other way up.

CHAPTER THREE

COPTIC EGYPT

From the comparatively plush suburb of El Maadi, a French-built Metro line sweeps along the banks of the Nile and under the heart of Cairo before heading off to the northern fringes of the city. The trains are modern, quiet and efficient; they are fast, frequent and cheap. But they are very crowded. By the time the train reached my stop I was thoroughly acquainted with every contour of the men wedged around me. This is a haven for pickpockets and perverts, and it is no wonder that two carriages are designated for the use of women only. Emerging on to the streets I was assailed by the noise and pollution, and discomforted by the fact that in many places there was no obvious place for pedestrians other than to walk with the raging traffic.

The tourist guides suggest that 'Islamic Cairo' with its long straggling trail of shops around the Khan al-Khalili is a good place to sense the atmosphere of Cairo. Struggling to find this great bazaar involved fighting my way through what felt like miles of streets from the subway station at Attaba along a thoroughfare called Muski. The whole route was jammed with parked vans, trestle tables and vendors leaving an almost impassable passageway down the middle. This narrow ventricle had many a thrombosis caused by children pushing carts, boys cycling with trays of baking on their heads, and occasional small pick-up trucks. On sale was everything from ladies' underwear to children's cycles. The noise level was raucous as salesmen were calling out to attract the attention of the shoppers. They were competing with one another and also with the 'ghetto-blasters' which offered a distorted concoction of disco-style Arabic pop.

Just when I thought I must have experienced all of Cairo – certainly a large proportion of its heaving population – I found the bazaar. Whilst it had its fair share of tourist traps selling perfume, alabaster pyramids and toy camels at 'very cheap' prices, there was in the bazaar a certain sense of dignity and history. Each area of the Khan specialised in one type of product. On the street there were some incredible salespeople and smooth talkers desperate for a chance to bargain, whilst standing slightly aloof were old established shops selling all sorts of crafted goods from exotic jewellery to the brass crescents that are fixed on top of minarets. I was lured into one shop. 'No need to buy. Just look around,' said the young man. It was a tiny shop selling all manner of perfume and this man saw in me an obvious client. Would I want to buy a present for my wife? 'You are married?' he checked, having asked. At the back of my mind was the need to resist because the last thing I needed at this stage of my long journey was a stack of presents for the family and others back home. Tea was produced and much appreciated. He kept putting dabs of perfume on my wrist. They all seemed similar: very brash and not unlike lavatory aerosols. Another glass of tea appeared. Every few minutes another young man would pop his head into the shop. A knowing smile in my direction would be followed by a shrug of the shoulders. I felt like a fraud so made to go.

'My friend, you must have some perfume. Business is not good.' His eyes implored me but I was determined. I did not want any perfume whatever it was like. How could I persuade him?

'I can let you have two small bottles. They weigh nothing. They can be for your son and daughter.' He announced with glee that they would be mine for only two hundred Egyptian pounds. As this was forty pounds in Sterling my determination to go was finalised. But the price came down as my determination rose, and eventually we agreed a price of twenty Egyptian pounds. For my part I had rested and been refreshed with tea. And I had two small presents called 'Tutankamen' and 'Lotus' to take home. From the vendor's part, he had made a sale. I am assured that he would not have sold at a loss so his honour was satisfied. We parted as friends and, once again, I was reminded of the need for a sense of upheld honour for both sides in a Middle Eastern transaction.

At the eastern end of the Khan is the huge El Hakim mosque. It was named after a fearsome Fatimid ruler of Egypt and has rarely been used as a place of worship. It was finished in 1010 since when it has been used variously as a prison for captured Crusaders; a stable for Salah ad-Din's horses; a warehouse by Napoleon's troops; and Nasser made it a school for boys. For a time it also was used as a madhouse. Dominating the surrounding area it affords an opportunity to gain height to see the city of Cairo. I paid the entrance fee and was making to wander around when a man in flowing robes came and introduced himself as Mohammed. A most appropriate name, I ventured, and then he disclosed that he was a muezzin. His job was to call faithful Muslims to prayer by means of the loudspeakers.

Although I considered that my guidebook was sufficient for my needs, Mohammed trailed me around the walls of the mosque. The scale of everything was spectacular. For example, the walls were so thick that it would have been possible to fit a tennis court on top of them. The mosque had a practical dual role when built in that it was to be part of the fortification of Cairo. Some of the walls were built using cut stones from the Pharaonic period and displayed hieroglyphics to prove it. French graffiti from the Napoleonic era had been carved in some places, presumably by soldiers eking out the boredom of being on watch. My aim of climbing a minaret to gain a good view was achieved and I was glad that I was able to shake off Mohammed at this point. As I climbed the circular stone stairway round the perimeter of the inside of the tower, he stayed at the bottom puffing away on his cigarette. The views were amazing because here was an opportunity to see Cairo life behind the facades of the shops and houses. Flat roofs were piled high with logs for fuel. Behind each frontage were small courtyards where women were cooking and washing clothes. It seemed as if the vista of urban squalor went on to the horizon. Millions of people lived in this Dickensian sink. It was both exhilarating and shocking to see.

Carefully picking my way down the staircase, climbing over places where piles of rubble blocked the steps, I was sorry to see Mohammed still waiting. With his cigarette clenched between his teeth he sidled up to me and asked for money. I protested that I had paid the entrance fee and showed him my ticket. He scowled. 'Money for muezzin', he pleaded. Now I have a few fond memories of some calls to prayer, but mainly they are brash and intrusive. This was not going to appeal very much to me. I asked him why I should give him money. He had only trailed me as I had a guidebook. 'Backsheesh', he argued. All this time we were walking down narrow steps to the street. Stopping at a particularly dangerous point, he began to make a scene. Rather frightened by this intimidation I offered him a tip of two Egyptian pounds, a decent percentage of the six Egyptian pounds I paid to go in. He then began to shout. 'Americans give twenty,' he yelled. Two of his colleagues rushed over and pretended to prevent him attacking me. I said that I was not American and he could have two pounds or nothing. His friends accepted the tip for him and I made a quick exit.

'Help the muezzin,' he shouted after me as I walked rapidly back along the street. I had not wanted to have a guide but had been expected to pay extra for one. We had not parted on good terms and, to make matters worse, I felt guilty because the muezzin was a religious man!

By now I was feeling tired and had decided to go back to El Maadi, when I noticed a Christian priest. In so-called 'Islamic Cairo' it came as a surprise, especially one as noticeable as this. Dressed in a black cassock with a Coptic cross dangling from his neck, this black-bearded man was ambling along the bazaar. This was my first 'sighting' of a Coptic priest and with excitement and trepidation I decided to make an approach. But how? Would it be perceived as brash or threatening? I had heard many stories of the oppression, even persecution, of Christians in Egypt.

'Excuse me, but are you a Coptic priest?' I ventured rather hesitatingly. I need not have worried for he broke out into a broad beam and replied in the affirmative. Explaining that I was in Egypt to experience something of Coptic Orthodox spirituality, he looked both surprised and encouraged.

'It is good to meet you,' he said. Then opening the door of a nearby jeweller's shop, he invited me in. Closing the door, he introduced himself as Father Mena Gad Girgis from a village near Luxor. His friend, the jeweller, was Marcos Maroos. Christians, it seemed, had been jewellers in the Middle East for centuries. Although Muslims now conducted much of the business in the Khan, the Christians held on to the jewellery trade.

Father Mena invited me to sit so that we might chat. Marcos made tea whilst this large priest opened up a plastic carrier bag full of beans. We talked about the situation for Christians in Upper Nile as we podded and ate the beans. Life was hard and many people were very poor. Father Mena was interested in helping with development work but could not see how to get started. It was difficult, he felt, as much of the hierarchy in the church did not understand the situation. If people were desperate and the church offered no help then should we be surprised that people turn to Islam when offered conditional relief? This was a shock to me. I had heard of some bad Christian missionary practice in places like China during the nineteenth century. In those times hungry people would only be fed if they became Roman Catholic, Presbyterian or whatever. They were known as 'Rice Christians' and would convert to whichever denomination had the latest supplies of food. I had thought that such practices were long consigned to the history books but here they were reappearing across the faiths.

Father Mena explained that whilst some Christian people were converting to Islam out of expediency others were converting out of fear. Atrocities against Christians were on the increase. In his area around Luxor the situation was very tense. As I watched this amiable man contentedly chomping his way through bean after bean it seemed inconceivable. 'Of course things are made difficult for us in other ways,' he continued. 'If someone were to change faith the other way, it would be very difficult. If a Muslim became a Christian his family would feel shame and ensure that he was killed.'

Here in the heart of Khan al-Khalili, I was beginning to learn first hand about the daily sacrifice of being a Coptic Christian. As Father Mena talked he held a silver cross in his hand. 'We live by the cross in the Coptic Church. We take up our cross every day. We die by the cross.' There was sadness in his voice but I sensed a resolution to go to the end. The Coptic Christians traced their origins to the arrival of St Mark in the very earliest days of the Christian Church. The Arab Muslim invaders came several centuries later and converted the Egyptians by fair means or foul. But as conversions were forbidden the other way round the Coptic Christians claim that they are not Arab but rather that they are directly descended from the original Egyptians.

Having had my fill of beans and tea I made to go. It was then that Father Mena mentioned the legendary Bishop Athanasias of Beni Suef. He had been one of my suggested contacts but Father Mena somehow ensured my going there because he gave me a letter to deliver personally to the bishop. He told me that Bishop Athanasias had changed the ethos in his diocese from being purely church-centred to reaching out to all aspects of daily life. Although he worked in a different diocese, Father Mena would write to see if the bishop might suggest ways of changing things in his parish. He reasoned that if I went to see the bishop I would be granted an audience whereas he might not. Then I could give him the letter. This seemed a good plan and one in which I was happy to co-operate.

The use of e-mail was a wonderful and fairly rapid method of contacting the Bishop's House in Beni Suef. Sister Agapie, a Coptic Orthodox nun, responded to my request for a visit. So a couple of days later, with a borrowed weekend case of Judy's, I boarded the early morning express for the fifty-minute journey up the Nile Valley. Once we had left the Cairo suburbs behind, the view of palm trees masking the endless desert beyond became a little tedious on the eye. Sitting next to me was a professor from Beni Suef University and we fell into conversation. Having asked what was bringing me to Beni Suef, a city that apparently saw few foreigners, I told him that I was going to experience the spirituality and lifestyle of the Coptic Church. He looked at me in disbelief and whistled through his teeth. 'You've got to be joking?' he queried. He did not consider Christians to be worth a minute of anyone's time. As the train slowed down to stop at Beni Suef he politely wished me well in my pointless task and we parted.

Stepping out of the air-conditioned carriage into the bright sunlight of the Nile Valley was like climbing into a tumble dryer. A breeze was driving the parched air from the desert and already the temperature was soaring. A policeman commandeered the one and only taxi in Beni Suef, an elderly Japanese saloon, and it was soon slowly bumping along the streets. The town had a dusty appearance and was very different to Cairo in that there were few vehicles but plenty of bicycles. I was taken to the cathedral church of St Mary, the headquarters of the Beni Suef Diocese. Sister Agapie greeted me like a long-lost friend. This smiling nun in late middle age had been seconded some years earlier to work in Crowther Hall in the Selly Oak Colleges, Birmingham, and felt a great empathy for England and things Anglican. I had an ally.

Being Lent there were plenty of services in the Cathedral. To touch something of Coptic spirituality this seemed a good place to start. So Sister Agapie took me into the Cathedral where they were about half way through the Eucharist. Immediately I was struck by the segregation of the sexes: men on the left and women on the right. This was a weekday and yet the service was full of worshippers, people coming and going without apparent rhyme or reason. The Orthodox Christians lay great emphasis on the Liturgy being conducted and have much less interest in who is there or for how long. Services are offered to God and Him alone and so the Western concern that people in the congregation should be involved does not arise. As cantors chanted the Liturgy from the front the only lay response seemed to be standing or sitting. Over the next few days I would become adept at anticipating when to sit and when to stand. The Liturgy ended with the priest walking up and down the aisles splashing Holy Water over the congregation. Babies greeted this with alarm but older children rushed gleefully to be in the way of the water as it was flicked out of the jug with a ladle. For the adults it was a very special moment as they experienced the water touching them. Having been brought up in a Protestant tradition my normal tendency might have been to dismiss such practices as superstition verging on idolatry. But watching the reverence with which these very devout lay people received this blessing I could not help being impressed by their sincerity. Of course it is possible to be sincerely wrong and I was going to require some convincing but, for now, I would leave that question for another day.

The wonderfully hospitable Sister Agapie scooped me up after the service. She took me next door to the Bishop's house. She had the key to his apartment and soon I was settled in a comfortably furnished room, with a refreshing cool breeze blowing through the open windows in the next room. The bishop's servant, Mahfouz, plied us with tea and cakes as we chatted. It had been a long morning and I could easily have curled up and gone to sleep but Sister had a meticulous programme for me. This had to be explained. I was to be given a room in the guest accommodation on the next floor and, over the next few days, I would be shown a great deal of how the diocese worked. To experience the spiritual side of life she alerted me to the times when the Liturgy would occur, and mentioned a few people who spoke English who might help me understand it.

My room was on the top floor of the bishop's house, reached by climbing a decrepit staircase that wound its way up the inside wall of a stone tower. At the top a rather dishevelled monk slowly opened a heavy wooden door. Wearing a black habit and bonnet, his piercing eyes gleamed out from chiselled features partly masked by a grey beard. 'Welcome! Pray for me!' he said, and then giggled. This was Father Justus. As Sister Agapie and Mahfouz showed me to my quarters, Father Justus kept burbling 'Pray for me!' followed by the same nervous laugh. It was mildly alarming and I began to wonder if I had come too far in my quest for Orthodox spirituality. My room had no lock, I noticed with a little apprehension. It was furnished in a spartan fashion, with a bed three feet off the floor and as unyielding as granite. Faded thin curtains flapped in the breeze as I lay down with a thud, my luggage flung on a nearby upright chair. The activities of the day had been exhausting. Moments later I was asleep, only to be awoken shortly by the muezzin in the nearby mosque calling the faithful to prayer. It was a sudden reminder of my encounter with Mohammed, the muezzin, in Cairo. Some Christians tell me that they find Islamic prayer calls to be spiritually disturbing. I confess that I do not. There is something attractive about the idea of proclaiming from the rooftops that God is great! However, when the call is both unmelodic and the loud speakers are in overload causing distortion, this is not pleasant. Also, as one mosque begins, it is joined by several others across the city and takes on the sound of miserable wailing. It becomes deeply jarring.

Over the next few days I would come to terms with the muezzin's wailing. The mosque had been built on a small piece of land separating the cathedral and the convent. I wondered why it had been built in such a confrontational place. The loudspeakers would burst into their call for prayer sometimes drowning out the chanting in church. The sense of architectural and verbal triumphalism of Islam over the Coptic Orthodox was painful to witness.

To see the Coptic Church in action was impressive. I visited church schools where Muslims and Christians learned side by side; I saw the development work amongst villagers; I experienced the hospitality of the nuns' convent; I saw the work amongst students; but I was still trying to grasp the indefinable spirituality. It was like herding kittens. And then I met Bishop Athanasias.

It was Saturday evening and I had just been to the convent for supper. Leaving the front door I noticed a four-wheel- drive vehicle drawn up alongside. Sister Agapie flew down the stairs behind me and, with all the excitement of a teenager seeing a pop star, she exclaimed, 'Bishop is here!' I was taken around the other side of the vehicle and the electronic window was lowered. Inside was a very frail old man, with his seat in almost a reclining position. From behind thick-framed glasses, his bright eyes beamed out to me. 'You are so very welcome,' he said, giving me his hand. Without thinking I shook it, as in Britain. He, of course, was used to Westerners but the correct procedure would have been to try to kiss his hand. In Orthodox tradition, to show respect for Christ as represented by a priest, monk or bishop, it is customary to try to kiss the hand but then, in a gesture of humility, this is withdrawn at the last possible moment. There were variations. Sometimes the hand would be offered and the priest would withdraw it with a nanosecond to spare. Or the layperson might lunge at the hand in order to make contact before it could be withdrawn. On such occasions it was reduced to a game of spiritual chicken. I guess that Bishop Athanasias was bigger than that.

Athanasias had been bishop for decades and had encouraged Christians to serve the wider community. Whilst in no way detracting from the spiritual order of his diocese he had actively encouraged Christian involvement in the community. This had reaped a harvest of goodwill amongst the majority Muslim neighbours as well as bringing much-needed education, health and employment amongst the Copts themselves. He had become a sort of local hero. He insisted that I travelled in his car round the block to his house. Sister Agapie came too, bubbling with pleasure. The car was almost mobbed by people who clamoured to see or have physical contact with the bishop. At one point a baby was thrust through the open window for a blessing. But once inside the church compound, with the iron gates firmly closed behind us, this wizened old man was carried upstairs and I followed, carrying his robes.

Over the next couple of days we had several conversations. Unlike Western tradition where a meeting with an important person would, more than likely, be conducted in private, perhaps across an imposing desk, here it was all very public. We would be chatting when someone would be brought in to ask a favour, tell of a problem, put forward a business proposition, or discuss an issue. Our conversation would stop and the other person would have their points dealt with, then we would continue. The two mobile phones would also be constantly jumping the queue! I was pleased to give Father Mena's letter to the bishop. He was most impressed when I told him of how we had met and how he had urged me to come. 'I will help this man,' he said reassuringly. One evening we were chatting when he asked Mahfouz to uncork a bottle of dark red wine. 'This is a new type of Communion wine,' he said. 'I wonder if you would try it and tell me if it is any good?' A glass was produced and filled with a dark rich red thick wine. It was very sweet and fortified, heavier than Port. I kept to one glass even though I was offered a refill. The Coptic clergy in Beni Suef generally do not drink alcohol. Lay people too are discouraged. This tradition has grown up largely as a result of the shadow of criticism from Muslims. Nevertheless, I noticed that Sister Agapie ran her finger around my glass and licked up the remnants. Then another nun, Sister Teresa, was invited in and given a glass of wine to take to her room. 'She was trained in a Catholic convent,' explained Sister Agapie. 'They drank alcohol and I think she misses it. Occasionally I give her a glass and she is so grateful.'

In discussing Coptic spirituality with Bishop Athanasias, I mentioned that I thought Britain had much to learn from the way the Copts and Muslims had learned to coexist over centuries. What advice could he give to the West, I wondered? He went into overdrive. Hauling his wasted little frame up on the chaise longue on which he was reclining, he said, 'For fourteen centuries we have been learning about Islam. You are playing with it. We have known terrible times and less bad times. But ever since the Arab invasions in the seventh century there has been a concerted attack on the indigenous Copts reducing their percentage of the population from 100% to 9% today.'

One significant aspect of Coptic spirituality attracted even the Muslims, he claimed. Leaning forward as if he were about to divulge a state secret, he said that the prayers of healing in the Name of Jesus produced results. Because Jesus heals, and the fact that this is consistent with Quranic teaching, Muslims seek prayer for healing in Coptic churches. He sat back, exhausted. But I was curious about this and pushed it further. If Muslims are prayed for in the Name of Jesus and get healed why don't they become Christian? 'Many people were healed by Jesus when He was on earth,' he replied, 'but not many followed Him.' He explained that there are probably many 'secret Christian believers' who have Muslim identity cards. It would be too dangerous to change their cards and might invite death.

'It won't ease up,' said the bishop, referring to Muslim pressure on Christians. 'We know them. They are out to dominate by force'. At that precise moment, with the sun going down, the muezzin broke out into their wailing from all across the city. It seemed to prove the point. 'Our way is the way of the Cross', Bishop Athanasias added from the shadows that were now filling the room. 'By serving the wider community regardless of what religion they follow; by love and then more love. They may hate us but we will live as Christ.' And seeing the way of the Coptic Church in Beni Suef it was almost tangible.

CHAPTER FOUR

STIRRINGS IN THE DESERT

The cold air had just a tinge of bite in its bone-dry stirrings just before dawn. I scuttled between the concrete buildings that lined the sandy streets of Beni Suef, avoiding the occasional cyclist who swooped past leaving the tantalising aroma of freshly baked bread from the tray he carried on his head. In a back street, outside the Coptic Orthodox Convent, a minibus was parked and alongside it was Sister Amelia. A small but amply proportioned lady of middle years, she looked kindly over her spectacles. She wore the grey habit worn by the nuns at Beni Suef, a very modern garment compared to that worn elsewhere in Egypt. Smiling with amusement that I was the only person who had arrived on time she explained that everyone else was using Egyptian time. I had been warned not to be late as we had a packed agenda, hopefully to include visits to what are reputed to be the oldest Christian monasteries in the world. Over the next hour various people turned up before we finally slid the door shut and left.

Our mixed bunch of pilgrims included a young nun, Sister Olagia. Normally hard pressed by the rounds of social care and religious observance, she had a skip in her walk and laugh in her conversation that told us all that she was very excited. I was to learn that the life for such women was hard, although the nuns would describe it as fulfilling.

Apart from the daily offices, which involved attending services in either the convent chapel or the cathedral six times a day, the nuns all had very exacting jobs. Some were teachers; others were social workers. A heavy work load was combined with running the convent including its cleaning and all the cooking. With the pre-dawn Mass followed by all the other offices throughout the day until late evening, it seemed as if the candles were burning at both ends. On the one hand the nuns were exhausting themselves with demanding professional work and tiring physical chores. On the other hand they were carrying forward the strange life of religious communities that see their main purpose in life as prayer throughout the day and night. It was not surprising that once the mini bus was in motion, Sister Olagia flopped into a deep sleep.

By the time our bus headed over the Nile Bridge into the Eastern Desert the sun was shining relentlessly and I was glad of the air conditioning. In between dozing I glimpsed the dusty scenery flashing past the window. In the distance, always in the distance, the big red mountain range to the south reared up forbiddingly. Occasionally one or two of us would be awake long enough to engage in a low-key conversation. Ros, an English girl, and Miriam, a German, both in their twenties, were volunteers working in Beni Suef. Whilst Ros had settled in to her work as a temporary teacher she was clearly looking forward to her return to Britain in couple of months. For Miriam it was more traumatic. She had come to Egypt only recently and was in culture shock. She was revolted by the Coptic veneration of what she referred to as idols. Whilst the Copts were clearly emotionally stirred by their faith, she could not understand it and felt excluded. Because it was not rational she was in danger of rejecting all she saw.

Miriam came from a Lutheran background but had allowed her faith to lapse. During her recent years as a student she had rejected all forms of her religious upbringing. She lived a totally secular life but had been persuaded to take a break by spending some time as a volunteer at the convent in Beni Suef. To leave the whirl of German student social life, her boyfriend, and her home culture, and then to be immersed in the life of the convent, its chores and the devotional worship, seemed cruel. She was a fish out of water. As she flapped on the bank, her anger was directed at anyone near enough to receive it. She was convinced that life in the convent was brainwashing. The services held day and night were nothing but a method of deprivation and making the nuns more obedient. The nuns themselves were from poor families and therefore knew nothing better. But she did! As I looked across to Sister Olagia, exhausted but with a smile on her sleeping face, I mused about how much Miriam did not know.

We must have driven for about two hours before Sister Amelia pointed out St Anthony's Monastery across the desert. She explained that we would go there later but for now we were going further south to the monastery of St Paul. Eventually, after what seemed an age, we reached the road that travelled north to south alongside the inviting waters of the Gulf of Suez. Turning right, we now headed due south, the azure waters of the sea and the bright sand of the desert combining to make the glare almost unbearable.

An Egyptian family was also on board. As none of them spoke any English at all we were unable to converse but made pleasant gestures. Gradually I began to understand a little about them. Bishop Athanasias had arranged this trip for them. The rest of us were the freeloaders. The wife, in her early thirties, had a terminal illness and was wasting away. She could hardly walk. Her husband was very caring and attentive to all her needs, which included trying to keep her comfortable in the minibus. They had two children, a girl aged nine and a boy aged eleven. They too were very attentive to their mother's needs whilst clearly resigned to the understanding that this long bus ride was a chore to be endured for her rather than a day out for them. This little family was to become very special to all of us as the day unfolded.

Just when I began to despair of ever reaching the monastery we turned inland and, entering a canyon began to ascend along a mountain road. Big gates across the road stopped our progress whilst Sister Amelia negotiated with the gateman. This was Lent and the monastery was closed, we were told. Excited discussions ensued and I heard the name 'Athanasias' being used frequently. The bishop had been concerned for us all to visit and had sent a letter to request it. This seemed to produce the required result and, minutes later the minibus was facing its biggest challenge yet as it crawled up the steep road.

Turning a corner I gasped as the monastery came into view. The Egyptians burbled with excitement. The atmosphere of anticipation in the bus was as if we were a party of children arriving at Alton Towers Theme Park. Built like a fortified town with turrets and thick walls, this was nothing like the kind of religious house that I had become used to in Britain. We left the bus and walked through one of the entrances. By now it was midday and the sun was baking the very stones around us. The climb, the brightness, the dry air, all contributed to a sense of detachment. It was as if I were peering through a window, or watching it on television. As the panorama unfolded I was conscious that we were entering a large square. The buildings all around were ancient. Some were churches, others houses and workshops. It was suggested that we might wander around and explore the monastery, as everything was open to us.

This site went back to the early days of Christianity in Egypt. Paul was a Coptic hermit who had lived in a cave for ninety years. At the end of his life, as strength was ebbing away, St Anthony the founder of Christian monasticism visited him. Realising that they would not meet again this side of death, Anthony walked back over the mountains to his own monastery before returning with a shroud. When he came back he found that the old hermit had indeed died. However as he had no implements with which to bury him, he prayed for a miracle. Just then two lions appeared. Instead of attacking Anthony, they dug a hole in which Anthony was able to bury the saint. This then became the site of the monastery.

Of course stories like this abound in Coptic spirituality. The writings of the Desert Fathers hold an interesting mixture of wacky stories and profound truths. To the literal Western mind it is easy to disregard such stories as irrelevant because it is hard to take them at face value. The 'How did they do that?' mentality can distort our ability to see into the truths that lie behind the story. The story of Paul and Anthony could be understood on many levels. But to this non-Coptic mind it boils down to this: if you put yourself into God's plan for your life, then things work out in the end. Looking back over almost two thousand years of Coptic history in Egypt it is clear that they have needed to be assured that there is more to life than what immediately presents itself. The monastery itself bore witness to this. On one level it was possible to walk around the campus in the overbearing heat trying to show interest, commenting politely about the original spring, admiring the old wine and olive presses, and observing the dusty old granary. But there in the middle was a tower into which the monks used to withdraw whilst under attack from Bedouins and Arabs. These people had held on whilst subject to privation, suffering and all sorts of desperate violence. It seemed that the more they had suffered, the more precious the witness of their monastery had become. The growth of the monastic calling seemed to run counter to anything I had experienced in the West. Across the Coptic traditions, the number of young men offering to become monks or priests is now at a higher level than at any time in living memory. My interpreter, a young monk with excellent English, used to be a photo-copier service engineer before becoming a monk.

The tomb of St Paul in the crypt under the main church is a highly venerated spot. To reach it I had to descend some narrow stairs behind the altar. Carved out of the rock, with ancient Coptic artwork painted on the walls of the cave, it was cosy with its carpets underfoot and candles providing warmth. After the intense heat and brightness of the desert, the atmosphere in the crypt was seductive. It touched all the battered senses and urged me to relax. It was then, as my eyes were growing used to the lower levels of light, that I noticed that the scatter rugs in this most sacred of Coptic sites were from the Disney stable. Here, where countless numbers of pilgrims had prayed down the centuries, visual stimulation to prayer was either aided or impeded by Donald Duck. And just where the Eucharist would be celebrated was Mickey Mouse. Contrasting styles that would be inconceivable in the West were a part of everyday life here. Where we are more concerned for the appearance of good taste, it seemed as if the Coptic spiri-tuality was more concerned with what happens inside a person.

Back in the daylight I sat for a while with Miriam. Her anger was unabated. As we sat in the shade of the guest-house we could hear the rhythmic chanting of the monks getting going with yet another Eucharist. What had this to do with real life? I ventured to suggest that the prayers of the monks might be important in holding back forces of unbridled evil. She laughed and, at that moment a crash and tinkling of glass came from inside the church. There was silence. We looked at one another, briefly debating whether to go into the church, when the chanting began again. It was quieter this time, and in the background we could hear the sweeping up of shattered glass. It under-lined the Orthodox priority that, irrespective of what happens, the Liturgy must be offered to God. He was waiting. This idea, of course, disturbed Miriam even more. Her inability to feel the spirituality of the Copts meant that it was false. I asked if she had ever felt anything of a spiritual nature back home in Germany. She explained that it was necessary to have an organ and a good choir like in her parents' Lutheran church.

I was beginning to see that the trappings of Christian spirituality are clothed in the host culture. Miriam was missing the music of Bach. The chanting of the monks was alien to my taste but what was at the heart of their devotions? It occurred to me that a thick crust of culture overlies the depths of spiritual reality. Many people never fathom the depths, preferring to remain content with their cultural comfort zone. To me this explains the reluctance shown by many Western Christians to being open to the spirituality of people from other races and traditions. I would need to try to swim underneath the cultural crust to have a possibility of touching the spiritual life of others. This sometimes would involve a suspension of credulity, an avoidance of judgemental attitudes, and an openness to receive a surprise.

It was time to move on. Just as we headed for the bus we were called back. A real life hermit had come down from his hermitage in the mountains and we were to be able to meet him. I was filled with excitement. Father Fanous, like his historical forbear, St Paul the monk, lived on his own in a cleft in the rocks overlooking the Gulf of Suez. His reputation for effective prayer was renowned throughout the area. It was understandable then that a cluster of pilgrims had gathered to meet him. Feeling a bit of a fraud, a sort of spiritual tourist rather than a convinced disciple, I joined the queue of people outside the guest house. Upon being ushered into a stuffy room full of monks and priests, it was easy to see which one was the hermit. An old man with a long tousled grey beard, wearing a dusty black habit, sat in an armchair. As people approached they tried to kiss his gloved hand but he would withdraw it at the last moment. That way respect for the hermit was shown but, equally, he showed humility in not receiving it. Mesmerised, I reached the front of the queue. Father Fanous offered his limp hand and I grabbed it, shaking it in true British style. Just as had happened with Bishop Athanasias, I realised my *faux pas* immediately but he smiled, saying 'God bless you' gently through his overgrown moustache.

Returning to the bus I asked Sister Amelia why Father Fanous wore a leather glove. 'Oh, his hand bursts into flames when he takes it off,' she replied in such a matter-of-fact way.

I had much to contemplate as we drove back along the coast to St Anthony's monastery. By now it was mid-afternoon and the effects of our early start were telling on us all. Even the driver seemed to be suffering from confusion because, having filled up with diesel at an isolated filling station, he promptly started to drive us back towards St Paul's monastery!

If St Paul's monastery had been like a small town, St Anthony's monastery was like a city. It spread out over an extensive area and included large commercial retail outlets and accommodation to cope with the thousands of tourists and pilgrims who visit every year. As we walked through the gates a genial old monk met us. Father Ruis Anthony looked like his namesake. It was as if he had stepped out of the painting on the wall behind him. Clearly he was prepared for the small family from Beni Suef and said that he had arranged for the bishop to anoint the mother with oil before we left. He also explained some background to the monastery. St Anthony, he said, had come from the Beni Suef area where he had become the first Christian monk. His ideas so appealed to people that others who wanted to adopt his lifestyle had thronged him. This was counterproductive so Anthony had abandoned his disciples and set up in the Eastern Desert, using a cave high up in the mountains. His disciples followed in due course and the monastery was established but Anthony stayed in the cave, climbing down once a week to ensure everything was well before climbing back with water and food.

Although the sun was now rapidly setting I was assured that there was time to visit the cave. Nowadays it is possible to reach it by a system of stairs but it must have been very difficult in Anthony's day. The two children, Sister Olagia, Ros, Miriam and I accepted the challenge. After an exhausting climb the small group of us reached the cleft in the mountainside and entered this holy place. About three metres inside there were some steps down and we entered a small chapel. By lighting the candles on the altar it was possible to see a little of how Anthony lived. There was room for a small altar upon which countless pilgrims had left prayer requests. But other than that there was nothing. In a way this underlined a different type of religious life when compared to that of the nuns. The hermit spent all his time in prayer. The only distractions would be his inner mind and it is not surprising that the tradition of Desert Fathers should have gained a twin reputation for both deeply piercing spiritual observation and also what verges on the insane. But it was a focussed life. The dual-purpose lives of prayer and service led by the nuns seemed more attractive to outsiders but, seen from Miriam's perspective, was little more than torture.

By now the sun had gone into its final nosedive into the desert leaving a pallid glow over the gnarled rocks. We decided that it was time to return to the monastery and made tracks as quickly as possible. Sister Olagia, ran ahead. By the time she reached the plateau area half way down she was already a long way ahead of us and a mere dot in the landscape. Just then she started to sing at the top of her voice, whirling around in excitement. She skipped and danced with her arms aloft. Her voice carried in the static air as if she were almost next to us.

'Reminds me of *The Sound of Music*,' I whispered to Miriam. 'What is *Sound of Music*?' she demanded. Like a hammer dropping on my toe I realised my *faux pas*, and did not launch into telling her about a nun leading children over the Alps to escape from the Germans. I muttered something about a popular film and made to catch up with the dancing nun. She was as high as a kite but was clearly experiencing a spiritual blessing. Her face had become radiant as she called out. She showed me that she was singing Psalm 121. 'I lift my eyes to the hills – where does my help come from? It comes from the Lord…' , Sister Olagia could sing of higher things than her personal circumstances would permit. Living a life of service for others under the shadow of Islam in a very urban situation, it was obvious why this place should bring release for her. 'Hallelujah!' she called out as she skipped on with her voice echoing back from the golden mountain behind us.

By the time we returned to the monastery it was dark. A meal was provided and we tucked in whilst those who had not been up the mountain talked with Father Ruis. Clearly they had been praying and the young mother was extremely emotional. This had an effect on her two children who scuttled to her side to be enveloped in hugs. But the prayers were to continue. Whilst we were given a guided tour of the monastery by night she was taken into a church for anointing with oil and prayers led by Bishop Yostos, the senior monk at the monastery. Once more I was confronted with the strange traditions of Coptic Christianity when shown the body of a previous bishop, apparently preserved, in a glass case. Far from being ghoulish, this was a major part of the monastic tradition. All monks remain in the monastery of their death. Their souls have departed and they are left to rot. Once the flesh has decayed and only a skeleton is left, they are stored ready for the resurrection of the body. But this particular bishop was so holy in life that when he died he never rotted away. He would be more ready for resurrection than the skeletons would! Every year, on his memorial day, Bishop Yostos opened the glass case and carried the body of the dead bishop around the monastery. It was in front of this dead bishop that the anointing with oil and prayer for healing took place. This was the final straw for Miriam. She withdrew, muttering accusations of raising false hopes.

With a three-hour journey back across the desert in the dark, we all had much on which to reflect. I was disturbed by Miriam's anger, even though I felt I could understand it. How were the issues of suffering dealt with? It seemed that the Coptic tradition allowed for suffering. It was the norm for many. Equally they were delighted but not surprised at supernatural intervention in ordinary lives. The legends of the Desert Fathers were alive today. They merged into what I had experienced. The hermit whose hand would ignite, the preservation of a dead bishop's body, and the possibility of healing from cancer were all part of the same world view. The cultural crust of English Protestant tradition overlaid with rigid logic and Renaissance scepticism had to be punctured if I were to understand these people's Christianity. If I were to swim under the crust of ice, I wondered, where might I come up for air?

CHAPTER FIVE

URBAN CAIRO

The car was being driven somewhat erratically along a hectic dual carriageway in the suburbs of Cairo. The driver, a senior Anglican cleric, was in high spirits. Humming favourite tunes from Gilbert and Sullivan, whilst other vehicles careered around us at breakneck speed, Huw was taking me to see another aspect of Coptic spirituality. He felt that this was an essential aspect to my being able to appreciate the life and tribulations of being a Coptic Orthodox Christian today.

After a few wrong turns we found our way to the outskirts of the city, to an area where rocky hills prevented the urban sprawl from expanding. This was Muqattam, the home of the Zebbulin. I had heard of these people, Coptic Christians who survived by reprocessing rubbish. From a Western perspective, and certainly from a distance, it seemed both laudable and environmentally beneficial. Here were people who sorted the mountains of waste produced daily in Cairo and so soft drink cans, plastic bottles, glass, paper, and all forms of scrap were recycled. The problem lay in the attitude behind it. These were the poorest of the poor. Many of the Zebbulin were reduced to eating what they could scavenge with all the consequent detrimental effects on health.

A small city had developed alongside the rubbish dumps. As the car slithered along its streets, thick with mud and slime, we caught the stares of people whose faces betrayed a life blighted by the curse of circumstances. I began to feel distinctly uncomfortable but Huw insisted that I should not be concerned. The Zebbulin were very warm people, he explained. The stench was overpowering and we closed the car windows. Open-fronted shops displayed their wares, including one with animal entrails dripping with blood. This acted as a magnet to a black swarm of flies. One type of shop was a surprise, a jeweller. Remembering that Christians tend to be the jewellers across the region, I was still surprised to find such a shop amongst the poorest of the poor. I wondered what use would the Zebbulin have for jewellery if it was a struggle to stay alive. I was assured that the jeweller had quite an active business because possession of jewellery, being a sign of affluence, is an important status symbol. If you have jewellery you are not on the poverty level and all can see that God has blessed you.

Eventually we arrived at a gate and Huw negotiated entrance. As if by magic we found ourselves in a totally different landscape. Walled in from the surrounding slums this was the place where the Zebbulin worshipped. Almost underneath a sheer cliff of limestone new offices and a conference centre had been built out of the local rock. In the bright sunshine and, especially in contrast to the squalor just experienced, the effect was dazzling. I had expected to meet local Coptic Christians but the place was almost deserted. A few children were playing in a picnic area whilst some women, dressed in black, kept a watchful eye.

Huw was eager that I might see the church. Two towers reminiscent of the old Wembley Stadium stood at the base of the cliff and it was between these that he led me, down a wide passageway and under the overhanging cliff. We emerged at the base of an incredible amphitheatre. Built in the entrance to a huge cavern, the roof of which was enormous, this stadium had seating for several thousand.

'The Zebbulin couldn't get permission to build a church so they converted a cave,' said Huw with a wry smile. 'And it is full regularly each week.' I just wished I might have seen such an event. Many of the Zebbulin came originally from Upper Egypt, drawn by the possibility of finding their way to a fortune in the capital city. Once they began their work of garbage collection and recycling they had been granted the area of Muqattam because it was out of sight and smell of the city, being tucked away in a fold of mountains. An alternative explanation to that of the city authorities preferring the Zebullin to be away from urban Cairo, was that of a vision of the Virgin Mary. Whichever, it was the result of someone's breathtaking vision.

Muqattam is also the alleged site of spiritual conflict from many centuries ago. It is told that shortly after the Islamic conquest, the Muslims taunted the Christians so much that the Church leaders were called out to meet the Islamic rulers. So convinced were they of the supernatural supremacy of Christianity over what they perceived as an erroneous sect, that they arranged a contest. The Muslims said that if the Christians could pray and remove one of the mountains, then they would believe too. Sure enough the mountain was moved although it cannot be said that everyone lived happily ever after. Stories like this, whilst having the air of incredulity to Western minds, are part and parcel of Orthodox faith. They fit in easily with Old Testament stories of Elijah and they fit Christian doctrine about faith. They assume literal belief and see no problem with the mechanics of how it was done. God is God and therefore nothing is impossible. Looking at it from the underbelly of society such belief and faith has much to commend it. But was it true? Again this is a largely Western concept. The Orthodox would just accept that God could have done it rather than embark on a search for proof.

The area in which the church was built was spectacular, with vivid bas-relief carvings showing biblical scenes. They reminded me of the heroic Soviet style of sculpture so I was intrigued to learn that the sculptor was a Polish Roman Catholic who probably owed much to the Russians in his training. Such breathtaking beauty was astounding. There were two more cave-churches, smaller but no less beautiful. I kept thinking of the crushed existence of the Zebullin, scrambling about in the filth for a living. Here they had something beautiful that they could call their own. This place could inspire worship. It gave them dignity.

As we ambled back to the car I walked over to where the children were playing. Before I left England I had been given various small toys and trinkets from Christmas crackers. The idea had been that they were lightweight and might be fun for poor children. I decided that the children of Muqattam might qualify so I gave a plastic frog to one little boy. No sooner than I had done this than three women leapt up from a seat and bounded towards me. Pushing the children aside they started clawing at me in an alarming fashion, pleading for gifts. I refused and tried to continue to distribute toys to the children but they became aggressive, trying to snatch my bag from me. By now they were calling out and I was shouting back at them. Huw came rushing over and between us we made a hasty retreat. I was visibly shaken.

How could these 'nice' people become so aggressive? I had only wanted to be a blessing to those children, trying to be even-handed but the mothers were trying to take the lot. The simmering violence that lay beneath a tranquil scene where small children were playing was alarming. But who would benefit from my distribution of the toys? I would, in that it would help me to feel better about snooping on the Zebullin and their poverty. Why had I brought the toys? It was only because they were surplus to requirements and gave me an opportunity to be magnanimous. They cost me nothing but the potential feel-good factor was massive. In short it was a picture of so much that is bad in charity work. It massaged the ego of the donor. I had not found out if discarded toys were the right things to give. I had not sought the permission of the mothers to give toys to their children. I could well imagine the feelings in a British park if a middle-aged Egyptian man started giving out toys to children. All considered I had to conclude that it had been inappropriate and that I had acted imperialistically because they were poor. I deserved the experience.

The church at Muqattam had seemed so surreal. It was laid out on a colossal scale but at the same time was almost deserted. All this talk about growth and renewal amongst the members of the Coptic Church seemed detached when I did not see the people themselves. This place might as easily have been an extravagant film set. Of course, I was pleased to know that the Coptic Church had active programmes for health and education, as well as training young people for jobs away from the rubbish dumps. I suppose that was why the place was empty during the week. 'One of the schemes involves farming', smiled Huw. 'Pig farming!' As the significance of that settled in I realised that the pigs would feed on the rubbish and that the presence of pigs would act as a deterrent to marauding Muslim gangs from the city. 'Best bacon you ever tasted,' mused Huw as he set his car on its nightmare journey back into Cairo. Humming tunes from 'The Mikado', Huw seemed impervious to the swearing and rage emanating from the fast flowing traffic as it swerved all around him. Earlier it had seemed incongruous but. following the sights I'd seen that afternoon, the ability to retreat into an emotional comfort zone became a sensible antidote to the impulse to break down and weep.

Whilst in Egypt I had been privileged to see the Coptic Church at work, and to experience something of its spirituality. But I had not yet found the origin of why it was in revival. Of course from a Christian perspective it would be easy to say that this was the work of the Holy Spirit but I needed to see the linkages of this. Everyone I met answered my query in the same way. 'Go to see Pope Shenouda' was the universal answer.

The spiritual head of the Copts, Pope (literally, the word means 'Father') Shenouda III, had an interesting pedigree. Choosing their leader by the same method that the New Testament apostles used to replace Judas Iscariot, the Coptic Orthodox cast lots. Three candidates are submitted: one is recommended by the Church; one is recommended by the Government; and one is recommended as sort of wild card. Shenouda was the outsider in the last election and won. A monk from one of the monasteries at Wadi Natrun he had always been noted for his fiery preaching and uncompromising stance. For a time the Government exiled him inside his monastery but eventually they allowed him back to Cairo. I had to hear this man!

It was dusk on a Wednesday evening. The squawking starlings were jostling to find resting places for the night as I looked up at the great statue of King Ramses mutely surveying the evening rush hour. The scene of bedlam that was unfolding beneath his mighty feet was very different from that of distant Luxor from whence he had come. Buses, taxis and trams seemed determined to wipe out hapless pedestrians who even dared to set foot in the roadway. Horns, shouting, bicycle bells and the constant roar of traffic seemed consistent with the thick soup of exhaust fumes that hung in the warm evening. And slowly, like a cancer, the pollution was eating away at King Ramses.

I had been advised to catch a tram to Demerdash, its second stop. The conductor was very excited at the idea of a foreigner on his tram. As the tram gurgled and lunged its way up the hill the conductor pointed out excitedly to a large illuminated cross towering over the rooftops. This was St Mark's Cathedral. It could not be missed, but it was no easy matter to gain entrance. A blank-faced concrete wall that would have done justice to Wormwood Scrubs surrounded the cathedral compound. Having walked round three sides of the perimeter wall I found what I thought was the way in. A quiet courtyard with a man sweeping dust in the glow of orange security lights was at least a way of getting on to the inside of the forbidding wall.

'Excuse me,' I said hesitantly realising that this man would not speak English. 'Pope Shenouda?' I added in the hope that he might recognise the name. He broke into a great beam and pointed me back to the street. I was dismayed. Was there no way within the walls? The sweeper was insistent and, had I stayed longer, I believe he might have swept me out to emphasise his point.

So there I was, back on the busy suburban street about to give up when I noticed that in the last few metres before I would arrive back where I began walking around the walls, a gate had been opened. People were going through. Police were checking some of them, presumably for security purposes, but it gave a heightened sense of doing something a little dangerous. Once through the gate I was amazed to see literally thousands of mainly young people – men and women – milling around at the base of some steps leading to an enormous barn of a concrete cathedral. Market stalls, lit up by fluorescent tubes were doing an enormous trade in CDs, tapes, books, icons, and posters. Pictures of Pope Shenouda were out-selling those of other religious subjects but, given that this was his show, it was hardly surprising.

The tomb of St Mark was housed in a small building at the foot of the steps. A steady stream of devout people was filtering through but I decided to take the opportunity to negotiate for some earphones on which I might hear a translation of the events in English. A priest took me up the steps and, whilst everyone was milling through side doors I was taken through the Great West Door. I was totally unprepared for what I found on the other side.

A vast building reminiscent of an airship hangar presented itself. The atmosphere was buzzing with excited chatter as thousands of young Copts were greeting one another. The lighting was not quite sufficient to dispel the darkness of the hot night that had settled outside. My guide took me up the central aisle, thoughtfully partitioned off from the bubbling congregation. We walked to the front row of pews and I was given earphones so that I might understand the proceedings. In front of me was an official delegation of Coptic priests from Eritrea. Whilst we were unable to communicate by language, I was left in no doubt that they were very excited to be there.

In front of me was a sort of stage on which various young peoples' singing groups were belting out popular numbers that certainly were appreciated by the congregation. The songs were heavily weighted with 'Hallelujahs' and I heard the name 'Shenouda' several times.

By now the building was full to capacity and the atmosphere was electric. At least a couple of thousand people eagerly awaiting the arrival of their spiritual leader. Without warning a door opened away to my right and a group of priests ambled through, including Pope Shenouda himself. At least I recognised him from the many photographs I had seen on my travels.

Some people knelt as he passed by, others rushed towards him. One man leaned across a security rope holding his baby aloft. One false move and the infant would have been injured but Dad was successful and the child received the papal blessing. After a lengthy series of greetings on the platform, Pope Shenouda sat down at a desk and looked at a pile of messages sent in to him. He grinned and made some joke. This seemed to cause the entire crowd to roar with laughter. He certainly had a way with words and quickly had his audience eating out of his hand.

He answered questions about whether someone should take out legal proceedings against a neighbour, and what to do if you think your priest is a crook. I suppose he was a cross between a chat show host and a Helpline. There was a great deal of merriment in the way he answered the questions and the audience was certainly gaining value from this part of the programme.

Just as it appeared that the agony aunt session was going into overdrive, he pushed his papers to one side and announced that his sermon was about fruits. For the next half hour he had all of us riveted on various passages from the Bible. His main thesis was that Christians should produce fruit in their lives to show that they are Christian. This clearly touched a nerve. It was about the reality of faith. Faith in Christ was supposed to make his followers act in ways that emulate their master. But did it? Pope Shenouda reckoned that most of the people who called themselves Christian were not producing fruit compatible with Jesus Christ. There was a great deal of shuffling, a little coughing, but mainly all was quiet.

'Then God says he will throw you on the fire. Even if you say you are Christian. Only by your fruits will you be known as Christians. Not by your family.' This was unnerving stuff. In a land where people suffer for being Christian, where Pope Shenouda himself has been under house arrest and publicly humiliated, he was telling these young people to adopt a radical faith. This echoed what I had experienced in Beni Suef and with the Zebullin.

After exactly thirty minutes Pope Shenouda stood up and almost rushed for the door. But he was not quick enough for some who dashed forward into his route of escape to receive the papal blessing. One little toddler was dropped on the other side of the security cordon only to wander the wrong way. How was he to know which of the thirty or so bearded men in cassocks was the Pope? His father was distraught with exasperation as the child ascended the platform long after the Pope had gone.

Outside again, and the stalls were in overdrive selling their paraphernalia. I chatted with two young men. They were university students and were surprised to find an English man in their midst. I asked what was on the two posters they had bought. They proudly showed me. One was of a dreamy-eyed Jesus whilst the other was of the Madonna and child. I did all I could to persuade them not to give them to me as a gift. I was left musing on the simplistic naivety that would buy such posters for student bedrooms. In England the posters would be of anything but this! The openness, the enthusiasm, the generosity of the Copts was something that endeared me to them. It was part of what I was beginning to see as a living faith, even when the chips were down.

CHAPTER SIX

NO ROOM AT THE INN

Travel between countries in the Eastern Mediterranean is never straightforward. If you get an Israeli stamp in your passport there are a number of countries that will turn you back at the frontier. Syria and Lebanon were two such countries, and I hoped to visit them after going to Israel. Seasoned travellers know to ask the Israeli entry officials not to stamp their passports. Instead they are given a temporary document to insert inside their passports; in return, they are often interrogated by the Israeli officials, sometimes in great depth. This applies whilst entering or leaving the country.

I thought I had it all tied up. Leaving Egypt by land I would travel from Cairo to Jerusalem, but a chance comment from a British businessman in Cairo was to change all that. He wondered how I would explain my Egyptian land exit stamp when I later presented myself to the Lebanese or Syrian frontier authorities. The truth slowly dawned. An Egyptian land exit stamp meant that I had used it for entry into Israel. Not having Israel in my passport was vital, but I must leave no clues behind. If I wanted to get into Syria or Lebanon I must not travel by land into Israel. It then became as clear as daylight that I would have to leave the Arab world by air so that my exit stamp would show an international airport. From there I might have gone to London, Los Angeles or Hong Kong!

This was the beginning of a complicated logistical exercise. Flying from Cairo to Tel Aviv would have been the answer but, as Easter was approaching, all the airlines were fully booked for days both sides of the holiday. Even flying to Greece or Cyprus proved impossible for the same reason.

On top of all this I had to visit the consular sections of the embassies of Jordan, Syria and Lebanon to obtain their visas. Each country demanded to keep my passport for anything from a couple of hours to a few days. This meant that I was effectively grounded in Cairo for nearly a week until all these formalities were completed. On one occasion, having found the address given for the Lebanese Embassy, I discovered that it had relocated. No new address was posted on the empty shell of a building. Fortunately a policeman nearby spoke English and was able to advise me. I was becoming used to shrugging my shoulders and saying, 'Inshallah'.

In the end I was to find a route travelling overland via the Sinai Peninsula to Nuweiba. From there I would sail to Jordan. A plane to Amman would leave me in place to fly with Royal Jordanian to Tel Aviv. Ironically, in view of the difficulties encountered in getting flights from elsewhere, this route was not heavily used and I was able to get a cut-price deal! For me, the bonus in this great diversion was that I would be travelling via Sinai. This was the inhospitable mountainous desert through which the Biblical Children of Israel wandered. In those days Moses was their leader and the stories about those days have remained strong in the region to this day. I decided that, as part of my quest, I would visit the ancient desert monastery of St Catherine.

Having obtained a new set of wheels for my suitcase, I caught the bus to Sinai. The journey from Cairo to the monastery took a whole day. Driving under the Suez Canal just as a ship was passing overhead was an interesting experience but did little to relieve the tedium of the

long journey. As we headed into the mountains, along wadis that could become raging torrents on occasions, we would glimpse the occasional settlement of Bedouin but very little else to indicate that humans lived on this planet. Whilst the sun dropped behind the huge mountains, the rocks turned into various livid colours before giving up and becoming shadows in the night.

Almost invasive in its suddenness, after the peace and darkness of the mountain pass, the tourist village of St Catherine's brashly presented its hotels, restaurants and floodlights. The bus driver took heart and romped his steed home. He was so eager to decant his passengers and park his bus that he made out that this was the terminus. However, five of us had tickets for the monastery and we were not going to walk! It took some persuasion and a little cash before the bus was urged back into life and we were taken up a twisting unlit road to our goal, the steps of the monastery guesthouse. All that lay beyond were towering mountains brooding above the fortified community. In contrast to the polluted odours of Cairo, the clear desert air was crisp and clean.

I had brought with me a letter from the Anglican bishop in Cairo. It was a letter of introduction and request for me to be given accommodation within the monastery itself. A young Bedouin carried my monster suitcase on his head as we ascended to the monastery itself. It was with a sense of anticipation that I was escorted through a small door in the massive bulwarks. After a wait of a quarter of an hour I was introduced to Father John. It was impossible to grant this request, he maintained. They did not allow visitors to stay overnight.

Nowhere to stay – and in this mountainous environment. My thoughts turned to the tourist village. The bus had gone and I could not walk that distance in the dark with my suitcase. However all was not lost. There was one room left in the guesthouse outside the monastery, I was informed. It took quite a long time to sort it out but eventually all was arranged. There was room in this inn...just. After supper I took a stroll outside the monastery. The moon had ascended and the buildings seemed to merge as one impassive sentinel at the base of a mountain pass. All around were huge boulders that had fallen from the almost vertical mountains. They lay in the moonlight looking for all the world like reposing prehistoric monsters.

I had to take an early night because I had to be up at two in the morning in order to do the tourist thing, joining a group ascending Mount Horeb (Jebel Musa – The Mount of Moses) in time to see the sunrise. This is reputedly the place where Moses received the Ten Commandments. Whilst there is no reference in the accounts of Moses to sunrise being an especially important time, I was up for the experience.

The previous evening, I had found out a little more about the monastery. It has been run by the Greek Orthodox continuously since the sixth century, being built in the time of the Roman Emperor, Justinian. But from even earlier times there was a religious significance about the spot. Not only is it at the foot of Mount Horeb but it also houses the Burning Bush. Honestly! A tradition of wandering monks and hermits in this area is documented from the third century. By the time that Christianity became the official religion of the Roman Empire, under Constantine the Great in 313AD, the area was already a major destination for pilgrimage. In 330AD, Constantine's mother, Helena, built a small church and a tower at the site of the Burning Bush to secure shelter for the monks.

When Justinian, who never visited the place, saw the plans after it had been built he had the architect executed for building it in such a ridiculous place. He felt that it was too vulnerable to attack. On the other hand the architect had built it round St Helena's church and tower on the site of the Burning Bush. It was clearly a no-win situation for

him. Over the years St Catherine's has been the subject of attacks by robbers and Bedouins but has survived. Perhaps its greatest threat came when the Arab Invasion brought Islam to the area. Fortunately the Sinai, and its holy places, is mentioned in the Koran, so this resulted in continued protection for St Catherine's.

The reason why the monastery is under the authority of the Greek Orthodox, rather than the Copts, lies in history. At one time the church was one body, but various schisms have seen the Eastern Church splintered into different factions, often over finer details of theological interpretation. The Greeks maintain that they are the original church whilst the splinters became much more associated with national identity. The monastery of St Catherine had remained under Greek control, and the patronage of the Roman Empire until the conquest by the Arabs. By transferring patronage to the new rulers, the Greeks retained control and maintained their protected status.

My alarm clock went off at two o'clock. I quickly got dressed and went into the sharp air outside. A group of young Italians was preparing to go up the mountain and invited me to join them. We set off at a great pace climbing steeply to the right of the monastery. Having gained some altitude I noticed little streams of torchlight on the valley floor but going in a different direction. Surely that was the way, and we were on the wrong path? When one of the girls fell down a small slope and twisted her ankle I began to wonder about the wisdom of what we were doing. I said that I would return to the monastery and join the other path but the Italians said that they would continue to follow the path they were on. Of course there was a pressure to this walk. Various guidebooks suggested around two and a half hours, but I needed to be on the top before sunrise. That was the whole point. So, once on the recognised path I speeded up and overtook a stream of what must have amounted to several hundred people.

Most had been driven in vehicles to the monastery in order to climb the mountain. I heard lots of different languages but no English so I pressed on at full speed.

From the darkness on either side a voice would call out 'Camila'. It would be a Bedouin trying to persuade us to ride up the hill on a camel. If there was one thing I was not going to do, it was ride a slowly lolloping camel in the dark as it picked its way along mountain paths! All the time the path ascended and all the time I was overtaking knots of tourists, each with their torchlight. At one point I was overtaking a camel when, out of the darkness, came another going speedily downhill for another fare. I was trapped between two camels as they brushed against one another but found, to my amazement, how pliable they are. I just pushed outwards and they gave way.

The last part of the hike was beyond the limit for camels. It involved climbing hundreds of stairs to the summit. The steep ascent up the narrow steps meant that the long line of climbers was limited to the speed of the slowest person in front. By now there was a distinct glow in the Eastern sky. Would I get to the top in time? I need not have worried. As I reached the summit with its tea and souvenir stall it was obvious that the actual sunrise would be some time. We were on flat rocks above a steep precipice. Looking over the edge it was possible to see more lights still coming up the path, but they were hundreds of metres below. The Greek Orthodox chapel was locked – probably very wisely. There was now nothing to do but wait. I found a perch near the overhanging rock and wedged myself in with an amorous young couple. No, they did not mind. They had been there all night and said that they realised that it would get crowded by sunrise!

It must have been another half an hour before the sun showed itself. During that time the heat of the hike had gone and my nether regions were feeling distinctly numbed by the rock I was sitting on. But as the sun came over the horizon a hush descended on the crowd. A

Korean group began singing 'How Great Thou Art' (presumably in Korean). The effect was electrifying. The beautiful harmonies cascaded around the still air as the sun's rays licked away the darkness of the mountains. After a few verses it was too much for some Australians who started shouting abuse and throwing beer cans. They had wanted silence and mystery, they maintained. Not this Christian sentiment! The Koreans quickly beat a hasty retreat.

The descent was much quicker than the uphill slog. Not only the favourable gradient, but the idea of breakfast appealed strongly. After cleaning up, I presented myself to Father John again. He was delighted to give me free access to all parts of the monastery including its world famous library. This is second in importance only to that of the Vatican in both number and value of the ancient manuscripts it contains. Father Justin was in charge. A very thin Texan with a long beard and twinkling eyes I was intrigued to know what had brought him to this remote spot. We agreed to chat after Vespers that afternoon.

The rest of the day was spent exploring the hidden parts of the monastery, normally closed off to outsiders. I was able to negotiate the tunnels built high up in the external walls. From there I could look down on the crowds of tourists heaving their way past the Burning Bush. The bush is a bizarre phenomenon. Somewhere in Sinai it is believed that Moses had his experience with a bush that appeared to burn but was not consumed by fire. Out of it came the voice of God. The story stretches credulity when offered to Western rationalistic thought but seems to fit very comfortably with a form of spirituality that expects God to intervene in the lives of people. The traditions of the wandering Israelites dovetail very neatly into those of the early Christians in the desert. I had already met a hermit whose hand would sometimes catch fire, allegedly. So why not a burning bush? And why not this bush?

The bush has flourished in this place as long as records have been kept. It was moved – once – to allow the building of an altar in the tenth century. But it remains the only example of its species in Sinai. All other attempts to transplant a branch elsewhere have failed. So to me, as to countless generations of pilgrims, this is **the** Burning Bush. And does it matter if it is not?

At four o'clock the bell rang for Vespers. Along with five others, I was allowed to occupy one of the stalls along the side of the Nave. A bus load of very elderly Cypriots occupied the chairs in the centre. Most of them were old women wearing black skirts and shawls. I learned that Greek Orthodox peasants yearn to visit this monastery and Jerusalem at least once before they die. Some of the women looked as if they might not survive the trip. This kind of pilgrimage, I understand, predates that of the Islamic hajj to Mecca and it is tempting to suggest that this might be part of the tradition that was learned by early Muslims.

The Liturgy began but the excited chatter of the ladies continued. Father John finally seemed to lose his cool and walked down the nave to scold them. This had the desired effect – for a time. I picked up a lot of 'Kyries' during the service but it was transformed when one of the elderly Cypriot men came forward and took over as cantor. Appearances can be deceptive. He looked like a farm labourer just in from the fields, unshaven and weatherbeaten. When he began to sing it was with the confidence and clarity of a lark. His voice seemed to transcend the heavy ornamentation of one and a half millennia in the church. It took me right up the mountain to that sunrise again. Here was praise to the Creator God who had made himself known to mere mortals.

After the service I was a little disappointed that my chat with Father Justin was not to be for me alone. I was joined by four Jewish women. They taught religion and wanted to understand better how the Christian faith had come out of Judaism and how they might relate it to the Jewish experience of God. Father Justin was able to articulate his faith clearly and in a way that connected with these Jewish enquirers. They were fascinated to see how many of the Christian rituals and beliefs had their roots in Judaism.

The Priest was evidently stimulated by this conversation and, in discussion afterwards, I gained an interesting glimpse into the way the Orthodox Church works. He was highly qualified as a teacher of theology and used to great effect in apologetics. As a 'reward' he was sent to Sinai to look after one of the most precious libraries in the world. Whilst he loved his new task he clearly missed the intellectual cut and thrust of theological debate. During his time there he had managed to get the library on the Internet and it was now possible to contact him by e-mail. The library, I discovered, was the only part of the monastery connected in this way.

At the end of our conversation I learned that Father Justin had been summoned to go to Athens to deliver a prestigious theological lecture. 'At least I'm not forgotten,' he winked as we parted.

Next day I travelled by servees, a shared taxi that operates on a fixed route to a fixed price, but only goes when the driver considers that he has enough passengers. The journey was across the desert to Nuweiba, from whence I travelled over the Gulf of Aqaba by fast boat to Jordan's only point on the sea, the port of Aqaba. After a night in a seedy hotel it was on to the capital, Amman, by plane. Here I was able to leave most of my heavy luggage to be collected two weeks later. Then on to Israel.

My plane to Tel Aviv flew at night. It took just one quarter of an hour and we were served drinks en route. The cabin staff rushed along the aisle and gave us all a small box of orange juice. The plane was, surprisingly, filled with young Israelis returning for their Passover. However their behaviour was alarming. Some called out racist taunts to the Jordanian cabin staff whilst one young man refused to sit down as we landed. Elsewhere this would have warranted official intervention upon landing but the cabin staff just allowed it to pass. Like many other examples I would see in Israel, it is often the young Israelis who would show arrogant disdain for the Arabs.

By the time I had been interrogated by Security at the Immigration Point, it was eleven o'clock. I looked for the Israeli version of the shared taxi, a sheroot, to take me onwards. The Jerusalem sheroot was half full as I climbed aboard. Soon we were heading along the motorway towards the hills. In the Bible, there are references to 'going up to Jerusalem' and I had once thought of this as being similar to the way, in certain areas of England, people go 'up to town', when referring to London. In Israel the term is meant literally. After crossing the coastal strip the road climbs steeply up into the hills. Even at night there is a great sense of anticipation. The route had security lighting all the way. Occasionally bombed out military vehicles could be seen parked strategically to remind travellers that the State of Israel had fought to gain every inch of this road. I was sitting next to a young Jewish San Franciscan. He was amazed at how similar it was to his native California. On the surface it was. Perhaps the driving was more reminiscent of Italy but certainly Israel presents a strong American identity. And well it might with so many Jewish Americans either in residence or having extensive business interests there.

Once all the other passengers had been dropped off around the various suburbs of West Jerusalem, the driver took me to his office in the centre. I had asked to go the ten minutes' extra drive to Bethlehem. But Bethlehem was in the Palestinian Territories and my driver was a Jewish Israeli. I sat in the minibus for a quarter of an hour whilst he checked the feasibility of taking me on. Eventually he agreed but it would cost a lot. I was between a rock and a hard place, but I needed to get to Bethlehem.

I had arranged, by personal recommendation whilst in Cairo, to stay at the Bethlehem Bible College. As it was the Easter holiday they had rooms available. I had booked it by e-mail but had not received acknowledgement that my midnight arrival was acceptable. As soon as the sheroot pulled up outside the college I knew I was in difficulty. High metal railings surrounded a substantial stone building. It was in darkness and there was no bell on the gate.

By now the sheroot had spun round and driven back to the perceived safety of Israeli Jerusalem. I shouted. I rattled the gates. But there was no response. A sickening sensation of rejection crept up on me. The street was deserted. Across the road was waste land; down the street was the Palestinian Police box. But next door was a fruit and vegetable store. I sat underneath its awning on a white plastic patio chair, wondering how I might pass the next seven hours or so. The wind chased a sheet of newspaper down the street. Floored in one, all my plans seemed to be as fragile as that bit of paper. And here I was in Bethlehem. No room at this inn!

Just as I was beginning to allow my morbidity take over something galvanised me into action. The police box. Surely they could help? I walked down the street and found a shy young officer who spoke no English. He called his colleague who turned out, surprisingly, to be a rather portly middle-aged black Caribbean. He wiped his hands on his trousers and continued to relish eating whatever it was that was in his mouth.

'What's the phone number?' he said in a disinterested fashion. I had no idea. I knew the address and I knew the e-mail contact, but not the phone number. Could we enquire through Directory Enquiries, I wondered. He grinned.

'This is Palestine, not England. We don't even have a directory.'

All the time both policemen were keeping a wary eye on the deserted street. I suppose that I could have been a decoy. After all we were less than a hundred metres from Rachel's tomb with its heavy Israeli presence. Eventually it was suggested that I walk around the corner to the Paradise Hotel. They might give me accommodation for the night. It was with relief that I walked into the hotel lobby to find a warm welcome from the proprietor. Pictures of Greek Orthodox patriarchs and other Christian trappings were evident. I felt safe enough to explain my plight. My new friend said he knew the college president and would telephone him immediately. When I said that I hoped it would not be too late I noticed that it was only a quarter to twelve. My watch was an hour further on. It was explained that the Palestinian Territories were an hour behind Israel, at least until Summer Time.

Returning now with a spring in my step I found the College lights on and the college president, Bishara Awad on the doorstep. How I thanked God for deliverance in the city of Christ's birth. But the little town of Bethlehem of the Christmas carol is only a dream. The reality, I was to find, is brutal.

CHAPTER SEVEN

JERUSALEM

The low moaning of the wind, punctuated by occasional lashings on the windowpane, woke me. It sounded like November in Skegness but as I opened the curtains there was no rain. The wind had whipped up dust and it was this that was hitting the windows. In fact the air was so full of dust that it had formed great clouds that even dulled the sun. Across the valley in Beit Jala men were busily working in small olive groves. This was a timeless Palestinian occupation that was rapidly vanishing under the advance of Israeli urbanisation. Away on the horizon the concrete viaduct spanning the valley carried a busy road. With its tunnels and viaducts this had been built to help Israeli settlers in the disputed area of Hebron avoid travelling through Palestinian built-up areas.

Bethlehem is only ten minutes bus ride from Jerusalem. But it is in a different world altogether. On the outskirts of the town was a huge checkpoint. It was being extended as I was there. The Israelis could close off Bethlehem at any signs of unrest and thus contain the 'problem'. As many Palestinians were dependent upon getting into Jerusalem for their work, any closure of the checkpoint caused major economic problems. The military blockades contrasted with the rather sad illuminations dangling from the street lighting. Stars of Bethlehem flapped in the warm dusty wind; aluminium

Christmas tree shapes dangled in a strange remembrance of a different season, for this was now Easter. At the checkpoint young conscript Israeli soldiers looked nervously around as they eyed every vehicle that came through.

I was travelling into Jerusalem on the local Beit Jala bus. Next to me was an old man, dozing. He could have been a shepherd out of a Nativity play. His care-worn face, the stubble on his chin, the headgear, all told me that this man was an Arab who had suffered. The bus ground its way up the hill to the checkpoint where it was stopped. A young Israeli soldier got on and looked at us all. Was he counting us? Meanwhile everyone seemed to pretend that nothing was happening. It was humiliation for the entire population. But nothing was said. The soldier jumped off and the old bus poured out its filthy exhaust as it struggled to regain its composure. Almost immediately we were in a different world of dual carriageways, illuminated bus stops, modern housing and busy suburban traffic. At one point our old bus pulled up at traffic lights alongside a new Mercedes environmentally-friendly Israeli bus. The occupants of the Beit Jala bus turned away to avoid catching the eyes of the Israelis. But I noticed that they too had averted their gaze. As the lights changed the new bus raced away and a moment's possible realisation that we are all people was avoided.

The bus decanted its passengers outside the Damascus Gate, one of the most vibrant entrances to the old walled city. Here, squeezing through its dark entrance in a heaving mass of humanity, it is possible to be either exhilarated or alarmed as control over destiny is lost. You have to go with the flow. Sometimes the human river would coagulate whilst a tide of equal strength would push in the opposite direction. Sometimes it would weave to one side whilst a youth would drive through the middle on a small tractor towing a trailer as though there were no obstacle in the way.

The object of my tour, to discover something of the spirituality of the indigenous Christians, had been lost in the crush but I composed myself and dived into an Armenian Catholic Church. The dignity as well as the cool atmosphere contrasted with the warm dusty street outside. An old priest sat near to the altar and exquisite harmonious music was relayed through the sound system.

Over the centuries, a minority of Armenians has turned for spiritual oversight to Rome. They are allowed to keep a reduced level of tradition and liturgy while Rome exercises control of the clergy. Most Armenians however still belong to the Armenian Apostolic Church which is classified in the Oriental Orthodox (or Non-Chalcedonian) group of denominations which also includes Coptic, Syriac, Ethiopian and Indian Malabar traditions. Armenians lay claim to having established the first Christian political kingdom way back in the fourth century.

After savouring the tranquillity of this church for a quarter of an hour, I felt recomposed. Back into the melée of the street I made for the Church of the Holy Sepulchre. It was built over what many believe is Golgotha and purports to house the tomb of Christ: as the place of the Resurrection event, it is the object of veneration of millions of pilgrims from all over the world and has often been the scene of conflict as crowd control has never been a delicate science in the eyes of the Greek Orthodox priests who normally supervise it. I had first visited this church in 1990 and had been so appalled at the behaviour of the pilgrims and guardian clergy that I had never returned on subsequent visits to Jerusalem. This time it was blissfully quiet: although it was the Wednesday of Holy Week for the Western Church, there were very few tourists or pilgrims and I was able to wander round the entire complex at my leisure.

The church was built over many years so it is difficult to describe it as anything other than a complex of chapels and churches that are interconnected. The Greek

Orthodox, the Armenian Apostolics and the Roman Catholics control it jointly. Various other groups have a foot in the camp. For example the Coptic, Ethiopian and and Syriac Orthodox are all allowed small chapels in the area supervised by the Armenians. Some years ago the Ethiopians were evicted from their nearby residence by the Copts and now live in tents on the church roof. Such is Christian charity. An argument has raged for years between the Armenian Apostolics and Syriac Orthodox about the state of the latter's chapel. Another controversy is over maintenance and repairs. A small ladder was put up to mend a broken window over a century and a half ago. The subsequent row left the broken window and ladder in place for all to see today. The result of all this is dirt. Millions of pilgrims, burning of incense and the activity of birds have left parts of the church thick with dirt. Ecumenism is so bad that Muslims hold the church keys, although this is also a visible reminder that for centuries Christians lived under Muslim law. However, in spite of all this, I was surprised to learn that the fine dome was built recently with excellent ecumenical co-operation (to a British design!).

The noise of worship echoed around the building. In this or that corner chanting might break out at any time. Just when one group was in full flow, the Roman Catholic organ would burst forth drowning out any other sounds. Peace, perfect peace! The cacophony seemed to spread throughout the building. Ascending a narrow staircase past Ethiopian chapels I eventually found myself on the roof and then, surprisingly, at street level. What was that sound, wafting across the rooftops? The noise of bagpipes warming up was coming out of the Coptic Orthodox monastery of St Anthony. On entering I found a young man in Scout uniform playing for all he was worth. Would I like to see the church? The offer from a monk seemed very kind and, having warm feelings towards the Copts following my Egyptian experiences, I accepted. The church was not very old and neither was it prepossessing but I felt at home, recognising icons from Egypt. I sat down to pray but the monk kept fidgeting. He adjusted curtains; he cleared his throat; he walked around the back of the church. Eventually he could stand it no longer and walked up to me, standing alongside where I was sitting. I glanced up. 'Ten shekels', he demanded. Was this Egyptian backsheesh or was I being asked for a contribution towards church expenses? Either way it was clearly time to go so I gave him the necessary coin and departed.

The sun was now a red circle peering through the encircling gloom of dust clouds and there was an increasing chill in the air. This first trip into Jerusalem was proving unsatisfactory from a spiritual viewpoint. Feeling tempted to go back to my room in Bethlehem, I decided that I ought to persevere. Surely there was some place I might find a glimpse of real spirituality? My *Lonely Planet* guide was generally cynical about Christian presence in the area and I could understand why, but one place that seemed to get full marks was the Armenian Apostolic Patriarchate of St James. Vespers was scheduled for three o'clock so I decided to hang on. In the meantime I had time on my hands so decided to go to the Armenian Apostolic seminary to see if anyone might talk to me about Armenian spirituality.

In the street outside the seminary was a poster highlighting the Armenian holocaust of 1915. The accompanying map showed that much of this had happened in Eastern Turkey and Syria – places that I was intending to visit. But alongside the poster was a security box and the words 'Strictly Private'. Undaunted I approached the box. A guard was talking to a young man dressed in a black polo shirt and black trousers.

'Excuse me,' I interrupted. 'Does anyone speak English?' The security guard looked blank but the young man smiled. He said that he spoke a *leetle* English. I explained that I was hoping to learn about the Armenians and wondered if there was someone I might talk to. The young man introduced himself as Sevak Assayan and said that, as a seminarian, it would give him great pleasure to be of assistance. We walked across a lawn and sat down on a bench. The sun even managed to break through the dust clouds bringing an immediate increase in warmth.

'We were the first Christian nation,' he said proudly, 'but for many years we have lived under the Muslims. For centuries the Turks dominated us. In 1915 the twentieth century's first Holocaust occurred when one and a half million Armenians were slaughtered by the Turks.'

I looked at him and he picked a blade of grass. 'I know it was a long time ago but it affects us today. The Turks in 1915 wanted to take complete control in our lands. They thought they could do it by forced evacuation and by genocide. But even today we look to the land as part of our spiritual inheritance. You know, it all happened so long ago that you'd think it wouldn't matter. It does because we can't visit our heritage'. By now Sevak was impassioned. 'Even today the Turks deny this happened. We don't want to get the land back. We recognise reality. But if they would just say that it happened, and that they are sorry, we would forgive.'

I could see a lawyer's feast panning out. An acceptance could lead to reparations. People could clearly demonstrate that their lives have been blighted as a result of the devastation of previous years. Apologies and forgiveness? These are Christian virtues but could the Armenians be expected not to press for reparations? I suspect that without the international community pushing for Turkish compliance, the Armenians might as well whistle in the wind. But Sevak was sensing my interest and pressed on. 'In what is now Eastern Turkey there is a big lake, Lake Van. The Armenian Holy Cross Cathedral was our main church from 1113. It is now a ruin.'

I wondered whether there were any Armenians left in Turkey. Sevak looked sad. 'I do not come from Turkey. I was brought up in Armenia. This is the part of our country that survived because the Russians took it over after the First World War. Although life was difficult under the Communists, we survived because to be Armenian is to be a member of the church – even if they are atheists. It is our national identity and our spiritual heritage.'

I asked about Armenians around the world. It seems that, as a result of the persecutions, Armenians have settled worldwide. Sevak was bursting with pride as he told me that his church was very strong today. 'We have forty seminarians here in Jerusalem. There are three seminaries in Armenia. And we have one in New York and one in Beirut. It is our church that has preserved our language. In the early days the neighbouring languages of Byzantium and Persia could have taken over. But because our church had the language written down it was preserved. And it is the language of heaven...' he drifted into eulogy as he smiled at my incredulity.

Time was pressing and we wanted to go into the cathedral. Sevak offered to meet me again as I wandered across the street to join the small group of tourists as well as a few old Armenian ladies waiting for the doors to open. The door opened at three o'clock precisely and a parade of young men walked through in an informal procession, chatting as they walked. A priest followed them. As they entered, the young seminarians put on black gowns and then we were invited to enter. A heavy carpet hanging in the doorway was lifted in order that we might go in. Alongside the door a seminarian hammered on a piece of wood. It was an interesting variation on a bell.

Entering the cathedral was a strange experience. Once our small group of visitors had entered, the carpet was dropped down over the doorway and we were in darkness. It seemed chilly after the weak sunshine. Gradually my eyes became used to the darkened space as candles illuminated the cavernous interior. Reflecting on a bejewelled pulpit the candles gave an interesting impression of the Biblical idea of the light in a dark world. Was this how the Armenians viewed the wider world, a place of darkness, of sorrow, pierced by tiny flickerings of Christian presence? The pulpit was projecting from high up the north wall of the cathedral. Its appearance was a little like a box in the theatre but it was where the Vespers began. A priest clad in a black cassock with a pointed black hood began reading the Liturgy from this location. As he finished I realised that the seminarians had formed two groups facing one another. Then for the next half hour they chanted in beautiful harmony. First it was the tenors on one side, then the bass singers on the other. In between times a priest or seminarian would step forward and read whilst facing the altar.

Finally the most eerie and beautiful tenor solo lifted the Vespers on to a new plane. Encapsulating both the sorrow of a suffering people and the love of God it seemed to transcend the place where we were. As I stood in the centre of the cathedral allowing the worship to wash over me like gentle water I was musing on how suffering produces such faith and such beauty. Who has not been moved by the wailing songs of the Jews? Or the Russian Orthodox? Or perhaps the male choirs of the Welsh valleys? It seems that suffering brings out a special kind of music that is both dignified and uplifting whilst reflecting deep distress. It made me think of the Psalms where we hear of people who are both shattered and still able to worship God. It is a realm of experience of which we see little in the Western world. Suffering for us is sometimes akin to failure and therefore hidden. It is much better to face suffering with honesty. This aids coping with pain.

Whilst I had been deeply moved by the service I had been a little distressed by the antics of the tourists. Far from being prepared to experience the service, some people walked around taking photographs. During the reading of Scripture a tourist walked up and took a flash photograph almost in the reader's face. Even with the sudden illumination, nothing would deflect the ceremony. After all, I remembered, to the Orthodox this Liturgy was offered to God and Him alone. If tourists chose to be profane it was on their own heads. The Armenians had faithfully discharged their duty.

Stepping outside into the warm air of the late afternoon I got a snack in the street before catching a bus from the Damascus Gate. It was crowded and I was fortunate to get a seat. The man next to me wore a smart blue suit and Arab headgear. In front of me were two teenaged schoolgirls eating strawberries. They giggled at the sight of a foreigner on their bus and offered me a strawberry.

My spiritual journey for the day was not yet at an end because no sooner had I returned than I was invited to a special cultural evening being held in one of the communal rooms downstairs. The evening was arranged for a group of Norwegians on a pilgrimage. As I walked into the room the activities were already under way. Palestinian college students were singing and dancing, drums were thundering. The sheer verve of this music was impressive. After the serious search for spiritual presence during the day this seemed like hitting the jackpot. The Norwegians had offered to reciprocate after the refreshment break and I looked forward to some kind of cultural exchange. What happened was community chorus-singing in English, followed by a sermon from the leader of the pilgrims. It was not surprising that most of the Palestinians drifted out of the room as the guitar strumming progressed. When the altar call was made no-one came forward. It was not surprising because the 'congregation' by now was almost entirely Norwegian. The event ended with the Norwegians hurriedly departing for their bus.

Later I was fortunate to meet three young Palestinian men in the foyer. In their early twenties and dressed fashionably in jeans, they chatted about life for Christian Palestinians. As I showed interest they were keen to let me understand how difficult it was. Nevertheless they were nervous and kept fidgeting so we withdrew to one of the comfortable communal areas of the college. They introduced themselves as Rami, Elias and Karim. Rami came from a Latin (Roman) Catholic background and the other two had a Greek Orthodox upbringing. They were angry about the nominal nature of their religion as children. Having experienced an evangelical conversion in their teenaged years they now had a new spiritual worldview. Elias put it clearly, 'Our life as Palestinians is good and bad. The good bit is our faith in Jesus but the bad bit is the Devil. He gets everywhere. He gives trouble from different directions. The Israelis attack us because we are Palestinian. The Muslims attack us because we are Christian. We do not fight back because of our faith. It is easier to emigrate.'

At this point the other two murmured agreement. 'Only this afternoon,' said Elias, I tried to go to Jerusalem to hear a preacher. I had to line up for forty minutes before the Israelis sent me back. If I had sneaked through and been caught I would have been beaten and sent to jail'.

Rami then mentioned that, before the Intifada uprising of the late 1980s, 9% of the Palestinians were Christians. 'Now it is 2%', he said gravely. Life is hard here but we feel that God calls us to stay'. I wondered how things had changed and was told that I only had to think of how the Millennium had been celebrated in 'Christian' Bethlehem. 'All the signs say Bethlehem 2000', Rami said. ' Where is Jesus Christ in that? Bethlehem without Jesus is nothing. Most people are only interested in making money out of pilgrims. They are Muslims or nominal Christians; the visitors don't realise'.

'We think we have two problems,' offered Karim. 'Jews and Muslims. But there is a third. I meet Christians from Germany who tell me that I should get out because God has promised this land to the Jews. I meet Christian Jews who say the same. They don't read the same Bible as me! What kind of Christians are they?' He explained how he had been mugged on the streets by Muslim youths because he evangelises. He had also been beaten by Israeli soldiers because he is a Palestinian. 'Can you see why Christians want to emigrate' he said wistfully.

Karim was by now itching to go. Had he said too much to this foreigner? 'I have a wife at home but my friends do not. I need to go and if they want a lift they must come too.' As they were leaving Karim volunteered, 'Nothing is fair. If you are young and not wealthy there seems no hope. If you are a Christian you get the worst of all circumstances. But we have the Lord Jesus!' With that they went out into the night and to a very uncertain future. I had met all shades of Christian conviction that day and none of it was a comfortable experience. How different it was from the Christmas card image of Bethlehem. Life for the Christian was cruel and raw.

CHAPTER EIGHT

EASTER IN JERUSALEM

The Western and Eastern traditions of Christendom use different calculations to determine the festivals. On the occasion of my visit I was thus able to experience Easter - from different perspectives - on consecutive weekends. On the first Good Friday, that of the Western Church, I was faced with a decision. I could go to St George's Anglican Cathedral for the Good Friday Liturgy with Veneration of the Cross, or I could join the Roman Catholic Franciscans as they walked the Via Dolorosa, re-enacting the Stations of the Cross. Still debating with myself, the Beit Jala bus pulled up and I climbed into its embrace. There was only one seat left, near the back. As it rolled its way towards Jerusalem I found it increasingly difficult to make a decision. I still had to make up my mind as I jumped off the bus at the Damascus Gate. Looking at the gateway to the Old City, the street market was in full swing, with the streets alive with bustling and excited crowds. Suddenly the perceived starched formality of an Anglican service seemed to hold no appeal. The Franciscans won.

My previous excursions into Jerusalem had been tantalizing in that I kept bumping into different islands of Christian spirituality but had been prevented somehow from gaining an overall picture. It seemed difficult to find common ground even in places that should have been symbols of unity, such as the Church of the Holy Sepulchre. Indeed this church had become a symbol of disunity. Most hostility seemed to lie in the division between the Western and Eastern traditions of the Christian Church. Well-intentioned theologians and others the world over might be trying to understand their Christian cousins but in Jerusalem there is what is little more than a stand off. The ancient divisions of the church over perceived heresy or power bases are probably too far advanced to be healed. In this area those of an Orthodox persuasion remember the malevolent intentions of the Crusades. They would incline towards trusting a Muslim Arab rather than an American Christian for example. The tendency of fundamentalist Christians from the West to support the State of Israel against their Christian Arab cousins is a very bitter point.

Many of those of the Orthodox faith perceived the work of the Western churches, ranging from Roman Catholic ('Latins') to the Protestant and Pentecostal denominations, as proselytism. Over the years the Orthodox have seen large numbers of their flocks transferring over to one or other of the Western churches. I had already met several Palestinians who had done just that. They had felt that the Greek Orthodox hierarchy in Jerusalem had no interest in helping their Palestinian congregations in understanding their faith or standing up for them in the conflict with Israel. To many Palestinians the situation was even worse: the Greek Orthodox Church had sold valuable property in the Old City to Jews. There in the Christian Quarter the Israeli flag now fluttered over buildings that had been Christian. In contrast the Latins had said that they would not sell real estate.

The Franciscans were Latins. I wondered whether this might result in tensions with the Orthodox but all seemed well as, along with thousands more, I crushed into the courtyard of the Omarie College for the start of this pilgrimage. One paradox is that the Stations of the Cross should begin in an Islamic institution. Fortunately the authorities allow their premises to be invaded every Friday for this purpose. Given that Muslims revere Jesus as the greatest prophet beneath Mohammed, and that they resolutely deny that he was crucified, it is to their credit that they allow this commemoration to begin in their college.

The good-natured crowd that gathered in the courtyard was not comprised of locals. I suppose that it would be evident that at Easter it would be international tourists and pilgrims who would make up the vast throng. That all contributed to a sense of carnival. Various groups had obtained large but lightweight wooden crosses to hold up as they walked along the Way of the Cross. I gathered with a group of Australians and wondered what was the significance of this Walk for them. Interestingly I discovered that three quarters of them were new immigrants to Australia. Elham, for example, was an Iraqi woman who rejoiced in her new Australian nationality. As an Iraqi she would not have been granted entry into Israel but now she could come to Jerusalem. This trip for her was to give thanks for being able to emigrate from the clutches of the Saddam Hussein regime, and to visit the most significant sites of her faith. She belonged to the Chaldean Church, in Iraq. As this church was in communion with Rome, she easily found that she could belong to a local church in Sydney. I asked about Iraqis in Australia. She smiled. 'Few of us can take up our professions in Australia, but at least we are free'. She threw up her arms with glee, and I realized that here was someone for whom freedom of conscience was far more important than economic comfort. Given the distrust of asylum seekers in many parts of the world I was reassured to meet Elham.

A group of friars arrived with a substantial cross and the noise level increased as people pushed their way towards them. One group of pilgrims was singing the old song 'Were you there when they crucified my Lord?' Coming from the tradition of the American slave 'spirituals' I was touched to think of Elham and others for whom freedom was a precious commodity. I thought also of those who still suffer for their conscience, and for their faith. Jesus, the reason for our gathering that day, had talked about his followers being set free from all that constrained them. It was with no small amount of irritation that I thought of the basic message of Jesus, which led him to the cross, compared to the organization and power of some manifestations of the religion that holds up his name.

A portable loudspeaker was produced by one of the friars and a Bible reading was broadcast in four different languages. This first one dealt with the trial and condemnation of Jesus. Then they were off – the friars vanished through the narrow gateway and it was up to us to follow. Of course it was impossible for the thousands who were there to be able to follow the friars all at the same time. The gateway became a horrible logjam of humanity as we all pushed and one by one were spewed out on to the other side. By the time I was catapulted into the street the Franciscans had gone. They were probably two or three stations further on so I decided not to queue up at each station but to speed along and catch them up. The streets were cordoned off to prevent the pilgrims from coming into conflict with the flow of tourists and local shoppers. People were pressing against the crush barriers to watch us go past. I was unsure what they expected to see because we were just a long line of people ambling along as best we could in the circumstances. At one point a professional TV cameraman got upset when one of the pilgrims walked in front of his shot. He shouted an obscenity and this caused an American pilgrim to retort, 'Don't be miserable. Jesus is alive!'

I'm not sure whether the reprimand was even heard but it set me to thinking again about the way religion is organized, and about how people view their faith. The fact that Christianity is based on the crucifixion and resurrection of Jesus Christ must make it unique and should make a difference in the lives of Christians. If Jesus rose from the dead, and is alive now, then these people should be thinking in terms of a relationship with Jesus Christ. Surely it is this, which differentiates Christianity from all other World Faiths? To me, on this walk, I felt a fraud. I was really there for the experience and was experiencing little of the true spirituality of what the occasion demanded.

Like an overcrowded motorway we went forward and then stopped in fits and starts, presumably caused by the Franciscans up ahead stopping for their readings at each Station of the Cross. I used each opportunity to nudge my way past stationary pilgrims so that by the time we reached the Seventh Station I could see the Franciscans in the distance. The shopkeepers put up with a great deal of disruption as we filed past their wares, many of which seemed perched perilously close to disaster. Occasionally a Muslim woman tried to walk in the opposite direction, attempting to do her shopping. Not an easy task with a human tide flowing strongly in the opposite direction. Only one shopkeeper seemed antagonistic. Whilst the walkers were dignified, many in prayer, this trader seemed determined to have his sound system on full blast, with speakers facing the pavement.

I had caught up with the Franciscans by the time they entered the courtyard of the Holy Sepulchre Church. Having been warned that most pilgrims would be left outside because of capacity problems in the church, I was determined to be one of those who gained entrance. This proved an easy task and I was whisked along in the slipstream through the great door. Climbing a steep flight of stairs we visited the eleventh station (Jesus nailed to the Cross). I was now in the midst of the Franciscans and this seemed a very special time. They accepted my presence without demur and soon they were whisking me on down the next flight of stairs to a couple more stations, ending up at the fourteenth. Two cardinals and a couple of friars went into the tomb – the place where tradition states that Jesus was buried. We stood at the entrance whilst the narrator read the final reading. Once the cardinals came out of the tomb it was if a dam had burst. Crowds suddenly surged forward and at one point I could feel my torso being constricted as the people from behind pushed whilst the people in front could not move. Greek Orthodox priests had the job of crowd control and showed the same pastoral insensitivity that I had witnessed on my earlier visit. Because only four or five people could enter the tomb at any one time it was important that a space was maintained for people to escape once they had been in the sepulchre. However the doorway priest seemed more concerned in preventing the use of video cameras than preventing people being crushed to death. On one occasion he allowed a mother and baby to come to the front but for the rest of the time he seemed to be haranguing those near him for pushing – as if we had any control over the hundreds behind us.

After about half a dozen groups had gone into the tomb I entered. Behind me seemed the whole of Christendom. In the antechamber two candles gave light but more strategically, were used to light pilgrims' votive candles. Inside it was a simple affair. There was just a slab of marble worn smooth by the touch and kiss of pilgrims over the centuries. Instinctively I knelt in front of the marble slab and prayed. This tomb was empty. Its significance lay in that fact so, in a strange way, it was the paradox that meant so much. No coffin. No body. No relics. There was just a marble slab. It was Good Friday in the year 2000. Whether we argue about Western or Eastern Church calendars, it seemed significant to me.

Leaving the tomb to allow more in was a bigger problem than I imagined. The surging crowd was turning vicious and pushing forward so I was going to have to use all my energy to go against this flow. Many of those pushing with great resolve seemed to be elderly Greek ladies. As I pushed my way out some of the women even fought back! Fortunately the crush was only around the tomb so, once away from that area, I was able to spend time in the rest of the church. Nearby I found a side chapel dedicated for quiet prayer. Sitting there, half watchful and half prayerful, I felt my energy and spiritual resolve return.

Leaving the main part of the church I visited the Ethiopian Coptic Chapel. There is something tragic about their situation. Evicted from their monastery some years ago by the Egyptian Coptic Orthodox, they set up camp in huts on the church roof and have stayed there ever since. Their chapels seemed very much in need of redecoration and probably huge renovation but they had no financial resources. Their monks appeared poor and threadbare, reminding me of the appearance of homeless people. As large numbers of people were coming through the narrow passageway in the opposite direction to me, I decided to sit with an Ethiopian monk. He was reciting some mantra under his breath and his eyes had a faraway look. Whilst I sat with him, partly in solidarity, I am not even certain that he was aware of me. He was deep into a mystical experience. Eventually I rose up and returned into the main part of the church before returning to the open air. The bright sunshine was such a relief. Why was it that the natural phenomenon of fresh air warmed my spirit more than all the religious activity of the morning?

Easter in Jerusalem seemed an exciting proposition but when Rami and Elias, my Palestinian Pentecostal friends, invited me to their Easter morning service in Bethlehem it seemed churlish to refuse. Anyway wasn't there another Easter weekend the following week? The church met in hired rooms and I discovered that it was a splinter group from an evangelical church in Bethlehem. They had divided over a disagreement about styles of worship. This group would maintain that they were following the leading of the Holy Spirit and that the other group was stuck in their traditional ways. Where had I heard that before?

I entered the basement room in time for the ten o'clock start to find a few musicians tuning their guitars but little else in the way of confirmation that I was even in the right building. After about ten minutes a genial middle-aged man came in, introducing himself to me as the pastor. He was most concerned that I should gain the maximum benefit from the service and so I was invited to sit on the back row where I would be provided with an interpreter. He was very excited that a notable Egyptian evangelist would be the preacher that day.

I was surprised that my friends, Elias and Rami, had not appeared by the time the service began at 10.20. After all, I reasoned, I was really only there as a result of their invitation. The first worship song began. It was deafening and in Arabic. I felt a sense of total detachment. By now, all across Jerusalem, churches would be filled with time-honoured praise. They would be celebrating either Palm Sunday if they followed Eastern Rites or Easter Sunday if of the Western tradition. But this service seemed to recognize neither.

By now a congregation of around sixty people had gathered. All were Palestinian and all were impeccably turned out in Western-style clothing. All were young people, either single men or married couples. There were very few children in evidence, although one sweet little girl of about three wandered around toting a toy revolver. The incongruity of that in a church service, and the irony of it in view of the Palestinians' political plight, seemed to shriek louder than the music. Rami arrived in time to join me after the first song had finished. He greeted me and said that he would explain what was going to happen. Several more songs were sung with great gusto. No words were available; I suppose they were known by heart.

A reading from Luke's Gospel about the trial, crucifixion and resurrection of Jesus reassured me that Easter was back on the agenda. We then entered a time of open prayer. Some was in Arabic, and I was grateful for Rami's interpretation, but some was in tongues, which made understanding more problematic! The Egyptian preacher was then invited to take the microphone whilst the pastor sat next to me to interpret in English. It would be beyond Rami, it was explained.

Whether it was the fact that we were in a warm, low-ceilinged hall, or whether it was the inappropriate use of an amplified sound system for only sixty people, I am uncertain but what I do know is that I began to feel distinctly unwell. The pastor roared into the microphone and his voice came out of the speakers in a distorted fashion. It was so loud that my friendly neighbour's translation could no longer be heard. My head began to thump and I thought of cutting loose and leaving. Yet I had been to lots of services where I was unable to understand the language used. In those cases I had allowed the fact that others were worshipping God to wash over me. My immersion had been a personal blessing. But here? I was irritated by the way I was being harangued in a language I did not understand and wondered how long I could survive it. Finally I broke. I briefly thanked the pastor for his help, and bolted out into the bright sunshine.

By now it was too late to go to any Easter services in Jerusalem. I suppose that I had needed a good dose of my own culture; perhaps joining in with a rousing version of 'Jesus Christ is Risen Today'? Whatever it was I felt that I had to make contact with Christian people on this first Easter Day of the new millennium. One option remained. I had seen a poster advertising a prayer meeting in the open air on Mount Zion to celebrate the resurrection of Jesus. An afternoon event it seemed as if this might be just the ticket. Leaving for Jerusalem at half past one I noticed that the Egyptian preacher was still at it. I was glad that I had not stayed.

The Zion Gate in Jerusalem is the point where some of the most ferocious fighting of the 1948 War took place. Israeli soldiers holding Mount Zion (on the outside of the City Walls) had tried to break through to relieve the besieged Jewish Quarter on the inside. They had attempted to dynamite the wall but Suleyman the Magnificent, who had overseen its construction in the sixteenth century, proved too much for them. The all-out assault ended in disaster and a memorial plaque to the fallen Israelis is inset into the gateway. The bullet-scarred façade still tells of the trauma of that time. It was here that we were to meet.

I suppose that I had imagined hundreds would turn up. By the appointed time of three o'clock there were half a dozen. The organizer, Donna from Scotland introduced herself to me and explained that there would be a delay owing to the traffic jams all around the city. This was not only Easter but the end of the Jewish Passover. Everyone, it seemed, was taking advantage of the holiday. Ever fearful of Palestinian reprisals, the security forces had been disrupting the heavy traffic to make their searches and this had caused virtual gridlock. Donna had been planning the event for three years and had been in Jerusalem for the previous six weeks to make the necessary arrangements. It was the result of a direct call from God, she assured me, as she would never have had the temerity otherwise to set about such a venture. It was to be supported by both Jewish and Palestinian Christians, as she had talked and prayed with leaders of both communities. But where were they? So far there were only people from Britain and the United States. I chatted a little to some of them. One couple had come from Yorkshire to live in Jerusalem to work with Messianic Believers. They were very excited about the possibilities of the prayer meeting as it held possibilities for changing the situation for the Jewish Christians who, they told me, were suffering great discrimination from both the Israeli Government and the Jewish community in general.

About ten minutes later than the advertised time a trumpeter arrived and it was deemed that we were ready to start. We now numbered a dozen people. Because we might block the pedestrian route from the Zion Gate we were led downhill into the police car park for the prayer meeting. Technically we were still on Mount Zion but it somehow lost a bit of the poignancy. The event began with singing. I was surprised that the repertoire was Western, but even more surprised that it was old-fashioned choruses that were current in the 1970s. The occasional person passing by would watch for a few seconds before hurrying on with their agenda. Every now and again a policeman would come off duty to retrieve his car. Did I imagine that slight look of disdain, or was it scepticism, as they wearily got into their cars after a long day's duty?

I looked in vain for any Arab Christians. There were a few Jewish believers but, otherwise, it was a European and American event. We had a time of open prayer and at first there was an expression of thanks for the resurrection of Jesus but then, almost imperceptibly, the mood changed. The lady from Yorkshire piled in with a plea to God about 'The Land', that no compromise would be made to the Palestinians. Another took up the cry, this time that the Israeli Government would come back to Scripture and stop negotiating 'real estate' with the Palestinians. Should I have weighed in? The venom with which these people were praying nauseated me, and I had thought we were there to celebrate the resurrection. I could not stay. Leaving the car park I spoke to a visibly distressed Donna. The meeting had been hijacked. Her dreams, the vision she had, were broken. I felt very sorry for her as I made my way back up the hill. These were Christians who were convinced they were right. The end would justify the means. I was shaken by the fact that it was the Gentiles in the group who were so vociferous.

In Jerusalem I had seen thousands of pilgrims. Most were there to soak up the atmosphere of the place and hopefully to experience something of God. The people I had met on Mount Zion seemed to have everything sewn up. They knew what God wanted and so they were determined to pray it through to fulfillment. Determination and faith are excellent qualities but I kept remembering St Paul's words where he said that if you have every spiritual thing that you need but have not love, then it counts as nothing. It seemed that love was the missing ingredient.

CHAPTER NINE

PLAYING WITH FIRE

J erusalem – even the name conjures up expectations. I meet any number of people who love it, hate it, can't see the point of all the excitement, or prefer Manchester. But everyone who has been has a view. On this day I had a special reason to go to Jerusalem, and it had nothing to do with the Israeli – Arab politics. Sevak, my Armenian Apostolic seminarian friend, had invited me to join his church group at the Holy Fire Ceremony.

This takes place annually on Easter Saturday in the Church of the Holy Sepulchre. It is something that most people in the Orthodox world would give their eye-teeth to attend. Based around the empty Tomb of Christ it represents the coming of the Holy Spirit and was described to me as being both terrifying and spectacular. It was an opportunity not granted to many who are not of the Orthodox tradition. So it was very special and I had been in no need of a repeat offer. My agenda for the day had been cleared!

When I got off the bus from Bethlehem at the Jaffa Gate there was an immediate sense that this day, Holy Saturday, was something different. There were far more tourists than I had seen before, and they seemed to be crowding around the Citadel with nowhere to go.

David Street, the narrow alleyway dropping downhill from the Citadel was clogged with a heaving mass of people. With daylight almost excluded by the overhanging buildings it can be quite oppressive, even claustrophobic. Trying to descend the steps whilst not wrecking the displays of wares spilling out of the shops was not easy. Jewish families who had been to the Western Wall, this being the Saturday of their Passover celebrations, were pushing up against the flow of tourists and Christian pilgrims going down. It was a logjam.

Trying to turn left into Christian Quarter Road my way was barred by crush barriers manned by Israeli police and soldiers. They were letting no one through. This required a spot of quick thinking and, as I consider myself almost an expert on the back routes of Old Jerusalem, I decided to approach from a different direction – one that was not frequented by tourists. This involved climbing back up the steps to the Citadel, battling against the flow of eager tour guides waving their little flags and umbrellas. At last I surfaced into the comparatively pleasant atmosphere of Citadel Square before diving into the narrow streets behind the Greek Catholic Patriarchate. They were deserted. But they were still blocked. I reasoned that the soldiers here would have time to debate whether to let me through the barrier. I would not necessarily be rejected out of hand.

'You may not pass', said the young soldier. He was probably about eighteen years old and suffered with acne. I felt sorry for him.

'But I am the guest of the Armenian Patriarch', I countered, elevating my friend Sevak a little higher than he would admit to.

'You have a written permit?' replied the soldier, his fingers scratching his face.

'No, but I have come all the way from England to write about the Ceremony. I must go through.'

'You're a journalist?' His interest brightened. He looked as if he had just uncovered an international espionage circle.

'No, a writer. It is very important that I take up the Armenian invitation.'

The young soldier conferred with his colleagues. They decided to let me pass but this only got me on to the narrow Christian Quarter Road. Another barrier blocked my way across it to the western entrance to the Holy Sepulchre Church. No one was allowed. I went through the same arguments with these soldiers but they seemed less pervious to the shower of good reasons that I was able to offer. No permit, no entrance. Just then a young police-woman walked up and asked what was happening. 'Sir,' she explained, 'they cannot let you through this way but if you go that way (here she pointed south along Christian Quarter Road) you can get in by the other entrance.'

Was this kind advice or a means of shovelling a problem on to another colleague? 'But that way is sealed,' I remonstrated.

'Not if you take the first left into Muristan.' So I followed her instructions and found myself in a bright piazza. What a relief it was to feel that at last I was getting close to my objective. But my delight was short-lived. At the end of Muristan Road a scrummage of people, maybe ten deep, was pressed against a barrier. I'd been shunted from one dead end to another.

Approaching the crowd I could see the police at the far end. But how could I get through the crush to negotiate?

'Excuse me, I need to see Security.' It seemed to work. The crowd obligingly swallowed me into its midst. I made progress until I reached the middle, at which point I found myself in a crush that was heaving forward. By now the composition of the crowd had changed from inter-ested tourists to aggressively purposeful Greek grannies. I tried once more to request access to the Security forces.

One of the diminutive ladies turned round with a face like Lucifer. Deftly she stamped her heel on my open-toed sandal and hissed 'Peess off!' I felt like punching her but reason prevailed. Apart from being wrong wasn't I trying to go to church? Before I changed my mind I withdrew.

Nearby a parallel queue made up of tourists wearing identical yellow baseball hats appeared a more attractive proposition. Perhaps they would be more obliging? All being under the care of one 'minder' they were less purposeful, trusting that they would get through in time. They offered no resistance as I manoeuvred to the front. The problem here was that there was no policeman or soldier with whom to negotiate. All that blocked my way was a waist-high pile of garbage sacks. When a policeman appeared I called out to him. Unfortunately he spoke no English. By now this crowd had taken up my cause and started encouraging me to call again. Another policeman came around the corner and it was as if the whole group called him over to speak to me.

'Where is your permit?' There was a leer of triumph in his tone. 'No permit. No entry,' he retorted, walking off.

A small group of Palestinians sitting nearby laughed and encouraged me to write about Israeli stupidity. Of course they were not stupid. I was presenting a compelling case and they were concerned for public safety. Neither were they were being bloody-minded. But I have learned that in both Arab and Israeli culture to give up is to be lost, to persevere is to win. And I wanted to win. Five minutes later the same policeman returned to announce that no more people were to be allowed through. There was no hope of admission. Pointing to the nearby Lutheran Church of the Redeemer he kept saying, 'Go into the church and watch it on TV.'

I thought of Sevak in the church waiting for me to arrive. I had to get in. Was the policeman better humoured than before or was I deluding myself? I explained once more that I couldn't reasonably be expected to watch this on television if I were to write about it and I had been invited. In a stroke of genius with which I am rarely endowed, I flashed one of my business cards in front of the policeman. It did the trick. He was not backing down: I was presenting a new situation.

'Okay, come over.' Easier said than done. It was no joke to climb over the barricade and then wade through squashy bin bags full of waste food and other junk. I slipped and almost fell backwards into a split bag of gunge. But I kept my feet and collected a round of applause from the tourists and Palestinians.

Not wanting to hang around, I hurried to the gate into the church courtyard. Another checkpoint here presented no problems but I was dismayed to find that the yard itself was jammed full of hopefuls wanting to get inside the church. A passageway was being kept free to allow the clergy processions to enter. A young soldier was guarding this. Flashing my business card again I said, 'Guest of the Armenian Patriarchate', and he let me through. In front of me was the great door to the church. Manned by police this was going to be a major hurdle. Just then I noticed a young Armenian deacon so I called out to him.

'Do you know where Sevak is?'

His blank expression made me realise that he didn't speak English.

'Sevak.' I repeated. A light dawned in his face.

'Ah, Sevak!' He beamed and took my arm. Leading me through the great door of Christianity's most holy site I entered the Church of the Holy Sepulchre. We walked between police cordons through crowds to the Tomb of Christ.

There was Sevak. He beamed as I approached. 'Ah, you've come.' It seemed like the understatement of the year. He showed me into the reserved enclosure for the guests of the Armenian Patriarchate. It was just eleven o'clock and the ceremony was scheduled for one.

'I have a lot to do but my friends here will look after you.' With that Sevak bustled off into the sea of people around the Tomb of Christ. His particular friends were two young Armenian women, Nadia and Edis.

Edis was very excited. She was an attractive woman of perhaps thirty. Born in the USSR she had left for California twelve years previously. This was her first visit to Jerusalem and coming to the Holy Fire Ceremony was the fulfilment of a life-long ambition. Her husband was in the enclosure on the opposite side of the aisle. Although they were in communication by means of hand signals it appeared that his prime function was to record the event on video. A subsidiary but important priority also emerged. It was to catch Edis' reactions to events as they unfolded.

On my right a portly lady in her fifties wanted to talk. Ain was an Armenian born in Bethlehem but who had gone to live in Canada thirty-five years previously. She had attended the Armenian Convent School in Jerusalem and this was her first return visit. Already she had met up with school friends with whom she had lost contact all those years ago.

For Ain this was a religious journey but also one of great nostalgia. She was angry that the Israelis and the Muslims were squeezing out the Christians in Jerusalem. 'The Armenians have been in this city for a thousand years. All those who have ruled here have protected us. The Arabs, the Crusaders, the Ottomans, the British. But since Israel took over life has been difficult. In 1967 there were 30,000 Armenians here. Now there are 3,000.'

Ain was a well-presented woman who would be a formidable person to argue against. But as she began to reflect on what had happened to Armenian Jerusalem she became tearful. 'My father was a jeweller here. His was one of many shops but today only his old shop is in business. It is still run by the man who took it over from him.' A touch of resignation came into her voice. 'You know, he never fully paid for it.' This last revelation was not bitter but it reflected the sadness, which had marked her life – and that of so many Armenians and others in the Middle East.

Brought up with the Western view that happiness is almost a human right I find it difficult to cope with the reality of the lives of most of the people in the world. Nevertheless whilst the Christian faith of such people might not give satisfactory answers or reasons for suffering it did give an effective handle for coping with it.

Meanwhile Edis was beginning to bubble with anticipation. Partly out of excitement and partly out of the need to talk she explained the ritual. 'The two Patriarchs – Greek and Armenian – will check that the tomb is empty. Then they will seal it. Once all the people are settled the Greeks will process three times around the tomb. One of the Greek Orthodox priests will put a bundle of candles into that cavity. When it comes out the whole bundle will be alight. It's a miracle!' Across the cordoned passageway we could see the hole out of which the Holy Fire would come. Edis was jumping with excitement as she praised 'the God' for sending Jesus to die for our sins. 'The fire is like the Holy Spirit. The Greeks and Armenians will have their bunch of candles lit at the same time and then someone for each will run with the fire up to the gallery'. Here she pointed up to the chapel at the top of a steep flight of stairs. 'Whoever can reach the gallery first wins the honour of heading the procession next year'.

Now, to me, this sounded like good spectator sport. However I could not fail to recognise that to these women it meant more than that. The Armenians have suffered greatly for their faith and have kept both it and their national identity intact. It was important therefore to try and experience this ceremony subjectively – as if I were an Armenian. We still had an hour to go before the ceremony would begin and I was beginning to feel like the child on the long journey repeatedly asking, 'Are we nearly there?' However I kept my thoughts to myself. We were in church so we couldn't sing 'Ten Green Bottles'!

A slow tapping of poles on the ancient limestone floor of the church heralded the arrival of the Coptic Orthodox procession. Neither the Copts nor the Syriac Orthodox have any official place in the Church of the Holy Sepulchre but small chapels are granted to them within the gift of the Armenians. The Copts have a shrine at the rear of the Tomb of Christ and it was to this grotto that the procession slowly made its way. As it passed by, the Israeli police tried to weed out those who were sneaking in with the Copts. This resulted in some strong-armed and rather unseemly tactics. More than once a Coptic monk came back to tug someone free from police control. A large dignified lady was frog-marched away from her husband and family. In despair she wept, as the policeman had to use his full strength. 'Abuna' (Father) she wailed to the monk. He rushed over and persuaded the policeman to let her go. Then the monk, arm around the still-shaken lady, led her back to her family. We all applauded.

Meanwhile the main doors of the church opened again and what seemed for all the world like football chants echoed around the building. This was the entrance of the Syriac Orthodox, known locally as 'the Syrians'. Not having a place of their own by right it seemed as if these people were going to storm the building. The Syriac clergy came first, just a handful. In front of them a pole with two brass horns was held aloft. But they were pushed and shoved along by a crowd of big young men. They all wore white T-shirts proclaiming them to be Syriac Orthodox Scouts. A few of these men were carried at shoulder height, acting as cheer-leaders. As the full procession entered the building the chanting intensified. I was told that they were shouting words to the effect that the Syrians had the one true light. Shouting, ululating, and a regular frenetic beating of drums swelled the noise to a fearful din.

As they forced their way past us, just the other side of the cordon, the police stood back to watch. The human tide surged up the passageway until it stuck. Of course the strong men had forced their way in, followed by families and children. It was these softer targets that provided easier pickings for the police, who then weighed in to remove them. One teenage girl was separated from her family and started to struggle to get to the other side of the police but they grabbed her and pushed her back. She became hysterical, screaming, shouting, and kicking. An Israeli policewoman caught her flailing arms in the face and that was it. The policemen piled in and the girl was physically hurled in the opposite direction to that of her parents.

It was terrible to have to watch this from the comparative safety of the other side of the barricades. The police had warned us that, at times of surges, we would have to push back on the barriers because if they gave way there would be serious injury. So, instead of objecting to brutality, we were more concerned with preserving our bit of sanity. It was lamentable.

Gradually calm was restored and we could all breathe easily again. I noticed that Edis was on her knees praying for peace in the church. Tears flowed down her face as she explained to me that sometimes the Syrians 'have stabbed people'. It was more like a football crowd than I had thought! In this period of peace one of Edis' prayers was answered. The Syriac teenager was allowed to rejoin her parents. Visibly shaken by her experience she walked back along the cordons to an emotional reunion.

That all this should be happening in what is arguably Christianity's most holy sight was inconceivable. Just listening to the noise was almost indescribable. There was the buzz of general anticipation; there was the 'laddish' behaviour of the Syriac men; there was the screaming and shouting from people fighting the police. And through all this came the incessant tapping from the ceremonial Ottoman-style guards as they processed the official lines of clergy to their allotted places.

The Armenians arrived next. Following their guards they sang in their unmistakably rich deep harmonies. They processed to the door of the tomb where the Armenian Patriarch, now with the Greek Patriarch, ensured that the tomb was both empty and sealed. The ceremony was about to begin.

With their actions frozen in mid-air the Patriarchs stopped as another rush of Syrians pushed its way into the church. Screaming, shouting and banging their drums, they pushed the police to one side. Edis was crying now as her hopes and dreams for this magical moment seemed dashed. The Fire should have been released but with the central aisle blocked by Syrians the Greek Orthodox procession was unable to commence its three circumnavigations of the Tomb. Gradually the Israeli police cleared a passageway so that a flotilla of banners might begin to sail around the far side of the Tomb. The procession had commenced.

By the time it reached us the procession was making intermittent progress. Each banner had a religious image woven on it. Tassels hung below. The flag bearers allowed the tassels to swing over the crowds behind the crush barriers so that those who were able might either touch or kiss them. Others would lift up their bundles of unlit candles to touch the tassels.

Behind the swaying banners were two groups of men, each chanting with great gusto. A very serious cantor walking backwards led the first group. Every time the banner-carriers stopped in front of him he crashed into them. This was the source of great mirth amongst the old men he was supposed to be conducting. Profusely perspiring and dressed in their best suits they were clearly enjoying every moment. It did not matter to them – or us – that they kept making mistakes. When that happened they just laughed and started again. As they bumbled their way past, their place was taken by another group of men. These were priests, again led by a cantor walking backwards. They seemed much more serious than the old men who had preceded them. But they looked just as hot.

Behind these chanting priests came a disorganised group of older clergy. Perhaps they were bishops. Wearing white capes, they seemed totally uninspired by the occasion. Chatting to one another as they shuffled past it looked for all the world as if they were ambling home for tea. The whole procession would lurch forward and then stop inexplicably. But this gave an opportunity to see the top of the bill: the Greek Patriarch carried aloft on a throne. Four giant men wearing traditional Greek costumes, mini-skirts, leggings and fancy hats surrounded him. The Israeli police stood back, arms folded, and stared at the huge men. Their expressions told all as their eyes ran up and down these magnificent specimens of manhood dressed in what some might think of as rather feminine attire.

The Patriarch looked very frail. He was dressed in white and wore an enormous gold crown. In fact with his white beard he looked more like a sickly Santa Claus. I hoped that he would survive the ordeal because not only was it getting extremely warm but also people were lunging forward to kiss his hand. At any moment he might have been catapulted out of the throne, such was the clamouring attention he was receiving from the crowds. This procedure was repeated twice but this time without the Patriarch. After the third time around the Tomb the banners and singers stayed near its entrance. The policemen started to reconfigure the barricades so that the two runners might have an uninterrupted passageway to the gallery.

Tension was mounting. After hours of waiting we had arrived at the moment for the Holy Fire. Edis squealed with excitement, slightly jumping up and down with anticipation. A priest stood next to the hatchway into the tomb ready to put his bunch of unlit candles into the dark hole. Behind the Tomb, the Syrians had just started warming up for another round of rebel rousing when, quick as lightning, the man pushed his candles into the orifice. He stretched as far as he could and then brought out a flaming torch made of the candles.

The two runners lit their candles from the original bunch and the race was on. Cheers, screams, and yells of encouragement accompanied the racing men as they shot across the church and up the steep marble staircase to the Armenian chapel on the gallery. Then the Armenian Patriarch appeared on the balcony with a bunch of flaming candles held aloft. The Armenians had won!

The screeching and wild enthusiasm that followed would have done justice to any football terrace. Edis' face was streaming with tears. She was so happy. Bells now started to ring loudly inside the church. Their syncopated rhythm clanged over the noise of excited people as the fire was now passed from candle to candle. Within seconds massive fires were blazing. Some people had brought immense bundles of candles douched in petrol.

The heat and smoke rushed upwards into the dome and out through a ventilator. This was so sudden that it caused a strong compensatory draught to rush in from all quarters of the church. 'Feel the Holy Spirit!' shouted Edis as the draught became a gale dislodging two pigeons from their roost in the dome above our heads. They flapped and circled around in the smoke. Another sign of the Holy Spirit, considered Edis.

Meanwhile back on the ground the Israeli police had produced aerosol fire extinguishers. Where a bunch of candles was deemed to be burning too vigorously, where a woman's hair was alight, and where candles were considered to have been alight long enough, the police would appear to leap across the crowds to extinguish the blaze. Order of sorts was restored once all the candles had been put out. Now it was time for the Armenians to parade around the Tomb. I was delighted to see my friend Sevak carrying the main banner right behind the Patriarch. Three times they processed round the great symbol of Resurrection, their unmistakable harmonies rising and falling as they sang praises to God. Each time they passed, a group of Egyptians and Syrians would cut loose and try and follow them in the direction of the door out of the building.

And then it was all over. The Armenians had 'won the cup' in this Millennium year, a week after the commemoration of the eighty fifth anniversary of the Armenian Holocaust at the hands of the Turks. It took on an extra poignancy.

I bade farewell to Edis and her husband, and thanked Sevak for all his help. They were going to a thanksgiving service on the gallery but I really could not take any more. It was already three o'clock and I felt a great need for space and fresh air.

How did this kind of activity square up with the Gospel? At times it hardly seemed to have dignity. The behaviour of the crowds, the jostling, the fights; all could be considered unseemly. Yet once the procession had begun it had a dignity of its own. From the Orthodox perspective, the Liturgy is offered to God and only God. It goes on whether there are no lay worshippers or thousands. This ceremony was similar. It could hardly be described as 'user-friendly' but was immensely moving. It was not for me to judge the hearts of those who attended but I came away feeling that in the midst of the chaos of that afternoon there had been a general recognition that Christ was risen from the dead and that the Holy Spirit was moving in the chaos of life. I prayed that it might be so for the people of this heavily disputed land.

CHAPTER TEN

CEDAR'S STORY

When the Israelis took East Jerusalem in 1967, they quickly set about unifying the city under one administration. There was to be no going back. Many houses were evacuated and demolished, and the former border was flattened under a new dual carriageway connecting West Jerusalem with the settlements planted in the disputed Arab East Jerusalem. In recent years a plethora of multinational hotels has sprung up on land adjacent to the road but a few old houses have survived. One is occupied by Sabeel, an ecumenical Christian movement that tries to make practical sense of faith issues for Palestinian Christians by helping them to act for justice within a framework of Christian belief. They call it liberation theology.

It was with some apprehension that I climbed the steep steps outside the old Mandate-era house. Would this be a hotbed of anger against the Israelis? Would it be difficult for me in that the British were clearly instrumental in the origins of the present difficulties? I need have had no fears. From the moment I walked in and was given fresh water to refresh myself, to the moment I left, it seemed as if I was being bathed in love. These people had cause to be bitter but found that the Gospel of Jesus Christ helped them to overcome this. Cedar Duaybis was typical, but not exceptional, as an example of this.

Cedar was a comfortable maternal lady in her mid-sixties. A Palestinian clergy widow she has had more than her share of suffering but when I met her she was struggling with the idea of giving an interview. 'Why me?' she would enquire repeatedly, needing reassurance that I wasn't going to misuse her story. 'My story is no better or worse than thousands of other Palestinians. I'm no one special'.

I tried to convince her that whilst many might have shared the events she had suffered, her friends had suggested that the way she had attempted to resolve the dilemmas was worth hearing. On condition that I emphasised that her experience was not unique and that I would not use the story to sensationalise the truth, she agreed to talk.

Taking a deep breath and looking at the floor she launched in. 'It began in 1948 when I was twelve years old. We were living in a mixed middle class community in Haifa. Our neighbours were Palestinians – both Arabs and Jews. The Arabs were a mix of Christians and Muslims and the Jews were people who had lived in the land for many years unlike the recently arrived Jewish refugees from Europe.

'Our family was Anglican. My parents and grandparents had been educated in mission schools and were practising Christians. We read the Old and New Testaments without any problem. The Chosen People were the Israelites and we didn't really connect them with our Jewish friends and neighbours.

'We lived in a house owned by my grandfather on a hillside. It was a good neighbourhood. Life was, as they say, 'normal'. Even in 1948, when tension began to grow, life for us carried on as usual. I still went to the Sisters of Nazareth Roman Catholic School. We felt safe in our nice neighbourhood.

'In April that year things took a turn for the worse. Fighting in Haifa between the Jewish Underground (the Haganah) and the Palestinian Arabs intensified. Shootings happened in our street and I remember bullets coming through the windows.

'We lived on a steep hill and one day some Jewish terrorists rolled a barrel of dynamite down the street. It blew up and demolished the house next to ours. Life was changing very quickly and it was more dangerous every day.

'My father worked for the British Mandate as an Income Tax Inspector. His job was considered critical but he felt that the rest of the family should move to safety. After the Deir Yassin massacre we became very frightened. My mother was already in Nazareth, in the Galilee, with my younger sister in a small house we owned there. So my father, who by now did not have a car any more, arranged for my brother and I to go to join them. He paid the driver of a vegetable truck to take us. We had to lie face down in the back with vegetables all around us. As we drove along we could hear shootings. I dread to think what would have happened to us if we had fallen into the wrong hands.'

Cedar breathed a deep sigh. She looked at me with pleading eyes and explained, 'Of course we didn't know what the Jewish plans were. It's easy to see it now. But we thought that in Nazareth we would be safe. Getting there, we thought, was the end of the nightmare. But it had only just begun.

'We had no way of knowing what was happening in Haifa. Especially we wanted news of my father and grandparents. As the weeks passed we began to fear the worst. Then on the final day of the British Mandate, May 14th 1948, my father appeared in Nazareth. It was like the resurrection. We were overjoyed but could hardly believe it.

'He explained that as the British pulled out they provided boats to evacuate Palestinians to Lebanon. They said that it would be for two or three weeks until the fighting was over. My father, my grandparents and eighty percent of the Palestinian Arabs of Haifa went to Lebanon. But my father didn't stay there. From Tyre he came overland to Nazareth.

'All the Arabs who had lived in our neighbourhood went to Lebanon. It was all so sudden. In some houses tables were set for meals, in others the bath water was left running, whilst in another the iron was left plugged in.

'As the summer advanced we realised that this was not a short absence from our home. The Jews were sending Palestinians to the Galilee. The final day of British rule was the day that the State of Israel was declared. A truce was established and armistice lines drawn up. The borders were arbitrary; just where the fighting stopped. And Nazareth was in Israel although, at that time, it had not surrendered.

'The Zionists surrounded our city and gave an ultimatum to the people to surrender or suffer the consequences. The mayor and an Anglican priest tied a bed sheet round a broomstick and the city gave in. We cowered in a corner of the room as tanks rolled down the street.

'From then on we were strangers in a familiar land. We realised that this was not a short war after which everything would return to normal. We were now called Israeli Arabs. The Present-Absent People,' She said this last phrase with a wince. I asked her what she meant. 'We were present in that we were there, but we were absent from our real homes. Our homes were lost to us. We were treated as if we weren't human beings. The Israelis saw us as unwanted strangers. From now on we lived under military rule. It seemed as if we had to get a permit for anything, especially if we wanted to travel anywhere beyond the Galilee. We certainly couldn't get home to Haifa. And that military rule was to last for the next sixteen years.

'All this time the Christians in the West were rejoicing. They said that Biblical prophecies were being fulfilled. But this caused a great problem of faith for the Arab Christian. We read in the Bible of the Chosen People of God, the Israelites. Until then we had not connected them with the Israelis who were brutalising us. Mother would get distressed. She would say that if this really was God's will then we had better go along with it. But Father would say that our God of the New Testament was not a God of Injustice. How could we accept that the Jews were promised the land at our expense? From then on as Christians we started to reject the Old Testament. Many Palestinians stopped going to church around that time.

'As a Christian community we had no way of dealing with this big theological problem. The Bible became our enemy, the source of our troubles. When it was most needed it seemed as if our faith was useless. For me it seemed as if I were in a desert without direction, neither believing nor disbelieving. I wanted to remain a Palestinian Christian but I felt empty. There was no firm ground and my parents were rootless too so there was no comfort from them.

'For a while I tried to regain my identity, my culture, by being a Palestinian. I pushed my Christianity to the background. But it didn't help. I was living a lie. Then I tried to find my faith again and forget that I was also Palestinian. That didn't work either. I am a Palestinian Christian. I am who I am and I must never forget it.

'Meanwhile I got married to Khalin, an Anglican minister in Nazareth. But my problems of faith got worse. Not just for me but for the congregation and especially for the children. I taught in Elementary School. I taught in Sunday School. And I had my own children. Our daily problems continued. Every day we had to queue for permits for this, permits for that. But on the tenth anniversary of the Israeli takeover the military governor said we could go anywhere for the day without a permit, as long as we were back by sundown.'

Cedar had been reliving so much that she went to get a drink of water. I heard her chatting a little with a friend outside before she returned. She had regrouped and was ready for the next part of the story.

'We used the day to visit Haifa. Our home was still there and we were admitted into it. Every room had a European Jewish family living in it. You might find it hard to believe but we actually felt sorry for them. They were miserable. But why was their problem solved by putting it on us? My husband was a Jordanian national. He came to Palestine because, as a priest, he saw there was great need. He came on a two-year contract and stayed for the rest of his life. So when the Church moved him to Haifa, to the St Luke's Compound, it seemed to him a great opportunity for service but I was still anxious.

'It was strange moving back to Haifa. Our old church of St John's had been built in the early twentieth century to seat a thousand worshippers. When we went to St Luke's we noticed that at St John's there were only twelve members left. At that time Khalin was the only Anglican pastor serving in the whole of Israel. He had to travel to serve the Anglican communities. Although he always had to get a permit, it remained a very tense time.

'Soon after we arrived in Haifa the 1967 War began. Our neighbours were Syrian Jewish refugees and I had made friends with some of them. Unlike the European Jews they spoke Arabic, ate the same food as us, and generally we understood one another. One particular friend was very worried as her conscripted son was sent to the Egyptian Front to fight. I prayed with her for his return. You see she was my neighbour rather than my enemy. The boy did return and we rejoiced together. Of course we had lost the War but my neighbour had come home. Always we are torn between human feelings and politics. When you are stripped to bare humanity, politics don't matter. We were human beings sharing a difficulty'.

I expressed amazement that in spite of all the anger there could be these moments. They remind us that the human soul can rise above the bestial tendencies of war. Cedar smiled politely. I had interrupted her flow.

'But then the Church needed someone to go to Nablus in the Occupied West Bank. It was as if we were back to Square One. By moving there we were stripped of Israeli citizenship. Although we had been second-class citizens we did have certain rights as Israelis. Now this was lost. We were Palestinians living under military rule again. All our meagre rights were taken away. I couldn't even go back to Nazareth to visit my family. I still had my parents, two sisters and my brother living there.

'Of course, once again, there were inconsistencies. As Arabs we lost our citizenship for moving to the West Bank, but Israeli Jews who settled in the West Bank did not lose their citizenship.

'You know, Nablus was a brutal city. By now we had four children and we were under curfew more often than not. Our church was in the Old City and for days on end we would be holed up there. Every four days the Israelis would allow us out to buy food but when there was a curfew the shops hadn't been stocked so there was very little to buy.

'I can't think that we ever had one church service that wasn't affected by the curfews. Sometimes people couldn't get from where they lived to church. Sometimes they couldn't get home. Some curfews were very localised. They used the loudspeakers in the mosques to announce the latest curfews and people would run away to get home as soon as possible. Sometimes soldiers would run into school to chase four and five year olds. All the children saw killings. There was never an ordinary day. If the Palestinian flag was flown or if there was a demonstration there would be shootings by the Israelis. My neighbours were killed. My neighbour's teenage daughter was killed right in front of me.'

The story was becoming very intense for both of us. Cedar was clearly becoming distressed and tears were flowing. Should we terminate the interview? However Cedar said that she needed to complete her story, having begun. She composed herself and continued.

'The Nablus nightmare continued. One day the Israelis stormed the school in which my nine-year-old daughter was a pupil. A soldier got hold of her and, although she was released, she was tongue-tied. I never knew that this could be a real condition but she was so petrified by the experience that she was unable to speak for three days.'

Hearing stories of daily brutality exercised on children, of schools being invaded, of daily beatings of teenagers, I thought back to my own recent visit to Nablus. The people in their teens and twenties who had been so welcoming to me must have included some of these brutalised children. Thinking of the recognised need for trauma counselling after war or disaster I wondered how these people had dealt with these issues. They had presumably buried their horrific memories in the hope that things might improve. But I was left wondering about what would happen if conditions did not improve or even deteriorated.

Cedar continued. 'Life at home was getting tense too. Khalin had brought us from the comparative safety of Israel at Haifa because he was convinced that only he could do the job at Nablus. He was right. But at what cost to our children?' She choked and tears filled her eyes again. A moment later she continued, falteringly. 'Khalin would say that although we experienced brutality we must love our enemies; we must turn the other cheek. This lies at the heart of the Gospel of Christ.

'But our children rejected it. Like all their friends they were becoming more and more political. How could the

Christian message have any effect? In a way they were right but I was loyal to Khalin. But then there was Salim.' At this point tears flowed and I waited silently feeling the tension of the moment. She struggled on, 'Salim was, he is, our youngest son. His way of coping was not to join in the fights. It was to try and be where the action was in the hope that a stray bullet might kill him. Our lovely baby boy only wanted to die. And nothing we could do or say could give him any hope.

'It was January 6th and Salim had to take an important exam. He was now 17 and the exams were on the other side of the city. But a serious curfew was declared. Anyone breaking it would be shot on sight. He decided that he would go to that exam and that if he died as a result of breaking the curfew then his problems would be over. I can see it now. It was raining. Salim came to say goodbye before eight o'clock, and then he jumped over the high wall at the back of our house. As he sneaked away down the narrow alleyways I thought that this would be the last I would see of him.

'Just then the phone rang. One of our church people had died. You know round here we have to bury our dead very quickly. Khalin had to take the funeral. So at the age of 60 he said he would also break the curfew. That meant he had to jump the wall and sneak across town. I was totally alone – my other children were away at Berzeit University. I'd seen both my men risking death by jumping the wall. I was very frightened and wondered if I would ever see them again.'

She looked wistful. The awful memories were in flood and she could not stop them now.

'Then I heard army boots coming upstairs to my front door. The Israeli army was searching every house following the stabbing of a soldier. Whilst they were at my neighbour's house I quickly made the beds. I was going to lie and say that I lived alone. Otherwise they would know that Khalin and Salim were absent during the curfew. But when the soldier came to search my house he wiped his boots before entering. I melted because I realised that here was a young man who had been taught to respect people and property. In an instant I decided I would trust this man. I asked him to be patient and he seemed to soften. He asked the others to stand in the entrance whilst he searched my home. Then I told him about what had happened. He decided to search the house himself. He was so careful. So often these soldiers, they wreck everything. When this one found Khalin's desk was locked, He asked for the key. Others would have smashed the lock. He looked at everything and then put things carefully back in their correct places. In Salim's room was a collection of used rubber bullets and spent tear gas canisters. These were harmless but illegal. The soldier never touched anything. He then said that this must not happen again and left.

'That evening Salim returned. He had been caught by the soldiers and badly beaten. His clothes were torn. When he entered our home he collapsed in tears. Outside we could hear the screams of other young boys being beaten, their heads being banged. You know, Salim was a tall boy, six foot two, but for days he would not go outside. He felt totally humiliated. He said that when he was seen by the troops it was only remembering his mother and father just in time that prevented him from provoking the soldiers to shoot.

'Later that night Khalim returned. He had succeeded in reaching the mourners and had stayed with them until it was safe to return. In the weeks that followed we tried to rebuild Salim. His school friends responded to being brutalised by resorting to further violence. But we talked with him and prayed for him. It was always about the need to respect human dignity, human rights. We pleaded with him not to respond by being less than human.'

It was as if she had surmounted a difficult obstacle. Cedar suddenly became less tense. She caught me with an imploring gaze. 'At times like these how do you encourage young people to hold on to faith?' she asked.

'In our case the answer to our prayers came in the shape of a Christian woman who visited us from the United States. She was here to make a film about the troubles. When she saw what a mess Salim was in she offered to arrange for her church in America to sponsor him to go there. He went and was slowly rehabilitated.

'Salim now has a Green Card in the USA. Soon he will be granted citizenship. He is settled there for good now and is engaged to a lovely girl. He is very tolerant and seems to have no bitterness. He even has Jewish friends where he lives in Los Angeles. But he won't talk about the past. This is a closed area of his life.'

I asked about Salim's faith. Had it strengthened or reduced as a result of his experiences? In what was the only time I felt that Cedar sidestepped the discussion, she looked rueful and said, 'He has faith but does not go to church.'

Rapidly getting back on course, Cedar wanted to emphasise again that her story was not special. 'All the children of Nablus could tell similar stories,' she said. 'But I want to say that it is when we face people as human beings that we begin to win through. Like I found with the soldier. Like I found with my Jewish neighbour in Haifa.'

'In 1986 we moved to Ramallah. The Intifada began in 1987. It was another terrible time for all of us. But my Christian faith had helped in Nablus and I believed that it would again. It was then that I discovered Liberation Theology: that there were practical ways that Christians could respond to injustice. This encouraged us to stand for justice. To resist but without resorting to violence. I felt called in a new way to serve the cause of all people but from a Christian motivation.

'Now I felt whole again. I was one person not two. The everyday Cedar and the spiritual Cedar were united for the first time in years. I learned from practical experience that God is on the side of those who seek justice, love and mercy, because these are His nature.

'Times remained difficult. Khalim was shot in Ramallah during the Intifada. He was hit by a rubber bullet and, although he was injured, he recovered. In 1988 he was arrested for ringing the church bells. Our home was searched three times during those years. Khalim died a few years ago from a heart attack but I feel that, with my faith in Jesus, I am able to carry on his work in some way.

'My eldest son, Ibrahim now lives in Canada and I believe that all my children have held on to their Christian faith. We have inspiration and hope in Jesus Christ. Without it I couldn't continue working here for justice and peace – for Israelis too. I have learned to forgive. I can honestly say that I feel no bitterness'.

The meeting was over. Cedar had exposed a great deal of herself and her inner feelings. She had been very reticent about sharing in the first place and I expressed hope that she didn't regret doing this. She gave me a hug, then she said, 'Jews and Arabs can live together. I am grateful for this revelation as a result of meeting Jewish people. We must work and pray for justice and peace for everyone'.

CHAPTER ELEVEN

PALESTINIAN ENCOUNTERS

As if claiming its birthright, the dawn was spreading its way across the little houses in Beit Jala on the hill opposite Bethlehem. Under the steel grey of the dust clouds that hovered menacingly I shivered as I waited in the street for George. I had been kindly offered a lift to Nazareth by a family of Palestinian Christians. They were going for family reasons but it gave me an opportunity to visit the town famed as the boyhood home of Jesus. The chilly air had managed to induce shivers before George's Mercedes minibus swept up to the gate. Collecting other family members in Beit Jala, I was intrigued that George took a back lane to join the new road built to connect Hebron with Jerusalem. That way we avoided going through the checkpoint. Even at this time of the morning, the suburbs of Israeli West Jerusalem were awakening. Although this was the Passover, and therefore many Israelis would not be working, the traffic was building up.

My travelling companions, George and his three sisters, Marlene, Judith and Hilda, were anxious. It appeared that they were going to Nazareth to sort out a matrimonial breakdown. It was not for me to pursue this but I was able to discover something that was a revelation to me. As we drove along the fast road towards Tel Aviv I learned that all four were part of the Palestinian Diaspora. In fact they had been born in Venezuela. They had returned to the land of their parents because of their Christian conviction that they had a ministry to their fellow Palestinians. They found their Venezuelan passports very useful in that this helped them to escape many of the difficulties faced by their compatriots. This was clearly the reason they had been able to avoid the Israeli checkpoint outside Bethlehem. But they were part of a Pentecostal church that believed in the Jews' return to the Holy Land as being the fulfilment of prophecy. That must be very difficult if you belong to the racial group who are being violated. I could imagine it would have been like a black person in apartheid-era South Africa upholding white supremacy.

George was pastor of a church in Jerusalem. He said that the tensions between Arab and Jew were inevitable but that it was important to find ways of reconciling them. Winning them for Christ was the only way to achieve this. His church, apparently, had an effective ministry with both Arab Christians and Messianic Jews in the congregation. Although there were inevitable tensions, he said that the benefits of cross-cultural faith sharing were huge. I asked whether the Jewish believers ever took up the human rights issues on behalf of the Palestinians. George shrugged his shoulders and kept his eyes steadfastly on the road ahead.

Nazareth was slowly coming to life as George dropped me on Paul VI Street. An Arab town in Israel it has seen a large influx of Jewish people since it fell to the Israelis half a century ago. The Arabs in Nazareth are thus Israeli citizens although the evidence would suggest that many feel second-class. For example, they may not visit the West Bank or Gaza (Palestinian areas) and if they choose to go and live in these areas they must surrender their Israeli citizenship. It was pointed out frequently that, far from losing citizenship, Israeli Jews are given financial incentives to live in the 'settlements' in the West Bank. It also seemed to be the case that Israeli Arabs are despised by some Palestinians for not rising up against the state of Israel. Within that group it seemed that Arab Christians who are Israeli citizens are considered the worst of all by the Palestinians.

With these thoughts I walked to the large Roman Catholic basilica. Built as recently as 1969 on the site of various older churches, its claim is to be on the site of the annunciation. This then was reputed to be the place where the angel Gabriel appeared to the Virgin Mary and announced that she would conceive the one who was to be Christ the Lord. The stark concrete of the exterior did not prepare me for the beauty of the interior. From the ground floor it was possible to descend a few steps and peer into a grotto where the annunciation was believed to have happened. But just as I arrived at the steps I was asked to wait whilst a group of Greek grannies went down. Were they the same ones I had run into at St Catherine's monastery? Were they the ones who had tried to block my way to the Holy Sepulchre? Whoever they were, they were unruly. Despite warnings about the need to be silent, this crowd acted as if they were at the funfair. Fighting one another for a peep through the railings to see what was, after all, only a stone altar, the grannies made a racket that echoed around the great basilica. Something had to break. With the speed of an express train a Franciscan friar rushed into the midst of the grannies and, clapping his hands and making a 'whoosh' noise, he hoped to calm things down. But he was totally ignored. The babble of excited voices and the popping of flashguns continued. The Franciscan shouted and gesticulated but the grannies only stopped their excited chatter once they had ascended the steps back into the church.

The second level in the church was used for services, and mass was under way as I approached. This time the grannies were excluded by an iron railing and seemed subdued. The service was being conducted in the round in front of the beautiful east window. All around were artistic representations, many as sculptures or bas-relief carvings, of the Madonna and child. Each represented a gift from a different country. It clearly expressed the universality of the Church. One, which I found particularly puzzling, was a case containing two large dolls in Chinese costume. The gift of the Republic of China (Taiwan) it was simply labelled 'Queen of China'. This left me with a number of questions but I could imagine the misunderstanding this could lead to in neighbouring China.

Behind the basilica is the smaller church of St Joseph. I have always felt an empathy with Joseph. He clearly had a great deal to accept. In the days when illegitimate children were not common, and when Joseph knew he was not the father, he had every reason to ditch his betrothed. The fact that he did not speaks volumes about the man. Of course, we understand that he heard from the angel Gabriel too, but all the same I think most men would have acted differently. Joseph clearly loved his Mary. The church honouring him was built over a grotto, which is reputed to have been Joseph's carpentry workshop. It is first century and I don't suppose that in those days there would have been many carpenters. So it probably is the one. Unfortunately it was stuffed full of Greek grannies! This time they were in the middle of saying their prayers so there was no way I could push through. Cutting my losses, I decided to get ahead of them.

To someone who can find the complexity of Christian denominations in the West confusing, the churches in the Holy Land can be mind blowing. Having left the church of St Joseph, under the stewardship of the Roman Catholics, I was confronted by a church-synagogue, the Christian part of which was administered by the Greek Catholics! Of course I had already come across the Armenian Catholics in Jerusalem so Greek Catholics were easy to compre-hend. They were people who had forsaken the oversight of the Greek Orthodox Patriarch in favour of Rome. In return they retained their Greek styles of worship but entered a world that seemed much more financially viable. The division of the historic Orthodox Church into splinter groups is something that has gone on since the early days of the church. Indeed it is an issue in the Acts of the Apostles. But there is a great sense of injustice felt by the 'classic' Orthodox against the activities of the 'Latins'. Much of this controversy goes back to the Crusades when Western rulers heeded the call of Popes in Rome to regain the Holy Land for Christendom. The trouble was that the Western invaders, often with naked commercial and military plans, did little to differentiate between Arab Christians (Orthodox) and Muslims. Later, when Roman Catholic missionaries came to convert the people of the area, there was a practice of financial carrots being offered. Thus the Greek Catholic churches appear to be affluent when compared to the Greek Orthodox.

The church-synagogue in Nazareth is a sort of semi-detached affair. The church is very much in the style of Rome rather than the East. Pews made of highly polished light coloured wood, Italianate pictures of the Virgin and child, and a generally bright ambience all spoke of Rome. But the altar was hidden behind a screen in the Orthodox tradition. It was a real hybrid but even more so when presented with the synagogue. It is suggested that this synagogue was the local one for Jesus when he was a boy. The argument is that its survival after centuries of being abandoned as an active worshipping centre for Jews, and its proximity to the Greek Catholic church must point to this. Now, I am no expert, but the synagogue seemed too well presented, too modern. But I may be wrong.

There are other places in Nazareth to visit if looking for spiritual inspiration. Further up the street I found a recently modernised piazza in front of the Greek Orthodox church of St Gabriel. To one side of the rather bleak square, whilst I munched some sandwiches, I noticed what appeared to be another grotto. Ambling over I found that it was a well, dried up, partially filled with Coke cans and covered with graffiti. This was Mary's Well. But had I not just seen the place where the angel appeared to Mary? It seems that there are two places where one event was supposed to have happened – and this was the Orthodox version. Walking across to St Gabriel's Church I was prepared for a re-run of what I had seen in the basilica. But it was very different. An old church, built to much smaller proportions that the Roman Catholic basilica, the entrance was thronged with pilgrims. Entering the doorway I walked down a few steps into a dark nave festooned with lots of brilliantly lit chandeliers. Priests and deacons were singing the Liturgy in fine voice. Cutting them off from the congregation was a heaving mass of sweaty humanity shoving its way at right angles across the church. On the far side of the church, the object of all this pushing was a grotto with a spring. At the front of the scrum was a group of my favourite Greek grannies. But they had improved their technique since I had last encountered them. This time the experience was interactive. They wanted to drink, to wash, or to fill plastic bottles and to do that they had to get to the front. The sight of these venerable women fighting one another and other hapless bystanders was terrible. I have seen pictures of American mothers fighting one another for the latest gimmick toys during the days leading up to Christmas, but this seemed even more shocking because the women were old and because this was supposed to be a holy site.

I withdrew and sat on a pew to the side of the altar. The old priest was ladling out the bread and wine to the few communicants, almost impervious to the noise all around him. Then he covered the chalice with a cloth, lifted it victoriously, and withdrew behind the screen. The mystery had been performed. As the deacon began another round of chanting I took my opportunity to leave. Behind me I had been conscious of someone who had sounded as if he were another worshipper. Turning around I found it to be a Jewish tour guide counting his money.

Of course, the Christians are not the only people in the area who have a high view of Jesus. Muslims too revere him as a Prophet. It is therefore natural that they should want a slice of the pilgrim opportunities that Nazareth can offer. For many years they have maintained a small mosque down the street from the Roman Catholic basilica. However, prior to my visit, tensions had run high over proposals to build a huge mosque on the main street blocking out the views and physical domination of the basilica. The Israeli authorities had granted planning permission and so, in one act, managed to divide the Arab population. Cynics argued that this was a classic case of divide and rule because they must have anticipated the demonstrations, the interfaith reaction, and the international concern that would be unleashed. But at least it drew the attention away from the Israelis so, for them, it was a clever move.

To be frank, I was pretty nauseated by the religious sites in Nazareth. The behaviour of the Greek grannies, the Muslim-Christian controversy, the dual claims of authenticity, all conspired to make me weary of my search for authentic spirituality in the home town of Jesus. I had begun my visit early and by now it was mid-day. I was thinking about returning to Bethlehem when I remembered a comment from my friend, Naim Ateek. He had suggested that I should visit the Nazareth Village Project. As a heavyweight in the ranks of Palestinian theologians I imagined that this would be an academic venture. After some initial difficulty in locating the Project, as it had not yet opened to the public, I was relieved to be welcomed by a member of the board. He explained that the idea was to recreate a small village in the style of first century Nazareth. With help from Jewish and Palestinian academics as well as international support, they were concerned that pilgrims and tourists should be given a taste of what life was like when Jesus lived in Nazareth, and that this would naturally enliven their understanding of the Bible. Authentic houses were being constructed with painstaking detail. Plans were in hand to demonstrate everything from sowing seeds to bread making, with parts of the village devoted to indigenous flora and fauna. But it was the cross that was so moving. Showing the usual method of Roman execution it was easy to see why the legs of the prisoner were usually broken after some time on the cross. This made him collapse, causing massive constriction on the lungs and suffocation. In the account of Jesus' death in the Bible the soldiers did not break his legs, as he was already dead.

I had encountered disillusionment that morning. But the sight of this awful instrument of torture and death was strangely uplifting. Whilst people were welcome to fight over holy water, or which site was more authentic, the memory of the empty cross touched base with my spiritual heart. As I left the Nazareth Village Project I could not help but wonder how a modern interactive experience would survive in a climate of fear and mistrust. The fact that Palestinian Christians had put this together, gaining the respect and support from some of the top Hebrew academics in Israel, was hugely encouraging but open to all sorts of misinterpretation in a land that appears to thrive on a ghetto culture.

By now it was early afternoon. A quick phone call to George told me that he would not be returning before the evening. I had been long enough in Nazareth and the thoughts of another six hours or more was too much. Simple, it seemed. I would travel by an Israeli bus to Tel Aviv in order to catch the express bus to Jerusalem. Nothing is ever that simple in that part of the world. What I had overlooked was that this was the beginning of the Jewish Passover and that the buses were off the road. But then there was the alternative of travelling down the spine of the West Bank, in the Palestinian Territories, through Jenin, Nablus and Ramallah. On all my previous visits to the area I had been advised not to travel in this area, as it was too volatile. But this was now the only option. So began a slow journey, by servees taxi and bus, but one which was to be most enlightening. The servees taxi was a large Mercedes limousine and once it had filled up, it took me as far as Jenin for a fixed price. Wedged in next to a middle aged Palestinian, I found that he was very talkative and wanted me to know how wonderful he thought the British to be. As the taxi roared along the road out of Nazareth, we came to the border with the Palestinian Territories. On the Palestinian side of this border the sides of the road were alive with market traders and small businesses set up under the trees. I must have looked surprised because my new friend laughed. 'This is our Palestinian economy,' he chuckled. 'Israelis drive out from Tel Aviv to shop here, to have their cars serviced, and to relax. It is so cheap for them and it is a good income for us.'

After years of conflict it was not surprising that Jenin, the terminus for our taxi, was very run down in appearance. Although it had been given grants by a number of European governments I wondered what it would have looked like without them. The streets were full of young men, and my Palestinian friend judged that it might be safer if he conducted me the few blocks to where the next taxi was waiting. On the way he pointed out the former British jail, dating from the mandate era. At least under the British the whole area was called Palestine, he mused. Having walked through a busy market and along dusty streets we arrived at the taxi for Nablus and, as I was the final person to fill the car, we departed immediately.

The journey to Nablus took us along mountain roads with breathtaking scenery. Ideal for tourists, there was scant evidence that anyone would have a holiday in this area. For someone to have a disposable income would probably involve being Jewish, and that would not be a good idea in this militant Palestinian area. It was not long before the young man on my left started chatting to me. Jawad was the Chief News Reporter for Radio Palestine, based in Ramallah, the administrative capital of the Palestinian Territories. As the car roared around hairpin bends he began to explain what life was like for educated Palestinians like him. Because he was a journalist the Israelis refused to allow him a visa to enter Jerusalem. But as a journalist he needed to be in Jerusalem. This meant that he had to sneak in by the back roads risking capture and imprisonment. I asked what his feelings were about Israel and was surprised at his moderation. 'Palestinian people want peace,' he explained. 'We have accepted just 23% of our own land but the Israelis won't accept this. The longer the peace process remains under discussion, the more likely we will see it break down totally. Then, unsolicited, he added a comment about the then Israeli Prime Minister. 'I believe Barak is a good man. If he can persuade the men around him, then we might have real peace. But there are many Israelis who want war.'

Jawad was clearly thoughtful but then he turned wistful. Looking me straight in the eye he asked, 'Why would a Jew living comfortably in Tel Aviv care about whether Israel or Palestine holds this area?' He gestured to the beautiful rugged countryside. 'Is it worth going to war?' As a media man himself he was convinced that the Israeli media machine was responsible for feeding the minds of people in remote Tel Aviv with the need to uproot the Palestinians. And as long as this attitude pertained he felt there was no hope. The lights of hope were going out but then he offered a different scenario. 'If we can have peace the Israelis can then come and have holidays, and trade in peace. We will all do well'.

Nablus is a city built along a valley with housing stretching up steeply inclined roads. I wandered around the souq, exploring the narrow streets. Everywhere I was greeted by friendly smiling faces bidding me welcome. It had been a long day and I was feeling extremely tired but a kind of honey soaked fritter was just what I needed to have a boost of energy before deciding to indulge myself in a Turkish Bath. Knowing that this would take some time, I reconciled myself to the fact that it would be very late before I got back to Bethlehem.

The Turkish Bath is a very special experience in the Middle East. Whilst Victorians in Britain imitated the idea as a kind of remedial treatment in spa towns, in the Middle East the tradition can be traced back to the Romans. But it was under the Turks that it was developed and, as it involves running rather than standing water, it was acceptable to the Islamic rulers. Over the years the baths have gradually vanished so that the one in Nablus is reputed to be the only one surviving in either Israel or the Palestinian Territories. The arrival of good water supplies to homes has dramatically reduced the patronage of Turkish Baths. I remember as a child that our local swimming pool had what was known as the 'Slipper Baths': cubicles where people could go and have a bath because they did not possess one in their home. Slipper Baths have gone, and it was understandable that the Turkish Baths would go the same way. Except for the fact that such baths, going back to classical times, have always been places of great social and business contact. Perhaps the telephone killed much of the need for that?

I was given a towel, a wrap, a piece of soap and half a loofa. Then I was shown the layout of the several domed rooms. In one section was a sauna with hot dry and hot steamy rooms plus showers. In the main section a series of cubicles had deep stone basins filled with water from taps, and aluminium bowls for douching. In the centre of the room was a heated stone floor on which to lie after washing. Connecting these two sections was a changing and resting area, and a massage room. I decided to sample everything. Going into the sauna area first I joined three young professional men in the steam room. They were all colleagues from a bank in Nablus. One told me with such eagerness that he was a financial consultant that I thought he was about to try and sell me a pension plan. In the dry heat room was a middle-aged man reclining on one of the excruciatingly uncomfortable wooden slat benches. I found I could only sit on mine. The experience was not pleasant so, after only a couple of minutes, I went for a cold shower. It was now time to try the washing room. The soap looked like the old-fashioned bars of soap that people used to scrub clothes with. I had read that it was produced locally and had extremely good properties for the skin and hair. Not having shampoo I risked it.

Once thoroughly clean, and having used the loofa, I lay down on the heated floor. Two young Austrians and a rather self-assured Jordanian were my companions at this time. We booked the masseur who called us through one at a time. The massage was done in a room with three other men sitting around in conversation with the masseur. Although not tall the masseur had obviously pumped iron at some point and I felt as if I was about to be massaged by Bluto from 'Popeye'. I lay face down and he ensured that my wrap was modestly covering all that it should before slavering me with oil. Then he started the massage. He found several knotted muscles, especially in my right shoulder, probably from carrying my camera bag. All the time he was chatting to the other men.

'So where are we drinkin' tonight, Ahmed?' Slap. Pummel. Fist up the spine. 'The George and Dragon? I've not been there in ages. Is it better than it used to be?'

I was turned over and my legs and arms pulled. 'Personally I prefer the 'Crescent' – landlord's a friend of mine.' Thighs and calf muscles were squeezed in a downward motion. I thought I'd cry out at one point. Then it was over.

Whilst it lasted no more than three minutes it did wonders for my neck, shoulders and general physical weariness. I went to shower off all the oil and then got changed. Returning to the entrance room I rested on a reclining seat whilst a cup of tea was brought. It is amazing how much a relaxing steam bath can do when you are exhausted. In some ways I felt it cleared my mind too. It was as if the heat of the day had been replaced by clear vision at sunset. And so it was. After another ten minutes I felt recovered enough to leave so, collecting my bag, I paid and went back to the 'servees' station.

The journey to Ramallah, through the area in which the legendary Samaritans lived, was accompanied by a wonderful glowing sunset. I felt as if I too were glowing, so therapeutic had been the bath and massage. But I was intrigued as to why this mountainous area of the Palestinian Territories should have such a good road, and was even more surprised when I saw that Israeli soldiers guarded major road junctions. Was this not this the Palestinian area? I talked to the old man next to me. Shrugging his shoulders he smiled. 'They talk of Palestinian Territories. But all they gave us was the Post Office to run.' In my perception of the hopes for peace, I saw another light flicker and die.

The short journey from Ramallah to Jerusalem would normally take no more than half an hour by bus. As we swung out into the rush hour traffic I looked at the people in the street. It was the kind of busy scene that could be matched in many places the world over. Shoppers were rushing around as if there were no tomorrow, traffic snarled up the congested streets, and everywhere were the neon signs denoting that Palestine too was part of the globalised economy. As the bus raced through the outskirts of the town there were signs of brutality. A burned out vehicle at the roadside, neglected housing, unfinished and seemingly abandoned commercial developments. The passengers sat in silence and you could feel the rise in tension as we approached the checkpoint at the approach to Jerusalem.

The bus growled slowly to the sentry box and an Israeli soldier flagged us down. As he checked our papers I noticed a Biblical text hanging from the driver's rear view mirror. It was headed 'Hear the Word of the Lord' and was a quotation from the prophet Jeremiah 32 verses 37 to 41. 'I will surely gather them from all the lands... I will bring them back to this place and let them live in safety... I will rejoice in doing them good and will assuredly plant them in this land with all my heart and soul.' The middle verses talked about inspiring the people of God to act as if they were His people. As I watched the Israeli soldiers I wondered about the way such verses are received. For many the prophet was speaking of the Jews but for many it was about those Christians who could be either Gentile or Jew. Nevertheless it seemed a remarkably insensitive verse to suspend in a Palestinian bus. The passengers might have interpreted it as 'your oppressor is right, says the Lord, so get lost'. Perhaps they did not read English?

After what seemed like an age but was truly only a few minutes, the soldier summoned two young men to get off the bus. Then he slammed the door shut, banged on the side, and we set off up the hill in a cloud of black exhaust fumes. The driver gritted his teeth. 'They talk about peace. But at our level there are no signs of it', he said to me. We drove on in silence, through the fashionable suburbs built for Israeli Jews on land still disputed by the international community. Volvos and Mercedes overtook, carrying their wealthy occupants into the city as our driver struggled to change gear.

At the Damascus Gate I managed to catch the last bus to Bethlehem. Buses stop running to the Palestinian Territories at a remarkably early hour. The bus was heading up the hill when a Police car stopped it. A loudspeaker was used to direct us to follow it into a side street. All the passengers had to get out on to the pavement. This took some time as the door was a narrow one with three steps to climb down. For some elderly passengers this was a slow process. We had to submit our documents and the policemen stood by their vehicle looking impassive. Then we were told to climb back on the bus and all our documents were given to the driver. As I got on the bus one of the policemen said, with a smirk, 'You see we check but we do not harass the people'.

The bus set off and our documents were passed back from seat to seat. Sitting near the front I was glad to retrieve my passport quickly. Going round a system of one-way streets we had just reached the point where the police had pulled us in previously when a soldier made us stop in a lay-by. This giant of a man climbed on board and demanded to see our documents. Wearily we submitted. Then with a gurgle of glee the soldier appeared to find an irregularity in the papers of two old men. He ordered them off the bus.

I watched as this huge man pulled himself up to his full height, dwarfing the two old men. They looked up at him from under their Palestinian headgear and he began to rant at them. Perhaps he spoke in Hebrew and perhaps they did not understand. Whatever it was, neither man said a word. This seemed to cause the soldier to go into overdrive. By now a group of tourists had gathered to watch. Cameras flashing, this was developing into the kind of story that might be used elsewhere so the soldier took the option of scaling down the incident. Shaking his index finger as if they were two miscreant children he then pushed them back on the bus. This driver said nothing. Neither did the passengers. We just drove to Bethlehem in silence.

CHAPTER TWELVE

CONVERSATIONS IN AMMAN

Perhaps I was getting a little too involved in the Palestinian-Israeli issue. Whatever it was, issues of justice seemed paramount in my emotions but where was that experience of the spirituality of the indigenous Christians? There were some who would argue that spirituality is not to be internalized, that it must be visible in every aspect of life. I agree with that but I was missing a sense of 'otherness' that I believe should accompany real spiritual experience. At one point a senior Palestinian theologian had commented that if the political problems were cleared up overnight some of the clergy would have little to preach about. It was with a sense of both relief and anticipation therefore that I found myself winging my way back to Jordan. Perhaps in an Arab country, especially one that survived on a political knife-edge with some of its neighbours, there might be a more realistic view of faith by the Christians.

Returning to Amman, the capital city of Jordan, involved another night flight. The twenty-minute flight took us over the West Bank. The Arab villages could be made out with their little necklaces of blue street lamps punctuating the blackness. In contrast, the disputed Israeli settlements, built on the tops of hills, were very clearly visible with their daylight security illumination. Their blue swimming pools in an area where some Palestinians complain that they have insufficient water was a story in itself.

We taxied in alongside an impounded Iraqi Airways Boeing 707. Perhaps the juxtaposition of an arrival from Tel Aviv alongside an Iraqi plane was a clear illustration of the fragile peace that Jordan is able to maintain with its strong neighbours. Certainly that was the impression I was given by Issa, a teacher from the Theodore Schneller School, who had agreed to come and meet me. As we drove into Amman in his old car he waxed lyrical about the wonders of his country. Whilst it is a country in which the majority of the population is Muslim, things were very relaxed between people of different faiths, he assured me. As a member of the Greek Orthodox Church he said that he had no difficulties relating to Muslims. The lack of tension in the atmosphere was almost tangible as we drove along the fast road into Amman. Compared to the military hardware on the streets of Israel this seemed to be the most relaxed country in the world. But impressions can be deceptive.

By one o'clock in the morning I was exhausted as Issa dropped me outside the guesthouse at the Theodore Schneller School. Thoughts of sleep were soon put aside when my attention was attracted by a jolly young man in jeans, T-shirt and baseball cap shouting my name and waving as he ran towards me. 'Mr Ian. Welcome. Let me take your luggage'. This was Thaeyr, the warden of the guesthouse. Although I was exhausted he was very keen to socialize. He had an empty house and no one to talk to. Scooping me up and welcoming me into the house, his welcome could not have been more of a contrast to my arrival in Bethlehem two weeks earlier. Within seconds he splurted out the fact that he was an Iraqi. Did I mind? He was genuinely concerned that British – Iraqi relations might result in my hostility towards him. Once I had convinced Thaeyr that I was delighted to be under his roof the floodgates opened and he told me about himself. He explained that he tried without much success to use the name John, rather than Thaeyr. His real name translated as 'Revolutionary' and he was concerned that others would see him as a threat. However I was soon to find that if I referred to him as John no one knew whom I meant. To them he was Thaeyr! This was a classic sign of insecurity and I was to begin to see why he felt this way. However I was exhausted and begged to sleep, a request that met with reluctant acquiescence.

The following morning I got talking to Thaeyr. He displayed great agitation and kept making nervous jokes. He was clearly unsure about whether I was friend or foe. True friends are a rare commodity in the world of displaced persons, and information about people is readily traded. Eventually I seemed to satisfy him that I posed no threat and he lay back on a settee before pouring out his story. Born of Chaldean parents in the north of Iraq near the Kurdish area, he had been an active Christian for as long as he could remember. The Chaldeans, he explained, have their own language rather than Arabic and this is used in church. The Chaldean Church was one of those ancient churches dotted around the Middle East that had split off from the main strands of the Orthodox and entered into full communion with Rome. As part of the arrangement they had been allowed to retain their ancient liturgies in their own language. It was this, Thaeyr explained, that gave him a real sense of being at one with God: hearing the Liturgy in his own language. Since arriving in Jordan he had missed the Chaldean Church and had explored Roman, Orthodox and Protestant churches but never felt that they pressed the right button. The way he described his faith, it seemed to me that it was more to do with cultural identity rather than a relationship with the Living God. This was the basis of his difficulties with other Christian denominations in that he felt that they could not offer him a spiritual comfort zone. What really sparked him off were the thoughts of being in a large group of Chaldeans worshipping in their own language. I could identify with that emotion and several times on my trip had been tempted to seek out services in English. Christian Spirituality had a great deal to do with the emotion, I was discovering. It was about non-negotiable dogma on the one hand but, on the other, it had to touch the feelings of the real person inside. This had then to be expressed in love.

Now aged thirty and prematurely grey, Thaeyr said that he had been applying to get a visa to live in Australia. He knew people there and felt that he might be able to use his professional skills as a Civil Engineer. As an Iraqi, he was allowed to live in Jordan but not to have paid work, so his professional skills were dying. His parents still lived in Iraq but he had taken his chance to get out after the Gulf War. Things were dreadful for the population, he explained, with shortages of everything. The secret police monitored so much that he felt he could not say anything more than pleasantries when he rang home.

'I was born in 1970,' he said. His nervous smile vanished as he folded, unfolded and refolded his notepaper. 'And what have I seen? War with Iran. War with Kuwait. The Gulf War. And now I am displaced. Every country turns me away. Jordan lets me stay but they could change their mind tomorrow and I could be sent back. I need a permanent visa. Australia rejected me, and let in Muslim girls. Why?' His irritation was very close to the surface. His life expectations had been dashed whilst he was still a young man. Nothing beckoned him forward because he was Iraqi and unwanted by the international community.

'I was a student in Baghdad during the Gulf War. The missiles came down all round us. It was crazy. I told my Mum not to worry. The Americans had told us that they were high technology missiles only aimed at military targets. But one day I walked past an ordinary house that had been bombed. I was going to take my final exam. They were carrying out a little girl that had been killed. I wept for her and could not take my exam.' He looked at me with distress in his eyes as he thought back to that day in Baghdad. The lies of the Americans; the lies of the Iraqis. He was broken by it all. 'I dream of the war. I wake at night shivering because of those bombs. People say they pray for me but it doesn't go away. I'm a wreck inside. What has happened in my thirty years? I'm here. They think I'm simple – let them think it. I'll keep my head down but in secret I am working on computer skills. I have my own e-mail address. The school hasn't even got that.' He frowned. 'You won't tell the Principal about the e-mail will you? Just let him keep on thinking I'm just Thaeyr running the Guest House.'

I asked if he'd had any trauma counselling after the Gulf War. 'I need to see a psychiatrist,' he confided. 'I'm a wreck. I'm a headcase. Sometimes I think of suicide but I won't do it. That would be a victory for the Muslims.'

'The Muslims?' I enquired, not seeing the connection.

Thaeyr looked at me with disdain. 'In Iraq there were many Christians. Many have emigrated since the Gulf War because life is intolerable. But it was good before. The West feels sorry for refugees like those Muslims over there'. He pointed through the window at a major Pales-tinian refugee camp established in 1967. 'I don't feel sorry for them,' he confided. 'They do nothing to help them-selves. You need to see how they wreck this country. True Jordanians are proud of their achievements. The Kingdom has been good to me. But those Palestinians, they grab every dinar they can and do nothing for the country that houses them. They are robbers.'

This was strong stuff. 'Most are Muslim', he continued. 'If you say anything to disagree with a Muslim you are in trouble. I once worked for a Muslim and mentioned my faith in Jesus as Son of God. I lost my job.' Thaeyr was clearly angry and had by now folded his paper into a little aeroplane, creasing it tightly. I enquired what would happen if he went back to Iraq. 'I'm not a refugee. I could go back at any time but would be called up as a reservist in the army. It would be hell. I could then not return here for two years. It's easier not to go back.' Here was a man living like a refugee, hoping to be accepted as one, admitting that he was not really one at all. I had to ask what would happen if Saddam Hussein and his regime were to fold. Would he go back? He looked rueful. 'My life is wasted till now. Iraq is always going to be fought over. It always has been. I need to get out of this mess and start again somewhere else. I can't even get married, as I've no prospects. I have an Egyptian girlfriend but she works in Dubai and I told her to marry someone with prospects. She will.'

Whilst Thaeyr was an extreme case of desperation, I believe he is typical of millions of people the world over who are unable to achieve what they ought because of political, religious or economic persecution. He was understandably bitter about the raw deal that life had offered him. Seeing people from the West staying at the guesthouse must have driven him crazy. In the West, it seems as if the United Nations Declaration of Human Rights includes a clause about the right to be happy. It is not so for many people the world over. Happiness is a rare luxury. On a later occasion Thaeyr admitted that he had paid a deposit to a person who had offered to smuggle him to Europe. The man had vanished and Thaeyr had never seen him or his money again. Perhaps this was just as well, but I could empathise with his dilemma.

My head was still spinning when I was invited to chat with Kamal Farrar. Born a Maronite (in communion with Rome) in a village in Palestine just south of the Lebanon border, by a tortuous route he had become Director of the Theodore Schneller School (TSS) in Jordan, and an Anglican priest as well. This large man, I quickly realised, was a tough cookie because of life's raw deal. As we chatted I could see that he ran the school without compromise. His standards were high and those of his staff had to match his aspirations. Nevertheless, when I saw him with the boys later I saw that they adored him. He was a giant who protected the defenceless.

As we settled down in his study, he explained a bit about the school. Its predecessors were founded by German Lutherans to provide éducation to poor but promising children in Palestine. They had a number of schools and offered education to boys regardless of religious affiliation. However the creation of the Jewish state in Israel proved a very difficult time. The school was perceived as providing education for the Palestinians, the enemies of Israel. At the same time Israel was distrustful of Germans as a result of the Holocaust. So the schools were closed and everything relocated to Jordan. In the 1950s it was becoming clear that private schools in Jordan were being taken over by the state, especially if they had no strong umbrella organisation to look after their interests. At that time the Anglican Diocese of Jerusalem and the Middle East offered to provide shelter. As Anglicans and Lutherans have traditionally co-operated with one another, this seemed a good answer. German funding still remained very important. The school was mainly, but not exclusively, a boarding school for boys who come from socially deprived or broken homes. Its success rate academically and in getting boys into jobs had been excellent. A Theodore Schneller School graduate was highly prized as an employee.

But I wanted to know the story behind this ex-Maronite, now an Anglican. Sitting formally behind his polished desk, Kamal drew himself up to his full stature. His eyes moistened as he remembered a troubled life. 'During the takeover of Palestine by Israel in 1948, I was a student in Paris. At that time the army came and evacuated my village. My family, along with all the other members of the community, was forced to live in tents a few miles away. Meanwhile Jews newly arrived from South America were given the homes evacuated by the villagers'. He gazed out of the window as he recalled those events of half a century ago. 'Over the next three years the village was evacuated again as the Jews were resettled in purpose-built accommodation. The Israeli air force then used the empty village for target practice. The place was flattened. Only the Maronite church remained. It was used as a cow shed by a nearby Kibbutz'.

Wistfully, Kamal turned back to me. 'Whilst I was out of the country as a student, I heard about these things and on my return felt that I could change the world'. A cautious smile broadened his face. 'I went to see various Israeli officials to find out if the villagers might have their church back. Everyone referred me to someone else. No one would take responsibility. Three years later I finally got to see the local Governor. This man wanted to see the church for himself so he took me in his official car. He was visibly moved and gave immediate orders to the local police to evict the Kibbutzim from the church and to force them to clean it before returning it'. By now he was smiling. Was it because of the success or because of my incredulity? 'We decorated it again. But can you imagine the joy we felt as we held our first services?' It was a moving thought, and one that once more tied faith and spirituality to cultural identity. Just as people, on hearing a beautiful Anglican cathedral service, joke that God is an Englishman, so the cultural button is pressed for people in other parts of the world. They may not value it when it is readily available but cut off the supply and it is deeply felt.

We got round to talking about Kamal's ecclesistical background as I was puzzled that he had been a Maronite Priest and now was an Anglican. 'I had a problem with the church hierarchy,' he confessed. 'Not a problem with

Maronite belief. You know I am still a Maronite, still a priest. Just like you are English, I am Maronite. We are a group of people. Part of the oldest church in the world'. So who are the Maronites? 'We are a part of the Church which descended from the Syriac Orthodox and in that sense from the New Testament Church in Antioch. That means that our lineage predates that of Rome. We were established in the first century and had a system of church governance a bit like the Anglicans today. We had women as deaconesses from the early years. Our Patriarch was recognised for his Godly leadership but was never thought of as infallible. But gradually things changed and in the Middle Ages we agreed to be in communion with Rome. I am happy with thinking of Rome as a symbol of unity but not of authority'. Here was a man who had grown up through the most awful upheavals that life might throw at him, and at the same time prepared to embrace the principles of the Reformation even though it meant cutting himself off from his culture in some senses.

'When I felt that I needed to move from one position to another, in a different diocese, my bishop forbade it. The only way I could object was to appeal to a court in Rome. Now I ask you, what has Rome got to do with it? We are Maronites. I should be able to appeal to our Patriarch in Lebanon. I looked around and I believe that the Maronite Church was reformed before the Reformation. So the nearest I could find to that ideal was the Anglican Church. We have a strong emphasis on the Sacraments but we are reformed in our teaching and governance. I was ordained as an Anglican priest but my own Maronite Church still recognises me as a priest too.' So that was sorted!

In a way I could see similarities between Kamal and Thaeyr. Both had seen their youthful expectations ruined but Kamal had ridden through the waves. Maybe it was because he had succeeded in completing his qualifications outside his native land, or maybe it was because he had more drive and less introspection. But both had striven to make sense of their displacement without losing their Christian faith. Of course their stories were but the tip of the iceberg: there were millions throughout the region who could tell similar stories of dashed hopes, of heart-break, and of being uprooted. In the midst of all this some were able to continue, like some re-run of the story of Job, to be faithful to their church and faith. God had not abandoned them but they were unable to make much sense of the events that engulfed them.

'Excuse me, Dr Farrar.' Kamal's secretary had just put her head round the door. 'George Masreki is here'. I realised that my time with Kamal was up but was delighted to find that he had arranged for my conversation to continue with a friend. George Masreki was ushered in and introduced. Like Kamal, he was a big man. By now it was mid-morning and he was in shirtsleeves with an open neck, reflecting the rapid rise in temperature. We strolled across to the guesthouse where we were able to chat in one of the lounges. George, I discovered, was a director of a tour company in Amman. He was a member of the Syriac Orthodox community, people who were originally from the area that is now northern Syria and south-east Turkey. His ancestors had fled from Turkey early in the Twentieth Century when the Ottoman Government was persecuting the Christians. They settled in the Holy Land. In George's case, his family went to West Jerusalem.

George was delighted to tell his story. 'We are not Pal-estinians. We were immigrants into Jerusalem. I was born in 1945 and three years later our neighbourhood became the scene of bitter fighting between the Palestinian Arabs and the Jews. As we were neither Jews nor Palestinians, my parents decided to lock up our home for the duration of the troubles and came as temporary refugees to Jordan. Like many at that time they thought they would be away from our home for a short time – until the United Nations sorted things out'. I asked about other non-Palestinian Christians who made the journey. He shrugged his shoulders and continued. 'Remember that some years earlier my grandparents had moved to Jerusalem to escape from persecution in Turkey. My parents, and their friends and relatives, saw this new move as necessary. But this time they felt the eyes of the world were on us, so it would only be a temporary arrangement. In the end about two hundred and fifty Syriac Orthodox families came to Amman.'

History records that the arrangement was not temporary and that there are now more people of refugee origin in Jordan than there are truly indigenous people. George told me that his faith and culture are intertwined and so it has been important to ensure that the upheavals do not destroy either or both of these. They set up a school to ensure that their faith and culture were passed on to the future generations. However, unlike the Armenians who preserved their own language in everyday use, the Syriac Orthodox use Arabic as their common language, with Syriac, a form of Aramaic, in their Liturgy.

'I am very sad when I look at what is happening to the Christian people in Jordan.' The change of direction was sudden. We were now on to his agenda. 'There has been a huge change. In the 1960s there was a population of nearly one and a half million people in Jordan, and twenty per cent were Christian. Today the population is four and a half million of which three or four per cent is Christian'. Was this surprising, I wondered? The majority of Arabs in the Middle East are Muslim. As Jordan takes in refugees I suggested that this would both increase the population and the percentage of Muslims within it.

George looked sad. 'You don't understand. They emigrate. I am against emigration from the Holy Land. If it is left to the Muslims who will take care of Holy Places? But life is difficult. And what of our children? Life might become worse. We have peace talks, but no peace. We have too many people. Peace is not possible when everyone is considered. But we still want a fair peace. It is impossible so the best option is to get out whilst we can'. This big man sat forward in his seat. He had really touched a nerve. The Christian community in Jordan was haemorrhaging to such an extent that it could die out in a couple of generations. Christians were often well educated and could therefore emigrate with comparative ease. With an alarming sense of immediacy he grabbed my wrist. 'We need the Christian church in the West to help us. Christians are not politically dangerous in Jordan so the Muslims don't see us as a threat. We are educated and prosperous.' At this point I wondered whom it was that he was talking about. I was aware of plenty of Christians in the Arab political arena. Equally I was aware of many Christians who were poor. It seemed as if many Christians were unaware of the situation of other Christians – or maybe chose to ignore it?

Then in complete contradiction to his earlier statement, he confided, 'You know Muslims think Christians are against them. They feel that they have to conquer everywhere. Things would be very difficult in Jordan if it were not for our king. He respects all minorities and ensures their rights. We are well protected in Jordan. So if a Muslim man makes an approach to a Christian girl he will be very well punished.'

After George had left I felt uneasy. His opinion had been that of a wealthy businessman with opportunity to see the wider picture. But he had appeared myopic in some areas. His unreserved praise for the Hashemite Kingdom may have been genuine, and even well deserved, but I felt that it was preventing a sense of realism. To George, faith and culture were one and the same. This insular view, not just confined to some brands of Christianity, is very exclusive and prevents that faith from sharing its message with others of a different race or culture. The Christian Church from its inception has always been missionary in that it can apply itself to any culture anywhere. What I was experiencing here was a culture that had overwhelmed Christianity. The language, the liturgy, the community, all seemed more important than living out the faith in a tangible and welcoming way.

After lunch I went to collect my laundry from Issa's wife, Aida. This provided an unexpected opportunity to hear a Christian woman's view of the religious situation in Jordan. As indigenous Jordanians, both Aida and Issa were proud of their country. The king was wonderful in keeping everything in check, and thus allowing the country to prosper. Aida was shy at first, but then with the confident language support of Shireen, her eighteen year old daughter, she began to share a lot. In complete contrast to the line taken that morning by George, she talked about how Christian girls are taunted the whole time. At school or in the street Muslim children accuse them. They are told they are blasphemous, or ignorant. Everywhere, Muslim men approach them. They make either indecent suggestions or offers of marriage – conditional, of course, on conversion to Islam. 'They don't realise that we love the Christ. They don't believe he died. But He is our Christ. He died and came alive again. We know He is alive.'

Shireen, sitting on the settee wearing a T-shirt and shorts, was nodding in agreement the whole time. The absolute picture of Western fashion, she would not be able to walk out in the streets dressed like that. Here in this lovely home, I was being privileged to hear about a woman's perspective. Men might find being a Christian in Jordan easy, but these women did not. Aida continued. 'The Muslims, they hate Christians. The fanatics from Iran, they're here already. They come through the Turkish mountains and into Syria. In Iran they have killed Christian children in front of their parents. We are afraid that they will make Jordan like Iran. Bad not just for Christian women, but all women.' Aida was expressing views that no one had shared with me. There was the anecdotal, there was the demonisation of Islam, but there was also a strong awareness that if Islamic ideas took a hold on Jordanian society women in general and Christian women in particular would suffer.

CHAPTER THIRTEEN

LOVE IN ACTION

A local bus journey of about half an hour from Amman brought me to the ancient city of Salt. During the Ottoman era it had been the administrative centre but lost out to Amman when the capital of Transjordan was being established. Consequently Salt has retained a charm that it would undoubtedly have otherwise lost. Built along a steep-sided valley that eventually tumbles down below sea level into the Jordan Valley, it reminded me of a Yorkshire wool town. High above the town, with commanding views, was the object of my visit. The Holy Land Institute for the Deaf (HLID) had an envious record of being the kind of place where I might experience Christian spirituality in a way that was both sensitive to the majority Muslim culture of the region, yet without compromising the message of the Gospel. This I had to see.

My error in staying on the bus until it reached the terminus resulted in having to climb up the ridge from the valley floor. In the heat of the day it was no joke but I was warmly received upon arrival. Matthew, a graduate from Britain, was helping with the administration. He certainly understood the needs of this dehydrated traveller and ensured that all was well before showing me to my accommodation in the guesthouse. After about half an hour it was noon and therefore lunchtime in the school. Staff and pupils dined together. Of the one hundred and fifty pupils, most were profoundly deaf and it was moving to see how the Muslim helpers were so involved that they even said Grace before the meal. This involved gently holding up a hand bell whilst everyone put hands together in a praying position. For a number of minutes, until gradually every child's attention had been attracted, the assistants stood waiting. Then Grace was said in sign language with all the children joining in. Lunch consisted of bread and cheese. Although it sounds a light lunch, somehow in the heat (around thirty degrees Celsius) it was just right.

The Director of HLID was a Dutch Anglican monk called Brother Andrew. Since he took over the helm in 1977 he has overseen some incredible changes. Whilst the Institute is overtly Christian it seeks to help deaf children whether they are Christian or not. It also aims to model best practice so that it might spawn imitations. From small beginnings, the HLID now has some fine medical facilities, and teaches children from an early age how to communicate. By breaking that barrier some have gone on to great achievements, both academically and practically. The carpentry and car maintenance workshops were evidence that people whom society had written off might earn their way as they grew up. It has to be said that HLID has been recognised for its groundbreaking work. Over the years funding has been forthcoming from a variety of sources, including Saudi Arabia and Yemen, yet at no time has the witness to the love of Christ been diminished.

After a cup of tea I got chatting to Brother Andrew. His vision was an enormous one. It was basically a development of the theme of service. As the Institute had expanded its work and gained international recognition, calls for its involvement in other areas of life throughout the Middle East have been numerous.

I felt honoured to be able to chat with Brother Andrew. This smiling man with his white habit and black skullcap was an enigma. He belonged to a monastic order based in

New York but was on permanent leave of absence. Over the years people had come to see that he was transparent. What you saw was what you got. That was unusual in the Middle East. Because Arab culture can be ostentatious, and that wealth and prosperity are equated with the blessing of God, the converse can also be true. If something goes wrong, God has cursed you. But who would admit to that? Thus anyone who has a child with a disability would prefer others not to know. Often children who are disabled are locked away, with sensory depriva-tion, for life. Sometimes they suffer other forms of physical cruelty and torment. Andrew's work has demon-strated that deaf people (and other disabled people by implication) can be a blessing. Over the years he has worked hard to persuade parents to release their children to the care of HLID. With some spectacular results parents now send their children from all over the Middle East. He has found that Jordanian royal patronage has been partic-ularly encouraging, as have visits by international digni-taries.

I could see that HLID was very much in the line of sac-rificial love and service that one might expect from someone in holy orders. But I wondered whether he ought to question his policy of no proselytising. Surely the Christian Gospel is about sharing Good News? Andrew roared with laughter. 'Who says we don't share? Don't you imagine that by showing that we have good news, that we are good news, that we don't witness to the love of Jesus Christ? If Muslims trust us, it shows that they accept that we are no threat. They accept us – and our Gospel – at face value.' He had a point.

Andrew talked much about the need for the Christian Church in the Holy Land to stop whinging about the need for the Church in the West to support it. He believed that it should be setting up works and institutions that serve the real needs of all the population. The emphasis should be on service and self-sufficiency. HLID was certainly an example of this but I was soon to see Andrew's big project. Taking a taxi to the other side of town we came to some disused buildings that had once been the old Anglican hospital and church. In fact the whole place was a period piece. It had been developed into a hospital in the nineteenth century under leadership from the Church Missionary Society. Since autonomy had been granted to the local church, the hospital had gradually declined. In fact the Government Hospital had taken over the role. A couple of decades later it closed and since then the premises had been vacant. For years the Diocese had been trying to sell off the site for redevelopment. Always the ideas had come to naught.

'We prayed for many years that this property would come to us,' said Andrew as he led me into an amazing project. 'This place is our STRIDE Project. It means Salt Training and Resource Institute for Disability Etc. We will use it to strengthen the Christian presence in town. It will be a centre from where we will train people from all over the Middle East in good practice. We will model excellence'. The old hospital was in the process of extensive renovation. Actually it was being gutted. What was rising like a phoenix in its place was an elegant facility. Andrew showed me the caves where the early CMS missionaries lived. He showed me the old church, now commercial property but scheduled to be included in the restoration work. It was urban renewal in its best sense and it brought to mind some excellent projects I had seen in Britain. But here in Jordan it was unusual to restore old properties. It was easier to tear down and build afresh. But Andrew was adamant. 'This is a place where people have lived, cried and died for the Gospel. It is hallowed ground. So by using it again for the extension of the Kingdom of God, we believe that we are keeping faith with all that has gone before.'

As we walked through beautifully restored rooms, which were both modern and in keeping with their

Ottoman architecture, I was amazed at the vision that could bring such elegance out of ruined buildings. As I was conducted around the premises it became obvious what a massive job was being undertaken. Girders holding up floors were in some cases wafer thin. A team of four Irishmen was providing the physical and technical skills for the replacement of the girders. Qualified tradesmen, they offered to give their time in order to go anywhere in the world (at their own expense) to do jobs like this. Also on site was Ruben Landgraf. This 22-year old from near Dresden in Eastern Germany had chosen to give 20 months service of this kind rather than 9 months' military service. A heating engineer by trade he was Site Supervisor. I was invited into his flat and he showed me pictures of his home and family. He talked about the days before the fall of Communism. He also said that because of the repression under Communism the churches in East Germany did little evangelistic work in the years following the Second World War. This meant that for his generation, in which there is a growing interest in Christianity, there are churches catering for old people but not younger ones. Thus he had attended a Youth Fellowship but not Church. Ruben was a natural evangelist. As a result of his experiences, he considered that the realities of Jesus Christ as his Lord and Saviour were to guide every aspect of his life. He spent a great deal of time praying for people and during my two days in Salt I came across two Muslims who were now openly Christian believers as a result of contact with Ruben.

As I sank into my bed that night there was much to reflect on. For so much of my trip I had been hearing Christians from a variety of backgrounds telling me that they had to preserve their culture, their religious buildings and practices. But here was a very refreshing approach. It threw caution to the wind and aimed for the highest. If Jesus Christ is alive then HLID was prepared to demonstrate it by loving the whole community. As a result of people prepared to work and pray, some even became believers. It seemed that HLID was doing things the right way round.

After breakfast I attended chapel. It was a simple version of Morning Prayer in English with sign language. About half a dozen members of staff attended and about twenty children of varying ages. It was very moving to see the children, none of whom were there by obligation or compulsion, as they joined in the prayers. Perhaps this was a further endorsement of the work?

During the day I was taken into the Jordan Valley to see the HLID's outreach work, as well as visiting the brand new audiology block on the HLID campus. Over lunch I briefly met Nader, one of the Jordanian workers. We had found ourselves sitting next to one another and before many seconds had elapsed this self-assured young man in his early twenties was interrogating me about the purpose and extent of my visit to the Middle East. However our conversation was brief and we both quickly became absorbed in chatting with others. I was aware from time to time that his conversation was about personal faith and that he seemed to be arguing with Bernie, a very keen Christian girl. Later that evening I found him in the common room of my accommodation at the Institute. He had an arrangement with Matthew, he told me, to come up and watch videos. I left him to it but when I returned half an hour later to make a mug of tea, James Bond was over and soccer was on television.

We chatted and he wanted to know about the difficulties I might be having in travelling between the countries on my journey from Egypt to Turkey. He'd travelled too, having been born in what was Leningrad of a Jordanian father and a Russian mother. By now the television was turned off and he was clearly willing to talk. A bright young man, now in his mid twenties, he had been brought to Jordan when he was six. The family had found it difficult to settle and so they returned for a while to what had become St Petersburg. By now Nader was a teenager and this proved even more disturbing for him. Finally the family moved back to Jordan, settling in Amman.

He returned to my travels, and once again was interested to know that I had to be very careful about which countries stamped my passport. 'My passport caused problems, you know.' Nader talked with a very pronounced American accent which he claimed came from watching movies and singing in a band as a teenager when the repertoire was American. 'A year ago I wanted to go to Israel. A friend of mine from here, Marco, was going to Jerusalem and I wanted to go too. I got to the King Hussein Bridge and it took a long time to get through Security. They kept saying that my passport wasn't valid. It was Russian, issued in 1994, but said USSR on it. By then the USSR no longer existed. I kept saying that I got it from the Russian Embassy in Amman and that maybe they wanted to use up old stocks. Eventually one of the Security guys took me to one side and said that foreigners are better crossing at the northern Sheikh Hussein Bridge and that I'd have no problems there. So I went there. It's about one hundred kilometres round trip but when I arrived they wouldn't let me through either. So I had to come back here.'

I wondered where this conversation was leading. Why did he particularly want to go to Israel? Nader continued, 'Brother Andrew rang up some contact he has in the Israeli consulate in Amman. They said I'd been turned down because I never brought my bank statement or my student identification. They never asked. Anyway I got through this time. And I was baptised on 1st January 2000 at the place where Jesus was baptised. What a place and what a date!'

So that was it. He had wanted to get to Israel in order to be baptised. This, of course opened up huge questions. Was he from the Christian or Muslim community? He smiled a huge but nervous grin. 'I am a believer in Jesus, baptised as a Christian. But my card says I am a Muslim.'

I was amazed. I'd heard of converts from Islam but, as I was only too clearly aware, under sharia law it was a capital offence. And here sitting rather anxiously in front of me was a young man who had done it.

'What do your parents think about it all,' I asked tentatively.

'They don't know. They'd be very upset and angry. Although they aren't practicing Muslims, they would see this as bringing dishonour to the family', he said. Conscious of the sensitivity of the issue I said that he must tell me to back off if he thought me intrusive, but that I would be thrilled to hear how it happened.

'I don't mind,' he said. 'It began when I was back in Jordan from Russia. I was about fourteen, just growing up, and I'd never bothered with being religious but my friends kept saying that I should go with them to the mosque. We used to go and pray five times a day. I was very conscientious. But, you know, I was empty inside. I felt nothing. I expected to find a fulfilling relationship with God but after truly practicing all my Muslim obligations, I never got any satisfaction or relationship. And I began to think that I could be as good a person not praying like this as by doing it. So I stopped being religious and it seemed to me that it made no difference.'

This was heady stuff. In spite of all the impressions that Jordan was a relaxed country, practicing religious toleration, I had heard enough anecdotal stories about murder of converts to Christianity to make me understand that this was a risky business. The very fact that all subjects carry an identity card, which shows their religion, must be intimidating to those who want to change. I was assured that it was possible to change religion on the card but it involved notices in the newspaper. When someone is murdered for converting to Christianity I was advised that the police were unlikely to follow this up.

Meanwhile Nader was anxious to continue his story. 'About the age of sixteen I fell in love. Hey, we were in love! And I found that if ever I was lonely or in difficulty all I had to do was think of my girlfriend and within two minutes everything was fine. It was wonderful. We went out for eighteen months and suddenly she dumped me.'

Nader smiled as he recalled the pain and the shock. 'It was better than if she had died – but not much. My world was shattered. So for two weeks I was broken and then I found a new girl and it was better than before. And once again I just thought about her and she made me feel good. But eventually the same thing happened. I got dumped.'

Teenage relationships, heartaches, they are the same the world over, I was thinking in my middle-aged 'sorted' kind of way. But Nader was an analytical kind of boy. 'These relationships never lasted,' he continued. 'Deep down I craved closeness but my mind told me that I needed protection from being hurt. So I decided just to be friends with people. No commitment. How empty is that? It gradually began to tear me apart. I had always depended on the love of close girlfriends but now I was on my own. It was hard and I was lonely.

'You might not understand this but I tried to make up my own philosophy of the world and use this to fill my emptiness. It convinced some people and they even believed it but it was nonsense really. If I lived or died it didn't matter so why should I live? Although I didn't recognise it, deep down I had begun to search for a meaning in life. I had been working for HLID for about a year and one evening I was invited out with Harry, Agnes and Marco, volunteers in the Deaf School. When we sat down at a table for some reason they sat on one side facing me. As I looked at them, all good friends, I felt and saw what I can only describe as a transparent globe or bubble around them. It was as if they were safe inside something and I was on the outside. They were friendly to me but I felt as if I didn't have what they had. I asked them about it'.

As he remembered that night, Nader's eyes filled up. The outsider had yearned to be inside but his friends were adherents of the 'wrong' faith, even if Nader had wanted one.

'They told me briefly about God, the Gospel, and Jesus. It really seemed as if they were contented in that relationship. But all this talk of Christianity didn't fit my framework of beliefs and ten years of Islamic teaching at school. I still thought about what they said but I felt I couldn't do anything. My cultural background prevented me, and my conclusion that religions are made by people for self-satisfaction was dominant in my thoughts.

'After that things went a bit quiet. I still saw volunteers from time to time and I would ask questions and share the difficulties of my empty life. They would always bring everything back to God, Jesus and the Bible. They suggested that I might find some answers in the Bible. Failing that, they said that I might try and pray. I tried both but they weren't much help. Reading the Bible without acknowledging Jesus as the Christ made it hard to understand. The statement of Jesus being Son of God went strongly against my background. I was still feeling lost but I knew some people were concerned for me and it made me feel a bit better than before.

'Over Easter 1999 a group of young people arrived from Jerusalem. They were foreigners working on a building project in their vacation. I met them briefly for ten minutes on Monday and my friend Marco, who was in charge of the project, invited me to have dinner with them to get to know everyone. Adam, the leader of the teenagers said that was great and suggested that I could share my testimony with the group. I did not know what this word 'testimony' meant so I asked him. He realised his mistake and tried to evade the answer. But still I found out!

'After Wednesday lunch I was sitting at the table and had a fairly deep chat with Bernie. It was about my hard time missing the love I had. She said she had experienced something similar. But I enjoyed the attention she gave. She suggested I read John's Gospel. I tried but it didn't mean anything. That evening I went for dinner to Marco's house with the guys from Jerusalem. We had the food and then moved to another room. They were playing music, some of which was Christian, and sharing the events of the day. Again I saw the transparent globe. It was round them. It was much more powerful than before. Again I was on the outside.

'This globe was more a feeling than a physical thing. It was a mix of happiness, satisfaction and love all in one. It was surrounding them. I wanted what they had. I realised it was what I had lacked all these years. I stayed about ten minutes unable to speak or move. All that time I wasn't noticed. In fact I was totally ignored. Yet something very powerful was affecting me. When I came to myself, I felt I understood and accepted the Gospel of Jesus Christ. It was amazing. I wanted to share this but there was no opportunity. Everyone was absorbed in what they were doing, passing the guitar from one to the other. In order to break in I had to ask for the guitar to sing a Russian song and this gave me an opportunity. I was just about to sing when I flipped the guitar over and put it on my lap. I had the attention of about 20 people so I started to tell them about what I saw in them, my past, my struggle with life, and the happiness I had in finding real joy at that moment.

Nader laughed. It was a great relief following the intensity of the previous few minutes. 'They all started to talk. They all seemed to have some advice. At that moment they put me on a chair, gathered around, and put their hands on me for prayer. One girl gave me a New Testament.

The picture in my mind of these young Christians realising that a Muslim had just had a powerful encounter with the living Lord Jesus was both moving and comical. I wondered how they handled it.

'The next morning the group went to Jerash. I was invited along too. Whilst sitting in the bus Adam asked me if I could see myself in the future making a commitment to Jesus as Lord and Saviour. My answer was that I thought I already had. He was bowled over with astonishment and delight.

'On Friday they returned to Jerusalem so I went to see them off at the Sheikh Hussein Bridge. At the border, Adam asked me to pray over them. It was my first public prayer'.

This story was very special. Given the circumstances in Jordan, Nader had not been able to share it widely. But there was more to come and my desire for questions was held back. 'After a few months I felt a need to be baptised, to declare my faith in public. As my birth certificate says I am a Muslim this could not take place in Jordan. So I mailed Adam asking him if he could arrange for me to be baptised in the Jordan River on the Israeli side.

I queried what status his identity card now showed. He admitted that, whilst he had been baptised, his documents still showed him to be a Muslim.

'My parents still don't know. I suppose I could be killed.' It was the real sense of relief in his new faith, yet resigned to his vulnerability, that made me sense that this conversion was for real. Nader had not changed his religion: he had begun a new relationship. He had little concern over cultural identity and so felt free to make this great crossover.

As a new Christian with personal experience of Islam I asked whether he saw the God he now worshipped as the same before and after his conversion to Christ. 'It's difficult to answer,' he replied. 'In Islam we are told to be afraid of God. He will punish us for lots of sins. We have to keep praying to prevent punishment.'

I then pursued this point. 'The Bible tells us that it is a fearful thing to fall into the hands of the Living God, so isn't it the same?' He didn't think so. 'Yes we will be punished as sinners but Christ has taken our sins away. God looks on Christians as if they were without sin. The relationship in Islam is based on Fear. In Christianity it is based on Love. We love God in return.'

It was getting late. On the one hand this testimony was riveting because it was out of the ordinary but on the other it was gripping because of its implications. I remembered hearing someone ask a Christian worker from a Muslim area in Britain why there were so few conversions from Islam. The answer given was that God was waiting for her and her friends to be prepared to take converts into their homes, to give them new families and jobs and self-respect. The same now applied to Nader.

CHAPTER FOURTEEN

ENIGMATIC BEIRUT

Flying into Beirut requires nerves of steel. Having flown from Amman, across Syria, and over the snow-capped mountains of Lebanon, the plane approached Beirut. After circling the beautiful bay, it rushed straight for the high-rise buildings built above the corniche. Having nearly managed to embed itself into the commercial heart of the city, it screamed defiance only metres above the roofs of some poor people living near the airport, before landing to enthusiastic applause from the passengers. I was very pleased to disembark, and be welcomed by an old friend, Colin Chapman. He was a lecturer at the ecumenical Near East School of Theology (NEST) in the heart of the city. Bearing in mind our flight path I could easily have saved him the journey out to the airport.

By now it was night and as we sped along the fast modern road into Beirut it was interesting to notice how wrong my pre-conceptions had been. Beirut is now a universal byword for devastation. Yet the civil war that had destroyed so much of the city had been over for a decade so it was unsurprising that much had been rebuilt. Before the civil war Beirut had been famed for its opulent citizens, for their *haute couture* and chique fashions but all that had been devastated during the war. The elegant yachts of the mega-rich, the casinos, the flamboyant celebrities and tycoons had long gone. Now Beirut presented a rapidly expanding impression to the world but it was a more sober face than the decadent image of old. Massive reconstruction was seeing offices and hotels growing at a rapid rate, whilst some of the war damaged buildings were being rehabilitated.

I was delighted to stay at NEST because it gave an opportunity to talk with young theologians who would one day become leaders in their respective communities. It would be interesting to see how their views of the recent past in Lebanon, and its tribal loyalties allied to religious affiliation, would shape their spiritual perceptions. Colin also was prepared to help me to connect with the Middle East Council of Churches (MECC) as they would have contacts with people who were more at the grass roots of life in Lebanon.

After a fitful night, punctuated by airliners skimming the rooftop, I was ready for action the following morning. My first contact that day was with the Academic Dean, George Sabra. In all my travels in the Middle East I never saw such a trim and articulate Christian leader. I suppose it was the influence of fashion-conscious Beirut, but I was feeling distinctly scruffy as I chatted with one of the few people I had met who wore a collar and tie. Perhaps his air conditioned study allowed it; certainly it gave a level of comfort that I had forgotten about. 'The way I see it', said George, 'there are two distinct views amongst the Christians in Lebanon. I'm not talking about denomination or even whether people have a living faith to which they are committed.'

George was a man in his forties, a man with purpose in his voice. 'The first group see Islam as a threat and the second group see Israel as the big problem.'

I was eager to know more and George could see that he had my full attention. He began his explanation. 'Here in Lebanon we have had waves of invaders over the centuries, but we have been able to maintain our Christian faith. But this is all changing. The growth of militant Islam, particularly that coming out of Iran, is not good for Christians. These so-called Fundamentalists want to impose their laws and customs on the whole community, not just Muslims. Over the last quarter century lots of Christians have emigrated to the West and so our proportion of the whole community has declined. We actually don't know the numbers because statistics are never published but it is our guess that there has been a huge decline in the overall population and amongst Christians in particular. We can see this in the Christian schools where, every year, numbers drop as a few families emigrate.' There it was again. Christians saying that they were in numerical decline because of emigration. I wondered about what happens to the Diaspora once they reach their new country. For so many, their faith and cultural identity are inextricably bound together. After a couple of generations absorbing a different culture, the ties to the faith would be lost. I suppose some might join other denominations but my guess is that most would follow the secularist tendencies of the West.

George reminded me of the second group of Christians in Lebanon. 'These are the ones who see Israel as the big problem. It is part of an historic problem that the West has been putting on us for centuries. There were the Crusades; there were the Western missionaries converting people from Eastern Rite Christianity; and there were European and American colonial and commercial assaults. These people would see the creation of the state of Israel as a European problem that was dumped on us, and now we are living through the consequences. Follow that logic and all you have to do is get rid of Israel, and all your problems will go away.' He gesticulated as if brushing crumbs off his trouser leg; then he smiled. I could see that he was expressing extreme views to make his point but which end of the spectrum did he veer towards?

'Of course both have some truth, but it is interesting to see how they are received in the West. I confess that my view inclines towards the first. I believe that Islam is more of a threat to Christians here than Israel. And I think that this view is probably held by the silent majority.' He looked irritated and then added, 'But the most often heard view is that Israel is our main problem.' I could see his argument. Certainly from a political or military perspective, Israel was undoubtedly a major threat. But it presented no real threat to the faith of Christians.

I wondered whether George had any kind of future projection of where all this was leading. He leaned forward, 'In the West there is a growing sense of guilt about the past. They helped to create Israel, they protected and nourished it, and it has become a monster. Now the West questions its creation. So there is great unease about what is happening. At the same time it is not politically correct for them to speak of Islam as a threat. They are into inter-faith dialogue. This is all very well on an intellectual level but at the grassroots the picture is very different. People are fearful of what might be.'

This was a helpful start in trying to understand some of the complexities of life and faith in Lebanon. The Christians, until comparatively recently the wealthier majority within the population, were now assumed to be the minority as a result of emigration to the West, the arrival of large numbers of Muslim refugees such as the Palestinians, and the tendency for Muslims to have larger families. George gave me a picture of a fearful Christian community. His belief was that Islam was the main threat. This tied in with my experiences earlier in the trip. In both Egypt and Jordan there had been the same underlying concern. It was only in Palestine and Israel, where Arabs of both Christian and Muslim faiths had united in their common Arab hatred of the state of Israel, that inter-faith tensions were less. But they had still surfaced, as I had found in Nazareth.

That afternoon I was invited to the offices of the MECC. As it was only a couple of blocks away it gave me an opportunity to stroll along the famous corniche before going to my appointment. Wandering along narrow streets I came out near the sea at the Phoenicia Hotel. This fabulously glitzy place had just recently been reopened following war damage. As a backcloth, the burnt out hulk of the Holiday Inn stood behind it. That warm and sunny afternoon seemed to offer an opportunity for all the young people of Beirut to go for a stroll. Whilst there was some evidence of war damage, the influence of globalised prosperity in the form of McDonald's and other well-known fast food chains was everywhere. There were hundreds of people, ranging from students to soldiers, from joggers to children on bicycles. They were the targets for the itinerant bread sellers, lottery vendors and purveyors of corn on the cob. Perhaps the most striking image of the present day clash of culture was a young Muslim woman, fully covered as her tradition demands, weaving in and out of the crowds on roller blades.

Arriving at the MECC offices I was briefly introduced to its General Secretary, Riad Jarjour, before being handed on to Alexa Abi Habib, who had oversight of their programme on Justice, Peace and Human Rights. She was based in Cyprus and was actually just packing up her papers before dashing to the airport. As she rushed around I was impressed that, even though I had arrived at an inconvenient moment for her, she wanted to try and be of help. Their programme was impressive. But, perhaps as a result of her mind being on her departure, it seemed as if we were not talking along the same tracks. I explained that I was trying to understand the spiritual energy of the indigenous Christians throughout the area and she said that I ought to see a video of one example of their work. As she left, setting the video in motion, she also gave me the address of some human rights activists in Beirut. And then she was gone and I was sitting watching a programme about the opening of a water scheme for villages in Iraq. There was a Chaldean bishop, there were Baath party members being praised, and there were lots of people eating food at a reception. It all seemed totally irrelevant to my search. But maybe this was an expression of being Christian? To facilitate the local Christian community in Iraq to relieve some of the causes of poverty, gives heart and courage to those people to go on. They are connected through their faith to others around the world even though they might feel isolated because of political oppression or military action. Is this a form of spirituality too? It was all a bit tentative and as I left the office, feeling a little flat, I realised that I still had the details of the human rights people.

Looking at the piece of paper I saw that the group would be meeting that night. I was to go to the ninth floor of the Starco Building for seven o'clock. This large new office block had been built near the docks in an area that had been flattened by the war. Standing defiantly against the evening sky it was built in isolation from any other buildings. Large roads with minimal traffic swept around the landscaped building. Eddies of wind from the sea picked up newspapers and fluttered them around the building in showers of dust. It appeared that the building was deserted. I entered an unmanned but swish vestibule and called a lift, which quickly deposited me on the ninth floor. A long corridor, lined by closed doors, stretched out in front of me. As I walked along I realised that there was someone in the end room. By now I was a little apprehensive. Beirut has a reputation for political kidnappings and I was treading in a grey area, investigating a human rights group in a country where free speech was actively discouraged.

A man was standing in the doorway of Room 921. I explained why I was there, and that the MECC had recommended me to come. The man looked me up and down, told me to wait, and vanished inside. A few minutes later he returned and beckoned me in. A large room with an incredible view of the harbour opened up in front of me. There were around twenty people sitting around a large table. At one end a young man was reading a report in Arabic but stopped as I entered the room. Wa'il Kheir introduced himself as the chairman of the meeting. A genial middle-aged man in a suit, he said that he was delighted that I should join this meeting of the Foundation for Human and Humanitarian Rights but wanted me to explain my purpose in being there. This could have been a problem. The truth was that I knew what I was looking for but I was unsure whether I was looking in the right place. Having explained my interest, the meeting was suspended so that individual members might talk to me.

Information about repression flowed fast. Young people who dissent from the Government line, I was told, were being repressed on a regular basis. But what did that mean. This caused some amusement. Could I be so dim? An example was given of the presence in Lebanon of Syrian troops. They had taken up their occupation to stabilise Lebanon and bring an end to the civil war. That was a decade ago and they were still there. Once seen as liberators they were often viewed as an army of occupation. Many Lebanese, it was alleged, were against the rape of Lebanon by Syria. It was perceived that the wealth of Lebanon was being shipped back to Syria in the guise of maintaining peace. This view had to be controversial, I conceded, but what had it to do with human rights? People were not permitted to demonstrate against it. At this point one of the young men showed me a wound on his back. 'We are beaten', he said. 'We were sent to prison with no opportunity to get legal help, and there was no limit set on our prison sentences. Some are still there.'

Emotions were now rising. It was explained that by spotlighting such tactics internationally and locally the Group had achieved a limited success. Since 1996 the

Lebanese security forces had targeted human rights activists such as Wa'il Kheir. At that point another young man explained that only two weeks earlier he had received a warning that the security forces were waiting in his house. That, he asserted, could only lead to a violent arrest. He had not been able to go home since then and he had heard that security men were following his wife. I was then told of a journalist who was taken in by the security forces and beaten up so badly that he had been forced to flee the country, seeking political asylum in France.

By now I could see that Wa'il was anxious to reconvene the meeting. The young man had taken up his place ready to read his report on human rights education in Lebanon. Clearly it was time to go. As I made my way back into the corridor, Wa'il followed me. 'Our organisation is not Christian. We are people of all faiths, but I think it might be helpful for you to know that a number of us are Christian. We see this as part of our expression of faith in this difficult time'. He then asked if I might be prepared to return on the following Friday as they were going to try and have a press conference. 'An international person might help calm down the activities of the security,' he said.

Walking back along the silent and now dark corridor, I could imagine the secret police in every doorway. Getting into the lift I felt little anxieties fed by innumerable scenes in movies. When the lift stopped on the third floor, for no one, I felt even more concerned. Leaving the air-conditioned building was akin to walking into a tumble drier. The warm wind had increased and the ropes on the flagpoles were flapping like chattering typewriters. As I walked towards the old part of town a black Mercedes swept past me. Only when I returned to the almost physical embrace of my room did I feel safe.

Over the next few days I felt unable to confide in anyone at the College. I had been warned that in Beirut even the walls have ears and, whilst I did not think I was worth the bother, I did not want anyone to be put in difficulties because of me. Nevertheless when Friday arrived I was both exhilarated and apprehensive. Chatting with two black Africans over breakfast helped to divert my thoughts. Gideon from Ghana and Lewi from Southern Sudan were students in the college. From the myriad of sub cultures and sub plots of the Syrians and the Lebanese, which seemed to inveigle its way into the lives of most, here were two men who saw life in a straightforward way. Gideon, for example, was exasperated that the Christians of the Eastern Rite could not allow God's Holy Spirit to move in their lives. I suggested that they might see it differently but Gideon was adamant. 'I was a Muslim but God showed me the truth in Jesus. My parents followed me into being born again. My father had four wives and thirty-two children. So far twenty eight have been saved!' He maintained that this was foreign to the ways of the Middle East. He was right; it was foreign. 'In Ghana, people talk about Jesus Christ and people respond to the Gospel, but it is kept as a secret here.' His Sudanese companion nodded and smiled. Later, Lewi told me that he had learned not to compare cultures but to try and understand them.

I found my way easily to Room 921 in the Starco Building that morning. In the light of day it seemed just as empty but not in any way as intimidating as a couple of nights previously. The room was full, and a significant press contingent was in attendance. One man walked round with a television camera. I seemed to feature in his shots quite frequently. I wondered whether these views would be used in evidence later, but put these ideas to the back of my mind. Wa'il told me that most of the reporters were supportive but that some would be spies.

Although the conference was in Arabic one of the charter members, Mona, gave me a synopsis of what was happening. She explained that the group was of one mind, that the United Nations Declaration of Human Rights should be adhered to at all times. They put aside personal religious and political views in order to achieve this. Mona was a Muslim, and had strong views about the future of Lebanon. These did not accord with some of her Christian friends but she was against any regime that repressed people or prevented freedom of expression.

The Foundation, she explained, was very concerned about the imminent withdrawal of troops from Israeli-held Southern Lebanon. In particular they were concerned for people who had been forced by circumstances to work for the Israelis. They had been forced by economic necessity but were viewed by many as collaborators. Equally there were anti-Israeli activists who were in a particular prison. The Foundation was concerned that if a pro-Israeli Lebanese faction got there first, there would be slaughter. It was this even-handed approach that was so appealing. If the ideas were put out in the newspapers or the television I hoped that their non-sectarian stance would be recognised as the pure gold it seemed.

Once the reporters had left Wa'il invited me to chat to two charter members of the Foundation. 'You need to hear their stories,' he said with a sense of grim compulsion. The first to be introduced was Antoine Alouf, a twenty five year old lawyer. A Greek Catholic by faith, he wanted to share what had happened to him, and some of his friends, as they raised human rights issues in Lebanon. He had some difficulties with English and had to keep asking for help. In some ways this prevented him from giving full expression to his feelings and I could see an immense sense of frustration come over him at times.

He launched in eagerly, 'I am a member of the Free Patriotic Movement. We are not given a licence to be party in elections because of our views. We want perfect authority; we want the Lebanese to govern independently. We don't accept others governing us. Because I hold these opinions the security people don't like it. Particularly at election times, if people can be persuaded not to vote it will show the election to be invalid.'

For clarification I asked about other political parties. All, it seemed, had to subscribe to the view that the Syrian presence in Lebanon was beneficial. All other parties in the elections, he asserted, had connections with Syria. Elections had taken place in 1992, 1996 and the autumn of 2000. 'So we give out leaflets. We are not violent. We try to tell people not to vote, and give them information. In every election the authorities came for me. They took me to the Intelligence Service. They tried to tell us to abandon this. But for us it is impossible. Sometimes those who told us this were not even Lebanese. Sometimes they were Syrians.'

By now beads of perspiration had formed on his face. One or two of his colleagues had joined us. They urged him to continue but I interrupted. I wondered what happened when, after being cautioned, they continued their peaceful campaign. Antoine continued, 'some members were taken to the Police Station. There were sixteen of them and they were tried by military court on charges that have no legality. They said that these people tortured the army. That is impossible! We are non-violent. But the army tortured us. These people were held in solitary confinement. They were tortured. Some went on hunger strike. Those who were not arrested held demonstrations to raise the case of human rights abuse. I am pleased to say that this resulted in all being freed.' He looked pensive, 'all except three.'

I asked how long these three people had been in solitary confinement. Had they been tortured, and were they still in prison on charges that were not proven in a proper court? Antoine said that it was now a month. I wondered whether Antoine had been imprisoned. 'No', he said. Was he apologetic or pleased? 'I did not go to prison because they cannot prove anything. I am lawyer, cleverer than they are. They don't try. The more international connections we have strengthens our case. The more people worldwide see what we do, the better. It stops them abusing human rights so much. But, you know, in 1996 whilst one of my friends was being tortured, a high-ranking member of the Syrian Intelligence Service said that Syrian Army would not withdraw until all the Lebanese are poor people. They take Lebanese wealth back to Syria.'

Hikmat Dib, a neatly dressed man in his mid-thirties, was an engineer. Also a charter member of the Foundation, he was a member of the Maronite Church. He had been imprisoned three times for holding opinions contrary to those of the Government. Realising that his confidence with English was restricted, he asked Mona to help him. 'I first was taken to jail in 1995 for distributing tracts about the sovereignty of Lebanon. I was taken to the Ministry of Defence Jail. It's known as the Torture Factory'. He hesitated, and looked sideways at Mona. 'They wanted names so they tied my hands behind my back and hooked me to a winch and pulley. Then I was hoisted off the ground in great pain, hanging like that for about ten minutes. I think my torturer was Lebanese. I was also beaten on my genitals. Then they hit my ears till they bled. This went on for five days with about four or five interrogations each day. Every interrogation I was tortured. Then I had to sign a document, but I was not allowed to see what was written on it. Everything was covered over apart from the place for the signature.'

Apart from looking extremely tense, much of what was being said was delivered by Hikmat in a matter-of-fact fashion. Perhaps this was his way of coping with it. 'I was sent to the Military jail after five days of this. Conditions here were very bad. There were about sixty detainees in a room four metres by five metres. We had just one light. It was so crowded that we couldn't sit down. Then, after twenty-three days I was released. I know that it was pressure from the international agencies that got me out. It is important that the outside organisations keep up the pressure.' He was over the worst in his story and I wondered if he was more circumspect as a result of his experiences. Not a bit of it. He explained that he had been arrested on two more occasions, but was not detained as long. He knew that the authorities had been after him at other times but had managed to avoid arrest.

Both these stories are the tip of the iceberg. Whilst many people in Lebanon are undoubtedly concerned about human rights abuses, they remain the silent majority. If those people remained silent for fear of bringing back the Civil War, then they were allowing their consciences to be seared. Such people allowed the Nazis to rise in Germany. Antoine, Hikmat and their colleagues were doing something positive about the situation. Peaceful demonstration and giving out literature should not be indictable offences. In Lebanon the regime seemed to think that they were.

As I rose to leave my new friends, I was shown a document. It was part of the Universal Declaration of Human Rights, signed by the governments of both Syria and Lebanon. It said 'Everyone has the right to freedom of opinion and expression; this right includes freedom to hold opinions without interference and to seek, receive and impart information and ideas through any media and regardless of frontiers.

'Everyone has the right to freedom of peaceful assembly and association.'

As I walked the streets of Beirut that afternoon, I kept wondering about Wa'il, Mona, Antoine and Hikmat. Their stance was an expression of truth. In a way it was a form of spirituality. I had not enquired how much their faith informed their actions. Somehow it would have seemed unnecessary.

CHAPTER FIFTEEN

THE EDGE OF THE VOLCANO

I suppose that I had not realised that the destruction of the civil war had affected the psyche of the Lebanese people so much. To try and find what might be perceived as 'normal' spirituality was proving difficult. After only a few days I was imagining listening ears behind every potted plant. The frustration of Gideon, the Ghanaian, seemed to underline my own dilemma. In the college I was aware that the teaching staff were trying to open up the students to new approaches and new perspectives. In fact I walked in on one such controversy.

Colin Chapman and I were walking near the library when a young man came up and assailed him. Colin had led prayers in chapel the previous day and had prayed about the manner of the imminent withdrawal of Israel from Southern Lebanon. Walid, the young man, was incandescent. It was not just Israel who should go, he maintained. What about the Syrian presence in the rest of the country? Of course, Colin had been praying specifically about the manner of the withdrawal and the political vacuum it would create. He had not wanted to detail every other problem facing Lebanon and explained that, whilst he might feel similar thoughts, it was not his role as a foreigner to make comments about the political situation of his host country.

'But Colin, you should have mentioned the Syrian occupation!' Walid was very agitated. Colin mentioned something about it not having been relevant in that particular context and the student looked to me. 'Do you not understand?' he demanded. At that moment Colin saw his way off the hook – for the present. 'Why don't you explain the situation to Ian?' he said.

We met in the Library at NEST after lunch in which I had a meal and he did not. 'I am trying to lose weight', he commented. A man in his twenties he was probably overweight, although he said that his diet was working. His broad face kept breaking out into a broad grin as he chatted although he also appeared to fidget at times. 'I am Lebanese,' he said, 'of the Maronite faith. We are an Eastern Rite church, aligned to Rome. Our heartland is in the mountains of Lebanon although we are scattered throughout the country. We see ourselves as a community'. He went on to explain how a person is born a Maronite. To Walid, being Maronite was the same as being Lebanese. That had significant implications for huge numbers of people who were not Maronite but lived in Lebanon. To the Maronite they would not be true Lebanese. With the Maronites possibly slipping into the demographic minority I wondered how they would react. Walid was strong in his opinions. 'Increasingly we are referred to as Arab. This we resent. We have our own language, which is based on Aramaic. We have our own Lebanese culture.'

Walid was the only Maronite studying at the Near East School of Theology. It must have been particularly difficult for him in that there were other Lebanese students who were Protestant, and certainly not Maronite. Were they true Lebanese in his thinking? Also there were Arab Christians from neighbouring countries, including the hated Syria. I asked him to tell me a little about his community. 'The Maronites are a sad people at the moment,' Walid explained. They blame themselves for losing the civil war and losing Lebanon. Since the war their position is much weaker and the danger of Islam is growing.'

I asked why they blamed themselves for losing the war. He shuffled around in his chair and said, 'because they feel that they could have tried harder. They divided up into factions during the war and sometimes fought one another. Most Maronites would have preferred to have peace with Israel. We are a trading people and we saw that as the way to prosperity. After all there are only five million Jews in Israel but there are three hundred million Muslims surrounding us. Maronites see Israel as a bridge to being part of Europe and America. We prefer that to looking east to Islam.'

I asked Walid to tell me more about what makes the Maronites a cohesive group. 'We are a mountain people,' he said. 'Whenever we have felt threatened throughout history we have gone back to our roots in the mountains. It happened during the war when most Maronites from Beirut fled to the mountains.' So who formed the main Christian grouping in Beirut? I had assumed that, because the Maronites considered themselves to be the major Christian denomination in Lebanon, they must be heavily represented in Beirut.

'Before the war, the biggest Christian group in Beirut was the Greek Orthodox,' Walid explained. 'But there were also Armenian Orthodox, Evangelicals and Maronites. The biggest danger from the Maronites today is that there is a growing demand for an autonomous 'Little Lebanon'. They want the Maronite areas in the mountains to break away from the rest of Lebanon and to be a Maronite country on its own. I see this as a result of an identity crisis. We consider ourselves to be Maronites not Arabs. A hundred years ago the Maronites in the mountains spoke their own Syriac language in ordinary conversation. My own Grandfather used this as his first language. The other problem is that the present Government is a puppet of Syria. Syrian troops force us to declare that we are Arabs. This causes much resentment and there is now a growing desire amongst young Maronites to learn and speak Syriac.'

It is almost inevitable that when a group feels that things are declining it looks back to the golden days and tries to recreate them. Forcibly imposing the Syrian line against the wishes of almost half the population might hold the line for the present. However, as soon as the grip is slackened, all the ingredients for a descent into civil war would come into play again.

Walid was now in full flow. He was a man of energy and passion. 'Identity is all about self-awareness. The Maronites were here before the Arabs. We were persecuted by the Byzantines and that was why we fled to the mountains, to Mount Lebanon. So the Arabs are new on the scene.' I am always fascinated by the perspective of history in the whole of the Middle East. Byzantine persecutions are seen as yesterday so that the Arabs are marginalized as immigrants. Whereas in other parts of the world new arrivals have been assimilated into the population, it seems that the religious affiliations of people groups in the Middle East have prevented assimilation.

Walid wanted me to know about a revival of spiritual awareness amongst young Maronites. 'The calling to become a monk is being grasped by many young men in a way we have not seen for years. We now have eight hundred Maronite monks in Lebanon. They are the conscience of the Maronite Nation. By looking to the church the young Maronites are resisting being diluted into Arabism'. This matched what I had observed amongst the Coptic Orthodox in Egypt. 'The presence of fifty thousand Syrian troops in Lebanon, and an officially enforced line that we are Arab means a lot of pain.'

I could see that the Maronite Church could become a rallying point for young people in resistance. This could be dangerous, I observed. Walid looked exasperated. He sighed and wriggled in his seat. Then lunging forward he looked ready to launch into a speech. 'Not really,' he continued with resignation in his voice. 'Our Maronite church hierarchy do not represent general feelings. I don't mean the monks. I'm talking about the bishops, priests and abbots. They tend to follow the Vatican and its policies too closely'. I asked if he could explain what he meant. As the Maronites were in communion with Rome, he explained, they had to follow Vatican diplomacy. That meant not rocking the boat. This was puzzling to me because if the Maronites were not officially part of the Roman Catholic Church I wondered how Rome could exert its influence through the hierarchy. Drawing his chair forward, Walid looked at the floor. 'They don't adapt Roman policies to our particular situation. For example they accept Rome's Middle East policy and its views on Islam. Our church leaders accept this but many Maronites find they cannot. We like the Pope but we don't like the interventions of the Vatican.' I asked why the Maronites weren't officially part of the Roman Catholic Church. 'We were only brought into communion with Rome during the time of the Crusades but we are much older than that. We still use an oriental Liturgy for example. Our priests may be married or single. But they cannot get married once they are priests. Our bishops are always unmarried. We have a long tradition of independence. The Pope is our symbol of unity not authority. But our church hierarchy is becoming authoritarian and remote from the people. They are becoming like Roman Catholic clergy around the world.'

During our initial meeting over lunch, Walid had mentioned something of a revival going on amongst the Maronite community in Lebanon. What did this mean? And how did it show itself? He said that he could not give evidence. It was a personal impression but he felt that during the war many Maronites lost touch with their spirituality. 'Religion was used as a tool of war,' he said. 'But now we have a need to return to our roots. We have an oriental spirituality not one dictated by Rome. Many young churchgoing Maronites feel that revival is necessary. We must get closer to eastern traditions and see where our history is shared. But Rome interferes. It refuses to appoint popular church leaders, just those who will agree with them. The priests love getting frequent trips to Rome. They are well educated and cultured. They want to climb the ladder of success and so are prepared to keep to the party line'. The universal nature of the Roman church with its concerns on international, literally catholic, perspectives was clearly at odds with a church that only identified with one culture group. Walid continued, 'Churchgoing is increasing. Of course this might be bigotry. It might be that going to church feeds our prejudices as Maronites. We find it difficult to separate the cultural from the spiritual.'

I was conscious of Gideon's frustrations with the Lebanese. They would not allow God to move in revival, he had maintained. But Walid was talking about a revival of young Maronites. Did I need to change my understanding? Was this revival? I had a mental picture of campaigns and opportunities to decide to be Christian. I thought of moves of the Holy Spirit with the miraculous never far away. An increase in churchgoing was hardly revival?

Walid laughed at my perceived simplicity. 'You have a western understanding of revival. For a Maronite, being a Christian, being a Maronite is part of his identity. This means that if he wants to regain his identity, as many did in the war, then a return to church is necessary. There are now many people praying at the holy places, for example.' So, to Walid a revival of the Holy Spirit was a western concept. A strengthening of cultural identity was what revival meant to him. Inevitably this involved a resurgence in church attendance. On reflection I remembered my experiences of the Coptic Orthodox in Egypt. Their revival was a coming back to the Liturgy, to the Bible, to prayer. There were changed lives. There were testimonies of the miraculous. Clearly this definition of revival was not a Western fabrication. But it was not the experience of Walid.

I was also interested in finding out more of Walid himself. What was it that had drawn him to a Protestant Bible College? The Holy Spirit, perhaps? 'I belong to a wealthy middle class Maronite family', he said. 'During the war I spent a lot of my time in nightclubs and the like. Sometimes there was shelling and the bombs exploded around the area where I was but I just wanted to have a good time. I seemed to have no fear; neither was I thinking much about eternal issues. Once, on a ferry going to Larnaca the Syrians started to shoot at the ship. We were all afraid but survived. But most of the time we would just accept all this as part of our way of life. Of course we were very political. You couldn't help it. We would demonise the enemy and once you do that hatred and bitterness are never far behind. But once the war ended I started to ask myself a lot of questions. Where was God? Why were so many people killed? My neighbours, my cousin, even my grandfather. I saw him blown up by a Syrian bomb. He was paralysed and died a few months later.'

These painful memories were still unresolved. He looked angry as he continued, 'I wanted to challenge God. Some parts of the Bible were helpful. I read Job, Ecclesiastes, and the Song of Songs. Job suffers greatly but in the end he wins through because he was faithful. In Lebanon today I don't see the faithful having won. The answer will only be seen when Lebanon is free. My family are church-goers. They attend church as Maronites not so much because they are believers, more because are Maronites. Like all easterners we are not so much believers, but we love our church. It is our identity. After the war when I was asking these angry kinds of questions I gradually realised that I was a true believer. I might not know the answers but I did believe. I began to want to know more about God and so Bible College seemed to be a good idea.

This was a refreshingly frank account of the way his life and his attitudes had shaped up. What did he want to do with his new knowledge? Did he intend to become a monk or a priest? At that he sat back with a big smile. 'No', was the emphatic reply. 'I came to NEST because afterwards I want to help my church in a new way of thinking. For us, the spiritual, the cultural and the political are all linked. Our faith is about the whole of life. But the cultural and political sides should be informed and guided by the spiritual'. This seemed such a refreshing view. Clearly he had not reached his own personal goal but he was conscious of his own shortcomings. What is more, because he was working at the problem from inside, he was best placed to help others.

I wondered what line of work he was in when not at College. Again he smiled. 'I am the son of the boss'. No line of business was explained. He was a young man with financial backing to study and to offer himself back into his community. Finally, I asked about his aspirations for Lebanon. He was very clear about this. 'Lebanon must remain multi-cultural. But we must be free of foreign forces. I cannot accept the idea of a separate Maronite homeland. We should cherish diversity and freedom. Let people be who they are.'

I wondered whether the Maronite church sought to recruit beyond its own people? Walid said that it was not an evangelistic church although it tried to teach and increase the spirituality of its own people. 'We are Maronites by birth,' he reminded me. How did he view other churches? 'Fine,' was the rapid response. 'But I do not like churches like the Baptists because they try and steal our people. Why don't they try and convert Muslims?

Such groups just cause division amongst the Christians. We cannot afford this. We want less divisions.' As we ended our time together I asked what was top of the agenda for the future of Lebanon. 'It is that we have our human rights and freedom, and that Lebanon should once again be the beacon of this right across the Middle East. It's my dream.'

I had much to ponder as I walked back to my room. Having resolved that the next day, my last in Beirut, should be spent reflecting and writing, I was delighted to receive an invitation to go with All Saints' Anglican Church on a coach trip to the south of Lebanon. It could be a form of relief after all the intensity of the last few days. This was to see archaeological sites and places of pilgrimage within the area close to the Israeli-held section. Not having been outside Beirut I jumped at the opportunity. The pilgrimage element of the trip was to visit places that may or may not have been associated with Jesus. It was as vague as that. But it was something different. The idea of going close to the Israeli zone had the same attraction as peering over the edge of a volcano.

All Saints' Church looked entirely new, as this area had seen some of the heaviest bombardment during the civil war. During that time it had been damaged and desecrated by Shi'a militia. Its rebuilding and reconsecration was like a beacon of hope. When all the redevelopment around it has been accomplished it will become a prime site in the business heart of Beirut. A group of expatriate members of the congregation, led by Nigel, their pastor, was already gathering. We were summoned into church for our initial prayers before climbing on board a luxury air-conditioned coach. Once it finally eased into the chaotic traffic on the corniche it headed south through the slums to the south of the city.

Arriving at the ancient port of Sidon after 45 minutes' drive, we were taken through a charming old Souq to the miniscule Greek Orthodox Church dedicated to St Nicholas. Next to it, in use as an office and souvenir shop, was the room where St Paul slept on his way from Jerusalem to Rome...allegedly! And that was part of the fun of the day. Nothing was really substantiated but a great deal of pilgrimage and veneration has been built on such flimsy evidence. But Paul did stay over in Sidon, so does it matter if we don't actually know which room it was that he slept in? We were swept back into the bus as we had a schedule to keep. We were next taken up a hill to Maghdouche overlooking Sidon. Here a magnificent monument and statue of the Virgin Mary looked out on the city and nearby Palestinian refugee camp. The reason for this spot was that it was where the Virgin Mary rested whilst her Son went into Sidon to preach. Of course! It was a very human picture but there was no evidence, only tradition, to back it up. We had a reading and prayer in a lovely cave church run by the Greek Catholics before climbing the monument. Unfortunately industrial haze and the flat lighting of the late morning made the splendid views a little less dramatic than they would otherwise have been.

We then drove south again to the ancient city of Tyre. First port of call was St Anthony's Catholic Church, looked after by an Egyptian Franciscan monk called Father Luke. It was interesting to find that he was also known locally as the Father of the Shi'a because a number of Muslims attended his church as well as Christians. This amazing spot of inter-faith work was intriguing but no-one seemed willing to explain it further. In this land of heated bigotry it was perhaps just as well that this gem of Christian service was kept out of the limelight.

In the church, Nigel celebrated Holy Communion using an amalgam of English and Kenyan Anglican liturgies. Joseph, a Sudanese Anglican clergyman, assisted him. A Kakwa from Yei in Southern Sudan, he was doing further training at the Mediterranean Bible College in Beirut. In his clerical black, dog collar and yellow 'Jesus' baseball cap he attracted a great deal of interest from people as we passed along the streets afterwards!

Tyre has magnificent Roman and Byzantine ruins. As the major Phoenician port it had been a hive of activity. We saw the remains of the Crusader cathedral, built on the ruins of the earlier Byzantine one. However, the backcloth of more recent war-damaged houses was a bit more poignant for me. I chatted for a while with some United Nations soldiers – from Poland and the Netherlands – before climbing back in the coach. This time we went to a magnificent site. A complete Roman and Byzantine city had been abandoned and then buried by drifting sand from the beach. It was just waiting to be uncovered. The reason for our visit was an obelisk, which had originally been located outside the temple. The local tradition was that Jesus had rested by leaning against it when he visited Tyre! During the Middle Ages, Crusaders had chipped lots of pieces from its lower quarters. Much more impressive was the hippodrome, which included the chariot racetrack. With its grandstands and central reservation it looked as if it could still be in use. In the mid-afternoon sunshine, with a cooling breeze blowing in from the sea, it was a most pleasant interlude. But, all too soon, we were being called back to the bus.

The journey now took on a very different nature. We left the big highway and headed inland into a hilly area. At times the road was unmade and we generated clouds of white dust as we bumped our way along it. People nearby would stop to watch us pass, sometimes giving a bemused smile. We passed a United Nations checkpoint manned by Ghanaians and were given a cheery wave from the soldiers. Then, going up what was little more than a lane we arrived at a small mosque near the village of Qleile. In open country surrounded by hills on top of which were

Israeli defence positions, it seemed as if we were in potentially dangerous territory. The previous night the lane along which we were driving had been bombed only a kilometre further on. Next to the mosque was a school, bombed out by the Israelis in 1996.

Next to that mosque stood the goal of our visit, the mausoleum for Nabi Omran. This is the name that Muslims give to Joachim, traditionally considered to be the father of the Virgin Mary and thus the Grandfather of Jesus. Inside the mausoleum was a tomb draped in Islamic cloths. It was suggested to me that this mausoleum was certainly not old enough to be that of Mary's father. Nevertheless it was a place that was venerated by Christians and Muslims alike and, as such, it was important to respect the spiritual power of such a symbol. On our way out of the mausoleum, one of the guides assured me that Nabi Omran was a good Muslim. This seemed to stretch credulity in that if he were a Muslim then he could not have been the grandfather of Jesus. I was thus able to dismiss this as being too far fetched. However I then learned something about Islam. Muslims have no problem in believing that Jesus and Mary were Muslims since, for them, Islam existed since the time of Adam.

This area was very sensitive militarily and had a heavy Hizbollah presence owing to the military occupation of parts of south Lebanon. We then drove to another politically sensitive area nearby. This was the village of Qana Jalil. Some people have claimed that this might be the Cana of Galilee where Jesus turned the water into wine. Of course this is highly improbable since there is a Cana just a few kilometres from Jesus' home village of Nazareth, in Galilee. But first we drove to the centre of the village where there was a mass grave for one hundred and six people who were killed on 18th April 1996. The Israeli air force bombed a United Nations post where local people were sheltering from the massive bombardments of 'Operation Grapes of Wrath'. Two soldiers from Fiji were also killed and the burned out kitchen was preserved as it was found as a grim reminder of what happened that day. Driving into the village we were watched silently by people in the street. This was a very different reaction to other people across south Lebanon. At the monument, we gathered around and prayed for the victims of war across the world. The long lines of tombs stood as silent testimonial to the dead. Small bunches of flowers had been placed alongside glass cases containing photographs and mementoes of children whose lives had been destroyed by this atrocity. Walking behind the graves to the bombed kitchen, about half a dozen teenage boys began shouting. Our local guide said they were upset that we had come to stare. Then a red BMW festooned in Hizbollah insignia screeched up alongside. The driver got out and started playing a tape loudly. This, we were informed, was a political speech about Israel and Lebanon.

Not to be unnerved I decided that I would go over to another group of teenagers. Four rather sullen boys were sitting near the graves. I noticed one had a soccer shirt. Introducing myself as coming from England I asked if any spoke any English. None would admit to it. I pointed to the boy's shirt and mentioned the word 'Football'. Immediately they all brightened up. The boy with the soccer shirt proudly showed me the Milan insignia and another boy asked 'Manchester?' I referred to Manchester United and we were away. All that seemed necessary was to mention football teams and footballers and they got very excited. One boy just kept saying 'Real Madrid'. After a couple of minutes of this, when I was running out of teams to quote, and was dangerously close to mentioning Accrington Stanley, we were called to the bus. As we drove away my four boys came to wave us off, all smiles.

We were dropped at the other end of the village. The street led up a hill with lovely views of the valley bathed in the golden light of a low sun. At the top was an excavation. The story here was that the local landowner worked in

Senegal where he met some missionaries. They asked him where he came from and when he told them that he came from Qana Jalil, they explained to him about Cana of Galilee and the miracle of water being changed into wine at the wedding. While home on holiday the man started to excavate his own land and found Roman remains. This confirmed to him that this was the real Cana of Galilee. The local tourist authorities were delighted to go along with this. The excavation had revealed some water jars and olive presses. Conveniently in the man's garden next to the excavation was a tree. We were told that this was the one under which the marriage took place. How it could even be considered to be at least two thousand years old demanded a huge stretch of the imagination. When we were then told that the miracle was performed at Jesus' own wedding, it seemed as if we were with Alice in Wonderland.

Walking back to the coach, I chatted to Joseph, the Sudanese priest. He was clearly enjoying the incredulity of all these so-called Biblical sites. I suggested that Southern Sudan might claim that Jesus visited Yei or Yambio at some point in his life. A tukl could be labelled as the one in which he lived and made available for visits. Then pilgrims might descend, bringing much needed revenue. He smiled and said that Jesus is there now, in the hearts of the believers. The story of the Sudanese church itself is testimony to the truth of the Gospel, he maintained.

The bus took us a short distance to a high point overlooking the valley. By now the sun was dipping behind the ridge, leaving large areas of the valley in shadow. Nevertheless it was still very warm and humid. Descending a rough track to a rock we were shown a carved central figure with 12 more around it. The suggestion was that this represented Jesus and his 'students'. By further stretch of our credulity we were told that thus it must have been here, rather than the earlier site, that the water was turned into wine. Informed opinion seemed to be of the view that the figures carved on the rock, and others in the vicinity, are *steles*, (Roman headstones on burial sites). If that were so then, if the base were to be excavated, it would reveal the remains of bodies and prove it. However that would then undermine the Jesus potential for pilgrim visits.

Descending further, we arrived at a cave. This, we were told, was where Jesus is alleged to have taken refuge from danger at home when the Pharisees were threatening him. We then climbed back on the bus and headed back to the coast. The drive back to Beirut through Sidon was uneventful and I was dropped off at the eastern end of Rue Hamra. The day's outing had been a wonderful antidote to the tensions of the previous few days. I reflected that spirituality is sometimes not objective. The Western pre-occupation with proof and logic prevents some people from experiencing anything more than the tangible. At the same time I was most concerned about integrity and truth. To me the sites of veneration were little more than baloney, and yet did they aid people to experience and to worship the Living God? My understanding of Jesus from the Bible is that he is the personification of Truth. If that is so then I could not reconcile the deliberate use of the phoney in pilgrimage.

CHAPTER SIXTEEN

TRAVELS IN SYRIA

On the dot of two, the 'servees' arrived. It was a massive Syrian-registered Dodge of about 1970 vintage. Capable of taking five passengers plus the driver it was a monster. The overweight and chain-smoking driver slumped across the bench seat flicking his column change gear stick as the car roared along. Racing through the Beirut suburbs the car was quickly heading home. I was most impressed not only by its acceleration but also by its hill climbing abilities. But most of all I was impressed by its deep melodic horn. In the midst of all the piddling little car horns of every traffic knot this car had the most regal of sounds. It was as if the king elephant had arrived in the harem!

On the way out of Beirut I chatted with the other passenger, a Syrian young man who in four weeks was due to emigrate to Philadelphia in the USA. He was useful as interpreter for the driver who spoke no English. Like many bright young men in Syria, he found that opportunities for career development were severely restricted in his native country. Emigration was the only option, he maintained. To do so legally involved payment of a not inconsiderable sum to the authorities, as he had to buy his way out of service in the armed forces.

Within a short distance east of Beirut, the mountains present a formidable barrier. This was no problem to our driver who relished the challenge. As we romped up a particularly steep climb in the suburbs, another young man flagged us down. He then joined me in the back of the car. He also was going to Damascus but he remained silent throughout the journey. Now the serious motoring began. Roaring up the hills sometimes we found ourselves overtaking three lanes of traffic on a road designed for two lanes each way. And this was sometimes whilst going around a blind bend. I was torn between the need to watch where we were going and the need to pray! Leaving the suburbs behind we entered a land of mountains and hill top villages. In one village the traffic was reduced to a crawl in order to overtake a platoon of the Syrian army as it marched up hill.

Once over the summit, the driver seemed as if he were bent on breaking some record – perhaps even the sound barrier. Then without warning, just before reaching the floor of the Be'kaa Valley, we pulled in outside a cafe. The driver then demanded his fare and went in. The other two men went shopping – for shaving cream and *Nescafé*! The stop was only brief and ten minutes later we set off again. After the mountain scenery the valley floor seemed very green. In front of us rose another mountain range and, part way up, the Lebanese frontier post. There was no queue as most people travel in the morning to Damascus. My passport was processed and I was technically out of Lebanon. I was therefore most surprised, on getting back into the car, to find that the car swung around and we were driving back into Lebanon. It transpired that our driver had learned of a Syrian army officer about a mile back who wanted a lift to Damascus. I may be wrong but suspect that someone was engaging in a bit of private enterprise. The army officer had no luggage other than cigarettes and I guessed that he would probably make quite a profit in Syria. Having collected him and a dozen or so carrier bags of cigarettes we then went back to the border where we entered the Customs shed. Did we have anything to declare? The Syrian army officer told the Lebanese customs official to let us through, and we were quickly on our way, driving along a well-aligned dual carriageway road for a few miles until, descending from the summit we approached a series of concrete arches and benign pictures of President Assad. We were in Syria.

Pulling up at the Immigration point, I had to have my passport processed. The others stayed in the car as I walked into the barn of a shed labelled 'Immigration'. Just as in Lebanon, there was no queue here either. Walking up to the desk labelled 'Foreigners' I found a soldier reading a book. He didn't look up so I stretched across to where another soldier was sitting. He slowly pushed a form over to me. Then the first soldier seemed to come out of his book and offered to process my passport. By now the driver and the two fellow civilian passengers were agitating to get going, so they came to join me. They left the Syrian officer reclining in the front seat enjoying one of his haul of cigarettes. The driver banged the desk and started to give verbal abuse to the soldiers. This did not go down well as they dug their heels in. Where was I going to stay? The address I had been given, All Saints' Community Church, was not a valid address. Remembering that Stephen Griffith, my friend in Damascus, had asked me to meet him at the Meridien Hotel, I offered this address. It seemed to suit the need. Honour was satisfied: the driver had speeded up the process but the soldiers had not been seen to succumb to his pressure. Moments later I was back in the car, passively inhaling the smoke of my four fellow travellers. The journey was now downhill at the most fearful of speeds. If there had been a puncture we would have been done for.

Damascus is situated in an oasis. Looking down on it from the mountains the desert stretched away into the distance but the oasis could be seen as a dark area. Very soon we were driving between lines of six or seven storey blocks of uniform flats reminiscent of Eastern Europe; no surprise to learn that this was largely a

Romanian development. The would-be emigree was dropped off in front of one of these blocks. An old lady squealed a welcome from the balcony as he ran across the road into the building. His mother would have her son for only a few weeks before losing him to America. Time was short for her.

The Meridien Hotel is a well-known meeting point for international visitors in Damascus. Its plush entrance and upmarket limousines provided a strange backcloth as the battered yellow Dodge roared up. Seeing the driver and I struggling with my gigantic case, a porter rushed up to help. I said farewell to my fellow passengers and thanked the driver for a safe delivery, before being ushered into a magnificent lobby. The porter was bemused that I did not want the check-in desk as I settled into one of the huge leather settees. After a few moments I convinced him that I was awaiting a friend. Not having any Syrian money at that point was a little embarrassing, but he left me to enjoy the air-conditioned atmosphere. It was not for long. Just having begun to do some work on my computer I heard a jovial voice demand, 'How long have you been here?' It was Stephen, dressed impeccably in a white suit, with black shirt and clerical collar. He was on his way to conduct a Sunday evening Anglican service for expatriate families in the Shell Centre and had called in the hotel just in case I might be there.

Stephen went and brought his car to the front of the hotel and I squeezed my luggage in the boot. We then drove off for the Shell Centre where a congregation of about 20 people had gathered. I sat next to the Brazilian Ambassador. Stephen preached on the Good Shepherd. He had a brilliant way of grabbing attention and then really being able to teach deep truths. He pointed out that usually, in the Middle East, shepherds were a bad lot. They were kept on the outskirts of society. For Jesus to call himself the Good Shepherd was a contradiction in terms. Equally, Stephen argued, many of the ideas of the Gospel were and are revolutionary in concept. The idea of God as Father, Stephen felt, was important. Just as many are embarrassed by the use of such a term because their experience of their father has been bad, so we needed to rediscover the 'Good Father'. God isn't any old bad father, he contended. Somehow, in the lands of the Bible, such exposition had added poignancy.

Stephen was an enigmatic character. Not only was he the chaplain to the expatriate community but also had to serve the spiritual and physical needs of the hundreds of Sudanese refugees who ended up in Syria. On top of that he was appointed as representative of the Archbishop of Canterbury to the Orthodox churches based in Syria. For this last responsibility his job title was the grand sounding Apocrisiarios. It was through his connections that I was planning to visit the Orthodox within Syria and then, hopefully, in Turkey. After the service we drove to the Old City. Passing along Straight Street we were assailed by smells of spices, perfumes, and coffee. Lights and noise were everywhere. Then we parked and walked down some narrow lanes. Damascus at night has a wonderful feel to it. This ancient city with its maze of streets, its bustling trade, and ambling crowds wandering in the balmy atmosphere, makes for relaxation. We entered through a small door, went along a passageway, and came out in a courtyard. This was the setting for the exquisite Jabri House restaurant. The traditional eighteenth century Damascene house was built with balconies all around the courtyard. Vines and other climbing plants added to the relaxing atmosphere. A waiter, who treated us as if we were the most important people in the world, guided us to a table. Over the next hour or so I found the rigours of the previous weeks unravelling as we ate a comparatively simple meal. It was good to relax and talk to someone who understood travelling in the region.

After the meal we drove to his flat, situated in a busy commercial street. He lived on the third floor, and there was no lift. My suitcase never felt so heavy. I was regretting the volumes of literature I had accrued along the way. Remembering the young man at St Catherine's Monastery in Sinai who carried it on his shoulder I really felt my age. The apartment comprised a lounge, two bedrooms, a kitchen, bathroom and study. My room was at the front overlooking the street and had a small balcony from which I could watch the antics in the street below. Although by now it seemed late, the shops and stalls were still doing a roaring trade. In this part of the world much business is conducted after sundown to avoid the heat of the day. At the other end of the spectrum, I found that the street was comparatively quiet in the morning so I would need my alarm clock to wake me up.

The following morning I spent wandering around the city and gaining my bearings. It claims to be the oldest inhabited city in the world, although Aleppo might have a rival claim. Having been fought over many times from its earliest days, there is evidence of many of its invading occupiers still to be seen. During the twentieth century the Turks lost control of the city to the French, who had a mandate from the League of Nations. Independent Syria was established in 1946. To the casual observer, the French left much in the ambience of the architecture of the city, although it is the Roman and Ottoman Turkish influence that is probably the most striking. Wandering through the Old City I tried to avoid the attention of the sales men. 'Come and see my shop. Have tea. No need to buy.' Maybe, but it was wearing and time consuming...

The River Barada looked disgusting. Being an oasis river it never leaves the oasis but dries up some miles to the east of the city. It was full of rubbish thrown over bridges and it smelt foul. The water itself looked a bluish grey. Yet it was teeming with croaking bullfrogs and small black fishes. As the river never leaves the oasis I wondered how the frogs and fish ever got there in the first place.

Returning to Stephen's flat I was introduced to Chol, his Sudanese driver. It might seem incongruous for a clergyman to have a driver but I soon realised that in a country where many of the indigenous population are unemployed, it is exceptionally difficult for a displaced person to gain a meaningful job. I was to learn and experience more of the Sudanese community in the days that followed. Chol would become a good friend and my means of entry into their midst. After lunch, Stephen said that he would like to show me some Byzantine ruins that were normally inaccessible to the public owing to military sensitivities. However, as his job gave him diplomatic rights, he felt that we might gain admission to the area. Chol drove us into the countryside west of the city, up the road along which I had come the previous day. The contrast between his careful driving and that of my 'servees' driver from Beirut was indescribable. Turning south we headed off to the lower flanks of Mount Hermon. The great mountain, still with snow in the gullies, towered ahead of us as we drove past lots of military camps. We were, Stephen observed, very close to the Israeli border.

Stopping at a military roadblock, a young major, who remembered Stephen from a previous visit, asked if he could come with us. Stephen muttered to me that it was important to be affable and so he agreed. Adham was a young law graduate from the south of the country. One of the supposedly elusive Druze people he seemed quite the opposite, positively showering us with attention. Following a red dusty road more suited to a four-wheeled vehicle, Chol eventually parked the car in an area called Burqus and we walked up a very steep hillside to a ruined basilica at the summit. Dating from around the 6th Century this Byzantine structure had proved to be something of a mystery. In particular, experts could not agree as to why it was built on top of such a remote hillside. This was most unusual as Christian cathedrals are associated with centres of population but there was no evidence of a settlement having been built there.

As we got to the top Adham became very excited. He wanted to try and find a hidden chamber that he had once 'discovered'. Like a child released on the beach he had us leaping from rock to rock until, with great excitement, he was calling us to follow him down a tunnel. This emerged on a balcony, overlooking a cliff, from which stairs descended. Going down we came into the chamber that Adham wanted to show us. After the heat of the climb the atmosphere inside the chamber was refreshing. 'Nice weather!' exclaimed Adham. We then climbed out and looked at the structure. The Byzantines had built a series of arched rooms over which the basilica was constructed. Beyond this were the remains of a first century temple. On each side of the doorway was carved a cross showing, Stephen observed, that the Christians had taken over an older site and christened it.

Beyond this was a Syrian military cabin. Adham took us to it and invited us in to meet two young men. They were conscripts, part of the Syrian air force, and their job was to observe any planes flying over. The cabin contained two beds, a gas cylinder and cooker, a military radio, a civilian radio and little else. We were told that they had been isolated by snow from the outside world for weeks in the winter. Their only method of passing the time was body-building. They gave us a drink of water. 'It's safe to drink water up here,' Stephen said as an aside. Walking down the steep grassy slope to the car my the sight of Stephen, the Anglican priest, walking hand-in-hand with Adham, the Druze Syrian major was unbelievable to Western thinking. However this is just a sign of friendship in the Arab world. Unfortunately, as this was a sensitive military area, I had been advised not to bring my camera! Approaching the car we could hear a flute being played. A shepherd was leading a flock of long-horned sheep down Mount Hermon. It all seemed so idyllic and biblical.

Reaching Adham's tent by the roadblock he insisted that we stop for a cup of tea. As it was already late afternoon we accepted. Inside his tent, sitting on Adham's bed I really felt empathy for this young man. He showed us the pistol under his pillow used for finishing off snakes that occasionally came his way. His reading material was all about improving his English. On the tent pole were two small black and white magazine pictures of ladies from very discreet fashion adverts. I mused on what I might notice in the tent of a soldier from the so-called liberal West. When the tea had been brought in we quizzed Adham about his life. He had graduated from university and then had to do two and a half years in the army. As a graduate he was an officer. Knowing that he was to go into the army he had tried to save beforehand.

'I worked for two months in Lebanon,' he explained. 'My salary from the army is very low. We are given food rations but it doesn't suit my diet so I buy my own.' If he, as an officer, found life difficult I wondered how the ordinary soldier might survive. I looked outside the tent to where his men were sitting around looking very bored. 'They go straight in the army after school and do four years, or much less.' The temptation for corruption was obvious. As they manned roadblocks, maybe extortion or allowing smuggling at a price would go on.

Both Stephen and I were interested to know a little about the mysterious Druze faith. As a minority religion in Syria their rights, like those of the Christians, were protected by the Assad regime, but there was always a fear of militant Islam. 'We Druze believe in reincarnation,' he explained. 'If a Druze dies in an accident or as a result of fighting in war, then the person is automatically born again. Otherwise he would go directly to the God.'

In Adham's own family, he told us, there was living proof. 'My uncle had died in an accident and at the same time in a nearby village a baby had been born. When the child was ten he came and found my family and told them that he was the uncle. He then took them to where he had been killed and told them to dig. They then discovered gold. So that is the proof of reincarnation.'

It had been good for me to have time with this sensitive young soldier. I had been concerned about the possible brutalisation of young men in the military forces. But here was someone who was unspoilt by his tough life. As we drove back down towards Damascus, Stephen and I discussed this. We came to the conclusion that these men are not particularly innocent, but they are naive. Adham's excitement when taking us to find the chamber in the ruins was so illustrative of this.

The next day I met another young man who was equally concerned about his future and his faith. Returning to the flat in the evening I was followed up the stairs by a young man. Introducing himself as Jihad Tafas, he had brought food for a meal and had expected Stephen to arrive shortly.

'This is my breakfast, I cannot wait,' he said settling down in the lounge. Before I could even ask if he had been fasting or something, he said that he had food for me too. He then produced a pizza, a sausage roll and a can of *Seven Up*. Stephen had told me of this brilliant young member of the Syriac Orthodox Church. He was a computer teacher who was in the process of writing a computer program for the Syriac language. Aged twenty-three, he had outclassed all computer experts in the Syrian universities and was hoping to get funding to do further studies in the West. He had hoped for a grant from the World Council of Churches but that had not seemed forthcoming.

Stephen arrived later and joined the conversation. Jihad had a strong faith and was prepared to express it. 'In my village' was how he began several references to the village of Sadad, near Homs, where his father was described as being an extremely active parish priest.

Jihad, a tall strong young man, had little time for ideas that did not help his church and country. He had extremely patriotic views about Syria. The infamous bombing of Hama in 1983 was fully justified, he felt. If left unchecked the Muslim militants could have destabilised the whole country. The President had no alternative after bombs had gone off in city centres, after tracks had been removed from railways to cause a crash. He was very concerned that 'my church' should be strengthened.

The Syriac Orthodox priests generally disappointed him. Allegedly they did 'nothing' to help their people. In contrast he cited the money flowing from Saudi Arabia to persuade people to convert to Islam. 'People in my village have been offered bribes to convert. They have refused but many are without work. In six months they may have a different answer. The church should help the people in difficult times.' He was very concerned that his cousin should have declared himself to be an atheist. He could not see any reason for this. To him God was so obvious! 'The best way for you to understand what I am saying is for you to visit my village', he declared. I was delighted to accept the invitation on the understanding that his parents were agreeable. We arranged to go that weekend

Stephen had been particularly keen that I should meet one of his friends, His Grace Saba Esber, the Greek Orthodox Archbishop of Suwaida, in the south of the country. This time Chol was unavailable so Stephen drove. It was not long before we left the green of the oasis behind and headed out across the desert. As we drove along Stephen explained that in the early days of the church there were no denominations. But the local Patriarchate was based in Antioch. As splits occurred and new schismatic denominations were formed they each claimed descent from the true church in Antioch. However the Greek Church is the original. It is locally known as the Roum Orthodox Church because when it was founded it was part of the Roman Empire. This is confusing to

Western people because it seems as if it is tied to the Vatican. It is not. Indeed it has had many problems from the Roman Catholics, who are known throughout the Middle East as 'Latins'. In the seventeenth century Rome recognised a breakaway group of Orthodox who retained their Orthodox Liturgy but aligned with Rome. They are now known as Greek Catholics. I had, of course, visited one of their churches in Nazareth.

The Roum Orthodox Diocese of Suwaida had been declining for a number of years partly as a result of corruption by its bishop. People had left to join the Greek Catholics in large numbers, pastoral care of the clergy and the laity was severely deficient, and funds were not released for capital projects. In 1999 Bishop Saba was appointed after the previous bishop was forced to retire. This man, in his mid-forties, seemed to have boundless reserves of energy. Stephen felt that I would be astonished when I met him.

The journey took us from desert to an area of fertile volcanic soil. Great extinct volcanic plugs were penetrated by massive quarries, which were eating out their flanks like a virulent cancer. The combination of black volcanic soil and water from the nearby Jebel Druze made this an important arable area.

We pulled up outside the Bishopric (Bishop's House) to be ushered into a pleasant lounge with a table featuring ornamental Easter eggs. Tea and biscuits were served before Bishop Saba entered. Dressed in a cassock, rather than anything more formal, he seemed very pleased that we had come. We were ushered into his fine office and he joined us sitting on armchairs on the visitors' side of the desk. Bishop Saba was clearly an enthusiast and proceeded to explain how the church was reviving. The Easter celebrations had been particularly meaningful. He had led the Maundy Thursday foot washing ceremony, a practice new to the Roum Orthodox. The idea of the bishop washing the feet of the lay people was as mind blowing as it was symbolic of the new regime. He told us that a programme of church building was encouraging people back to church. We were shown a new guesthouse and conference centre that was being converted from an office block next to his cathedral. The cathedral itself had been gutted and restyled in an attractive way.

Bishop Saba then took us out to Kharrab, a small rural village. On the way we were shown a former monastery in Suwaida that was given to the Druze by the ruling French in the 1920s. During that time Druze people had settled in the area to avoid persecution by the Maronites in Lebanon. As France backed the Maronites in Lebanon it was considered that it would be helpful to encourage the Druze to settle in southern Syria. The Maronites were aligned to Rome, and to populate this area with Druze would inevitably hurt the Roum Orthodox, who were no friends of Catholicism and were considered by many French minds as dispensable. This remained as a large running sore in the minds of the Roum Orthodox, an unhappy reminder of the French Mandate era.

We crossed vast plains of waving crops to the small village of Kharrab. It was suffering from population loss to larger towns, especially Damascus. Some houses were used for weekend occupation and holiday letting but there was a real sense of decline. Bishop Saba took us to the old St George's Church, not now used. It was unlocked for us and we saw how it was beginning to fall into serious decay. Holes had appeared in the roof and it would probably not be long before it began to collapse. Stephen pointed out several architectural features that suggested that parts were definitely Byzantine from the sixth century. Bishop Saba said that he wanted teams of volunteers to come to restore the church so that it might be used for occasional services. Within this small village there was competition for the loyalties of the Christian population. We were shown the Greek Catholic and 'Evangelical' (Presbyterian Protestant) Churches, but Bishop Saba was keen to show us his new church. With a banner declaring (in Arabic) 'Blessed is he who comes in the Name of the Lord' it was a splendid building with a dome. Adjacent to the church was a derelict site cleared recently by a bulldozer. The bishop pointed sadly to this spot. Until the 1920s, this had been the location of the Bishopric. The bishop of the day had given sanctuary to some men on the run from the French authorities. He housed them in a Roman ruin with extensive cellars. The French response was to blow up the entire Bishopric. Stephen suggested that with a story like that it might be useful to invite the French Government to send a team of archaeologists to excavate the site. We then drove back to Suwaida where we said our farewells. I was given three kisses by the bishop – the first such occasion for me!

Later that day we visited the small village of Ezraa. Our purpose was to visit the sixth century Roum Orthodox church of St George, so named because it had a tomb reputed to house the body of the actual saint. There are many such claims throughout the Middle East as this saint was probably a Roman soldier in the region to the north. But somehow it did not seem to matter whether the real St George was in residence. What made the difference was that the story of George and the dragon was a picture of triumph over evil. Similarly, in the face of invaders over the centuries, faith had always seen Christians through.

Over the west door of the church was a Greek inscription dated 515. Translated it said: 'What was once an abode of demons has become a house of God; where once sacrifices were made to idols, there are now choirs of angels; where God was provoked to wrath, now He is propitiated.' The point of the inscription is that this had been a pagan temple, and had been 'baptised'. Even its octagonal shape harked back to its earlier role. It is one of the most ancient churches still in continuous use anywhere. As it had been largely unchanged by its changing fortunes, it gave a glimpse of the style of what the ruins in other places might have looked like before they were destroyed.

Driving back to Damascus at high speed along the dual carriageway, we took in a wide vista: way over on our left the Golan Heights leading up to snow-capped Mount Hermon, on our right plains rolling towards Iraq. Somehow this encapsulated the compact dimensions of the lands of the Bible. The hatreds and the wars they had spawned seemed so futile in the light of that sunset. If only these traditional enemies could learn to live in peace... but then who was I, a mere visitor, I was in no position to tell them how it should be.

CHAPTER SEVENTEEN

LIFE IN SADAD

There is something both appalling and yet compelling about poverty. I remember as a child visiting friends who lived in tumbledown homes we euphemistically called 'slums'. Giving them an emotive name like that gave justification to the violent way in which vast swathes of vibrant cities were destroyed and communities smashed. All in the name of progress. They were certainly terrible places from the point of view of comfort, hygiene, appearance and many other indicators of what we call 'good standards'. But they were homes.

I had arranged with Jihad Tafas to visit his home village of Sadad. Stephen drove me to Jihad's apartment on the other side of the city. 'Many of the people here are from my village,' said Jihad as Stephen drove his car into a jungle of ramshackle buildings, along narrow alleyways. Eventually we reached a right angle that his modest sized car could not be expected to negotiate so we just left it blocking the alleyway and walked the last hundred metres. Faces stared out of every doorway. Small children ran away from us. The houses seemed to oppress all their inhabitants and I felt relieved as we reached the door to Jihad's accommodation. It was a one-roomed bed-sit. He shared a kitchen and toilet across a courtyard. In his tiny room a computer on a desk seemed out of place. Jihad told me that he had never seen a computer until four years earlier but now had succeeded in learning all that could be taught in Syria about programming.

He collected his bag and then we went back to the car. I sympathised with Stephen, as he had to reverse the car along the alleyway, trying to avoid the stone steps protruding into his way. He succeeded on all but one occasion. At last we reached the bus station from where the bus to Sadad would leave, having three quarters of an hour to wait before departure. The bus was a high-wheelbase vehicle, more like a lorry chassis with a bus body. I had to let the driver take my passport details whilst all the passengers had to give their identity cards for inspection. Upon leaving the bus station, the sheet with these details was given to the police. Jihad explained that this was for security purposes. His village was totally Christian and the police needed to be certain that no troublesome people would go there. I mused that if I were a 'troublemaker', I would not travel by bus! Jihad went on to praise the security of the government because it prevented Islamic fundamentalists from planned excesses.

Jihad explained that in 1983, when the government had bombed the Muslims in Hama, it was only after repeated warnings. He seemed to be repeating a well-rehearsed mantra. He was very patriotic and felt that his government was doing an excellent job in both protecting the community from wickedness and liberal ideas from the West as well as from the malicious intentions of Israel. As the desert flashed past the windows I tried to say that hating countries was not a valid Christian response. It was important to love people whilst perfectly reasonable to take exception to their government's policies. I even went as far as saying that there are good Israelis. This was a bit near the bone so I backed off.

At one point on the slow journey we pulled up in a small town and the driver got out and started to change one of the back tyres. Crowds gathered around, with each person seeming to offer advice to the driver as he exchanged one tyre for another. The new tyre looked no better than its predecessor. Both seemed bald. After two hours, gradually climbing from the oasis on the plain, we reached a desert plateau. Sprawling out ahead of us was a dusty village 'My village', Jihad said proudly. This was Sadad.

The drop down from the bus was about half a metre, and nearly sent me sprawling on the rubble. I managed to regain my footing just in time. 'Sorry, Father', called Jihad. Calling me 'Father' was, he explained, a term of respect. In my dishevelled state, trying to recompose myself in the cloud of dust thrown up by the departing bus, I had never felt less respectable. But then respect is an honour granted rather than dependent upon the feelings of the moment. Jihad grabbed my overnight bag and led me along a gravel road to his home. By now the sun was baking the road and I felt dazzled by the brightness. Sadad seemed to stretch out over a large area. After walking for about five minutes Jihad announced that we had arrived. There in front of us was a stone house. With a flurry of excitement, Jihad's parents, Abdullah and Hapsa, welcomed us at the front door. They were clearly excited to see their son come home. Their delight was eclipsed by that of Wasim, their ten year old youngest child. He went into ecstasy at the return of his elder brother. Two of his sisters, Mary and Widat were there along with Abdullah's widowed mother. Mary was unmarried but Widat had her two children, Sandra and baby Simone with her. This was quite a reception party. I was warmly invited in and shown into a gracious room with ornately carved upholstered chairs around the perimeter. On the walls were tapestries of St George, the Virgin Mary and a woman in a nightclub!

Abdullah was a priest in the Syriac Orthodox Church. A school teacher until his ordination, aged 45, nine years previously, he believed this to be the highest of all callings and had found it extremely fulfilling. His pleasant home was a reflection on the way he had saved his money as a teacher prior to ordination, including spells in both the USA and Yemen. Abdullah was careful to explain that the Syriac Church was very poor and so he was able to maintain a certain lifestyle only because he had made savings in earlier life. Shortly after our arrival, Father Abdullah (Arabic for 'Servant of God') had to depart for a neighbouring village where he was to take the Saturday evening Liturgy. We stayed at home and Jihad showed me around his garden with great affection for it. There was the vegetable plot with tomatoes, beans, cabbage and wheat. There were trees laden with ripening fruit, and there were lots of vines stretched across a series of trellises. Also very much in evidence were hens and a cockerel, as well as rabbits being bred for food. Jihad looked in vain for his two tortoises, which, he assured me, were there just to eat spiders!

Food kept arriving at surprising moments and I never quite got into the swing of what was mezze and what was likely to be the main meal. After eating biscuits and drinking Arabic coffee we launched into a meal of salad, fried chicken and chips. Hapsa found it difficult to understand that I could not compete for appetite with her twenty three year old son. To offer food to a visitor was a sign of welcome. To refuse food could be misinterpreted as being an insult. How could I survive the generosity? I noticed Father Abdullah was careful with what he ate and he explained that this was to avoid putting on weight. My hesitance was the same, I explained to Hapsa. We older men had to be careful. She smiled, accepting what I meant.

'Now I show you my village,' said Jihad. It was six o'clock and the sun was in terminal decline but it seemed pleasant outside. In fact it was not unlike a breezy summer's evening in Britain. The wind had got up and was flapping at any loose curtains, washing or flags. Away to our left we could see the mountains of Lebanon standing starkly against the setting sun. Looking like a transparency, curtains of rain were cascading from the red clouds over the mountains. To the south and east chilly grey clouds announced the approach of night.

Undeterred, Jihad showed me around 'my village'. Most of the houses were constructed of breezeblocks coated with desert mud. To the untrained eye they might be hundreds of years old, or could have been built last year. Sadly there were gaps where houses had been demolished or were collapsing. Rural depopulation was a major problem in Sadad. There were not enough jobs for the people, and those that could work, such as poultry farmers, often found that the price for their products was often insufficient to support a viable living.

As we walked through the village, Jihad told me that he had left Sadad at the age of eighteen. 'I needed to gain qualifications to work abroad. I want to learn lots of skills and then return to marry and bring up a family in my village.' The main village church was having difficulties, Jihad said. Having resisted Muslim advances for centuries, the village remained one hundred percent Christian but there were clear signs that all was not well. For a village that considered that it could trace its origins even to the Book of Genesis it seemed that its Christian cohesion might fall apart owing to apathy.

I was aware that Jihad was awaiting the outcome of an application through the Syriac Church for funding from the World Council of Churches to do Computing Studies in the West. If it turned down this request where would this young man turn? 'I want to use computers to help my church.' He said this with such eagerness, but it was also the sound of desperation.

We saw not only vacant plots where houses used to be, but also many walled fields that were 'dead'. Jihad commented, 'Our spring of water dried up about ten years ago. Those fields could produce crops again, but we need help.' Jihad sounded a note of sadness once more. Where were they to turn for the aid they so clearly needed?

Darkness was encroaching as we made our way back along the white dusty lanes between the mud-covered houses. The lights were on in the Tafas home as we came into the main entrance room. The entire family was sitting on the floor round the walls. The television was showing a nature programme about crocodiles. Hapsa was busy kneading dough for the next day's Bread of Thanksgiving. Rather than disturb the television, Jihad and I went into the main lounge, where we might sit on chairs. We talked about the situation facing the Syriac Christians today. 'It is very bad, Father', said Jihad. 'Because there is no good life here many people go to Damascus and other places for work. But they don't go to the Church. They think the Church is only for the rich. That it doesn't care for them.'

'Is that true?' I enquired.

'Yes it is', he said sadly. 'And without the Church they get to do bad things. The Syrian Catholic Church used to give cash to our people if they would join them. Now it is the Muslims who bribe people to convert. Our church should be on its guard. If people feel that our church won't help them, but that others might, then it should watch out'.

This reactionary view, almost dog in a manger, was slightly alarming. Jihad was seeing his culture and his faith being assailed on all sides and it was easy to throw blame. I tried to suggest that the people of Sadad were possibly drifting away from church not so much because of Islam but because of economic pressures. The inexorable lure of the city for jobs, the difficulty of making a living in agriculture, and the secular forces of the media, were all contributory factors to decline in rural worshippers in many countries.

Sunday morning provided an opportunity to experience the rural Syriac Orthodox church for myself. Even though it was only half past seven, the sun was shining strongly in the clear desert air. I joined the family for breakfast of Arabic coffee and a small unleavened bun, part of the bread of thanksgiving that Hapsa had been making the previous night. Abdullah had already gone to the church in the nearby village for which he had responsibility. Jihad and I walked to St Sergius' Church near to the family home. It took ten minutes during which I was delighted with how clean the air was, compared to Damascus.

The Service of Divine Liturgy was in full swing by the time we reached the ancient church. As I had already learned, in Orthodox tradition there is no sense that one has to be there for the entire duration of the service. The important thing is to be there for some of the Liturgy. After all the service is for God, not for the congregation. We had a few brief greetings at the door before Jihad led me inside. A church capable of seating possibly a couple of hundred people, it had maybe half that number in attendance. Without warning me as to his intentions, Jihad asked me to follow him. We walked straight to the screen at the front and then through the right hand opening, drawing the red curtain behind us as we went through. Standing behind the screen it was fascinating to watch the priest as he said the Liturgy, with his back to the people in front of the altar. He was very conscious of the need to use the microphone effectively.

Every now and again a deacon would read from the Bible or chant a prayer. But the thing that made all the difference, as Jihad reminded me, was that this was all in Aramaic, the language spoken by Jesus. One of the deacons motioned to Jihad and he took me into the vestry where we were both kitted out with an alb. I was given a white one with frilly cuffs and told that I would be one of the 'angels'. Jihad also had a sash and became involved in chanting some of the prayers. The consecration of the Host was high drama with the priest waving his hands over the elements while Jihad and one of the deacons would wobble tambourine-like dishes on poles over the altar to make a fluttering noise. This was to represent the effect of the cherubim. At this point, as in other parts of the service, incense was liberally offered around the church.

Eventually the bread was intincted into the wine and then laid out in pieces making up the shape of a cross on the paten. At this point everything seemed to stop and I thought the priest was giving out the notices. But no! Jihad told me that this was the sermon, based on John 3. The message was that the congregation could not assume their salvation. They must be born again. Then the service quickly came to an end. The bread of blessing was given out to the congregation and we went into the vestry to take off our albs. When we emerged the church was empty, just a haze of incense giving away the fact that five minutes earlier a service had been conducted.

As we changed, one of the old deacons came over to tell me that thirty years ago he had spent three days in England: one in London and two in Loughborough. He then went on to tell me that Cherie Blair had given birth to a boy. I first heard it in St Sergius' Syriac Church in Sadad!

The priest, Father Termer Awil, was a short man in his late fifties. He was very pleased, even proud, to show me the historic artefacts belonging to the church. The most important was kept in the cupboard on the altar. It was the finger of St Sergius.

Sergius had been martyred as a soldier in the Roman army in 303AD. Although his death was in what is now Northern Syria, his finger had arrived in Sadad at some time shortly afterwards. It became an object of great veneration. Around 1200AD, at a time when the village was threatened by invaders, the finger was hidden and lost for centuries. During the 1980s whilst studying some ancient handwritten books in the church, a reference was found to the hiding of the finger where the spear of St Sergius touched his horse's mane. An ancient fresco in the church showed St Sergius on a horse and for years people had commented that one hair of the horse's mane was wildly out of place. In fact it crossed with his spear. It suddenly made sense so they opened the wall at this point and found the casket containing the finger.

Next to the vestry was a cool room in which antiquities of all types and quality were kept. These ranged from illuminated handwritten Syriac lectern bibles to a 1999 calendar showing a photograph of President Assad. I am sure that a museum curator would have been overjoyed at some of the artefacts and appalled at others. To the people of Sadad this was not a museum but a storehouse of their collective faith memory. President Assad was there because he was seen as the one who protected their faith from onslaught.

As we left the church I was introduced to the senior deacon, a young man of 22 called Abraheim Farah. He and Jihad were close friends and we went to Abraheim's home for coffee. As we walked Abraheim explained that he was the 'Direct Manager of the Church Youth Team'. By any other count he was the youth leader and his work was very important in keeping the teenaged children connected to church. His parents' home was clearly a bit more 'up market' than Jihad's with its furnishings more luxurious. His mother brought a tray containing Arabic coffee, biscuits and courgettes. As I had not had any 'real' drink to quench my thirst all day, I found the courgette, which I skinned, to be very refreshing.

Having walked back to the Tafas household, I discovered that the remainder of Sunday was to be a relaxing time. Jihad prepared a barbeque which involved building a bonfire of branches about two inches thick. These were burned until they became glowing embers and then were shovelled into a barbeque tray. Hapsa arrived with a large round tray containing flat round wheat cakes containing a mixture of minced lamb and cabbage. Jihad then barbequed these cakes and filled a large pan with the finished product. All the while he was smoking 'hubble bubble'. The packet of red substance he used was made in Egypt and described itself as 'Molasses Tobacco'. He also produced a bottle of Araq. This was a home-brewed spirit which, when mixed with water turned milky white. He said they made it from their own grapes, which were then fermented before adding some spice. The taste was aniseed and was not unlike Pernot. At last all the cakes were cooked and we went back inside the house to join the extended family for Sunday lunch. Father Abdullah had returned from his church where he had not only had a service of Divine Liturgy, but had also taken a children's class afterwards. In addition to the barbequed lamb cakes we had a tomato and courgette salad in olive oil, a sort of suet with meat, and I was given a glass of fortified red wine. Jihad stuck to the Araq.

After lunch it seemed to be siesta time. The options seemed to read, watch television or sleep. It was dusk before Jihad surfaced. The Araq had been effective! Abdullah and Hapsa had been busy in the garden and had just come inside as Jihad said that he would like to take me round to another part of the village. The wind was now quite brisk and the temperature had dropped significantly. However this was a walk with a purpose. We were to meet Hapsa's mother. From a narrow unpaved street we entered into an archway off which were two rooms, one each side. The entrance area would have been large enough to bring livestock through. It led into a small courtyard covered with wires along which vines grew. Other rooms led off the darkened courtyard. We went into the right hand room in which five women, all dressed in black, were chatting, sitting on the floor. The eldest one got up from her seat on the floor and kissed me on each cheek. She was clearly very pleased that I had come.

Having sat down, nuts were offered as a snack until tea was brought in. None of the ladies spoke any English so whatever conversation occurred had to be through Jihad. I asked why the ladies were all in black, with Granny wearing a shawl over her head. It was explained that her husband had died nine months previously. In such cases it was customary for the widow to wear black for at least a year, and for friends and relatives to keep her company every evening. For this they too had to wear black attire. The community gathering round a bereaved person seemed to be very foreign from the way things are done in the so-called sophisticated West, but it was so supportive. I was pleased to have experienced this short interlude.

After about half an hour we set off on our return walk. The moonless night meant that the stars were very clear. Street lighting in Sadad was minimal. Trudging and stumbling along the darkened streets I reflected on the weekend. The Christian community in Sadad could trace its origins back to the early days of the church. Situated north east of Damascus it was probably established in the first century. Certainly the village had been shown to be extant hundreds of years before Christ. But now it was dying. The springs, which had been its lifeblood over all those centuries, were drying up one by one. The desert was encroaching into the fields. Although it remained a Christian village, its population was in decline and there was little evidence that, relocated in the city, the Christians connected up with a church. I could feel Jihad's pessimism.

Great excitement greeted us on our return. We learned that the former Prime Minister of Syria, subsequently arrested for corruption, had died in custody. The Syrian television news blandly informed the population without any comment on the death. In a totalitarian state it was not normal for the population to debate such matters but I felt I had to ask a rhetorical question. Did he jump or was he pushed? This opened the floodgates. Jihad was convinced that this was suicide and he was very disappointed that a trial would not now occur. His aunt and Mary were sad as they thought he was not guilty. They believed he had been murdered. So even within a totally loyal household speculation was rife. Later Stephen told me that three bullets had been used, so it was hardly likely to have been suicide.

Early the following morning we had to leave Sadad. By six o'clock the entire household was in full swing and, after a breakfast of Arabic coffee and biscuits, Jihad and I set off for the bus. It was late and, whilst waiting for it, Jihad explained that the church ran the bus service. When I expressed surprise he explained that there were a number of activities in rural Syria that the church had taken over rather than risk losing them. One other example was the village shop in Sadad. To me this seemed a remarkably positive venture. For the church, which purports to be concerned with the whole of life, to be involved in meeting the community's needs in this way was a very good model of service.

Just then the old bus rattled up to us, stopping in a cloud of dust. We climbed on board with great rounds of greetings from all and sundry. And away we went. Sadad was soon just a speck on the horizon in the desert but I would not forget the warmth of welcome I had received there. As we rattled along the road towards Damascus, I asked Jihad to explain some more about his feelings about this ancient Syriac church. I wanted to understand why a young man, now very much involved in modern information technology, would hanker for traditional ways of expressing his faith. Why, for example, would he not be attracted to more contemporary Western styles of worship?

It was as if he could hardly believe that I had even asked the question. He gasped and said, 'I really love my church. When I enter the building, or hear Syriac music, or pray to God, my heart not my ears are hearing. My spirit responds. On Good Friday I saw many kinds of churches in Damascus, but I never had the same feeling that I had in my own church in Sadad.'

So, for Jihad, it was the emotion of his village, the things with which he was familiar?

'The interesting thing is that we pray not in our usual way of speaking or language, but in an old language. Aramaic is special because it is Jesus' language. We know that old is simple but new is complex. You need to be simple with your God'.

I asked what difference being a Christian made to his lifestyle. Jihad had difficulties in life, particularly his financial prospects. He took a deep breath and looked at the desert flashing past the bus window.

'I know I had very hard circumstances. Sometimes I don't know what I should do. I get so busy with my job, with my studies, just trying to live that I have no time to have a social life. But, even with all of that, one night or just one hour with Jesus will put everything back to normal. It is easy to carry a difficulty if you compare it with the cross of Jesus. And every great trouble is not a trouble if you do what Jesus would do.'

He looked hesitant, as if far away, and then decided to share something personal. 'Three months ago I lost my cousin in a car crash. He was twenty-seven years old. After he finished his studying and his army duty, he had three years with his work. He decided that he had his own home and he had the money to get married. He told his family and he found the girl he needed. Then he was killed. What could I say to the family? I told them all that this young brother has spent all his years in Lent, but now God wants him to share in Heaven. This is a thing of beauty for him but very sad for us.'

Jihad was struggling with language but his conviction of the ultimate goal of God and the transience of life was clear. 'After this I decided that there is nothing important in this life and God takes us to Himself at the moment He wants. He is careful and brings happiness. He knows the right moment to take this man from us into heaven. I tell all my friends these things. They make my faith strong enough to believe in God. Our faith gives us power to live. If I have any problem I read the Bible and I find a solution.'

I was both impressed and disturbed by the expression of faith. The idea of God using violent means to bring a soul to Heaven seemed incongruous with a God of Love. This was reawakening the dilemma about a loving God and a suffering world. As the bus jogged along I knew that there would be no resolution to this conundrum.

CHAPTER EIGHTEEN

THE MOUNTAIN OF
GOD

Travelling by myself it had been comparatively easy to make decisions. But after nearly three months apart, Carol was going to join me for the final leg of the journey. This would take us from Damascus to the Syriac Orthodox heartland of Tur Abdin, in southeast Turkey. For centuries the Christian community in Turkey has been repressed. I had already experienced something of the Armenians in Jerusalem and was aware that they had been subjected to ethnic genocide in the earlier years of the twentieth century. The Greek Orthodox had been forcibly evicted in the 1920s. The Syriac Orthodox had been subjected to massive persecution that resulted in their numbers dropping from two million to two thousand over the course of that century. As they inhabited an area that was very tense, partly due to its proximity to Iraq and partly to the presence of large numbers of Kurds, I was aware that the authorities might not be too keen to have me investigating the situation. Having Carol with me converted our visit from fact-finding to tourism.

Such was my excitement that I even thought Carol was coming a day sooner than planned until I realised that the flight did not operate that day. On the right day the faithful Chol arrived just after midnight to take me to the airport. As we stood waiting for her to emerge from

Customs and Immigration I began to think that we had still got the wrong date. But I need not have worried. She was virtually the last person out. Hers had been the last item of luggage to be handed over.

Driving back along the almost deserted Airport Road and then along the silent streets of Damascus, we were catching up on the news of one another whilst Carol tried to catch glimpses of this alluring city. Later that morning, not wishing to miss any opportunity to experience Syria, we went with Stephen to Seidnaya. Driving up, and up, the long twisting road from Damascus we eventually arrived in a large wide valley in the foothills of the Anti-Lebanon Range. Stephen took us directly to the new Syriac Orthodox Monastery at Seidnaya. Bearing in mind all the impressions I had been given of this as the poorest church in the Middle East, the excellent facilities at Seidnaya came as something of a surprise. The large new monastery, built out of limestone, occupied a commanding position overlooking the valley. It had a magnificent church alongside, tasteful and simple in concept.

The 'abbot', Matta Abdalahad, who joined us in a reception room, welcomed us. He and Stephen were old friends and it was amusing to see how they joked with one another. Stephen, in his role as Apocrisiarias, was wearing a black cassock. Matta, similarly attired in black also sported a bushy black beard. His eyes twinkled with mirth and jokes were passed to and fro. Matta came from the strongly Syriac area near Qamishly, on the far northeast border of Syria with Turkey. He was both interested and pleased that we were to make the journey to Tur Abdin as he felt that more people from the West should be aware of the sufferings of the Christians there.

This monastery housed the seminary for the Syriac Orthodox Church in Syria. All priests and monks were trained there. The library had just been transferred from the Patriarchate in Damascus and there was a great sense of well-being and optimism. We were told that the seminary had students from European countries such as Sweden, Germany and the Netherlands. Later that afternoon we came back for Vespers. The antiphonal chanting to untrained ears might be thought of as gabbling. It was raucous compared to that of the Armenians in Jerusalem so I tried to focus my mind on God and allow the sense of worship to wash over me. But I was not very successful and my mind kept wandering all over the place. I wanted so much to enter in to the spirit of worship but I felt I was becoming weary.

Having completed nine weeks on the move I was certainly weary of moving on, weary of living out of a suitcase. But not weary of the excitement of new pastures. Not weary of new people. It was the physical effort of packing up and moving. Starting early in the morning was an added disincentive. But the faithful Chol was there for us. The trailing of two bulky suitcases down four flights of stairs was a rude awakening for anyone's sensibilities so, having given Stephen our fond farewells, we were fully alert as we were driven to the airport. Chol, as ever the dutiful chauffeur, was silent. Then he told us that he would miss us. I was glad that the United Nations had granted him refugee status and hoped that it would not be too long before he could find a decent host country.

The Passport Control were all for charging us a Syrian exit tax until I reminded them that, as far as I was concerned, Qamishly was still in Syria. With that the officer grinned widely and said, 'Welcome in Syria'. Eventually we were called to board the bus to take us out to our plane. As we drove across the tarmac, past Boeings of various sizes, I noticed that our plane, the furthest away from the Terminal, was of a different shape to the ones we had got used to. It seemed to be more slender than the chunky Boeing 737 nearby. It turned out to be a Russian Tupolev 134B-3. It must have been about 20 years old, a hangover from the days when Syria was very much in the pocket of the Soviet bloc. The inside of the plane was a surprise with tip up seats, and safety belts that were suspect at best.

The flight took us across the deserts of eastern Syria before we crossed the Euphrates and gradually descended to Qamishly. Once on the ground it wasn't too reassuring to taxi alongside wrecked planes. A DC3 with a broken back, a small jet airliner lying on its side with its wing broken! Fortunately our plane survived the ordeal. As the door opened the searing desert heat smashed in like a wave. We climbed down steps on to the runway but our luggage was decanted from the hold. Carol's case was only marginally smaller than mine and so we had to attach wheels to take our luggage on. There was no terminal through which to leave. The exit was just a gateway on to a roadway crammed with people either waiting to meet passengers or trying to sell them a ride in their taxi. A taxi was necessary as the Turkish border was a few kilometres north of the town. We negotiated a fare with one man whilst others kept trying to demand that we went with them.

The yellow taxi was a venerable monster that claimed itself to be a Chevrolet. With great fins on the back it would not have seemed out of place in an American movie made in the early 1950s. It was very battered and the driver told us that it had received new (possibly reconditioned) engines over the years. The ride at no more than 20mph took us in sedate fashion through the surprisingly large city of Qamishly to the frontier post. Would we come and have tea at his home? The driver felt that we would appreciate meeting his family and having lunch. The offer was tempting, and typical of the hospitality etiquette of the Middle East. I suppose that it would also have given him a certain amount of status amongst his neighbours if he could show that he had friends from the West. However, we knew that we had to get through the border and that the Turkish authorities sometimes closed the border for hours, even days, at a time. I thanked the driver but said we must press on.

At the border we had to fend off porters. Unfortunately I was having difficulty with my auxiliary wheels so this delayed us. Even when I had succeeded in getting them affixed they didn't seem right. Nonetheless we managed to get through the first security gate and away from the swarms of porters. We had to go to Emigration and this involved great excitement for the police on duty. Our passports were taken away and we were asked into the office of the police captain. No explanation was offered and it all seemed a little sinister. Then a young officer brought in some tea. This was hospitality, not detention.

After some minutes the police chief limped in. He was a big man who seemed to be suffering. It transpired that he had noted Carol's profession as nurse. He then wanted to explain that he had great pain with a rheumatic knee. He showed her his medication and wanted assurance that this was good. The tablets were of an unfamiliar brand and the instructions written in Arabic. They seemed to be anti-inflammatory so were probably reasonable. Keep taking the tablets, Carol advised. This seemed to satisfy him and we parted the best of friends.

Next we had to pass through a gate, which was locked on both the Syrian and Turkish sides with no sign of anyone with a key. A Syrian woman with loads of baggage was waiting as we approached. Then seemingly out of nowhere a soldier appeared and unlocked both gates and, having had our passports checked again, we passed through. A Turkish soldier checked our passports on his side of the gate and directed us to the Turkish Passport Police. This involved a slow pull up a hill. By now my luggage wheels were being far from co-operative. They seemed to want to tuck themselves under the luggage bringing the case into contact with the road. We struggled on.

Once inside the Passport Office, a young woman showed no signs of dealing with us as people. Not even catching our eyes she took our passports and put them to one side as she then dealt with easier Syrian customers. Eventually we were escorted to another office, much plusher, where a senior police officer was reading a newspaper. In the background was a television showing cartoons. He used his remote control to turn down the sound as we entered but otherwise showed no notice of our arrival. We sat down and unzipped a couple of bananas but still he carried on reading.

Then with a rapid movement he folded up his paper and sat up. 'Where is money?' he demanded. I imagined that he could have been a villain in some play but he was real. It dawned on me rapidly however that he was talking about the cost of the visa. It was ten pounds each. Laboriously he wrote out a receipt for this. He then took an age to copy our details into his logbook. When this was done I asked about the location of a bank to change money.

'No bank. Change here.'

He then looked up the exchange rate and showed me from his paper how this was a better rate than I would get in the banks in the town. As we left, armed with millions of Turkish lire, it occurred to me that I had just engaged in a spot of black market trading. We then had to take our passports and receipts back to the first police office for them to have the entry visas recorded and stamped. Then we were free to go...or so we thought! In fact we had only gone a few paces when we had to take our luggage up some steps into the customs shed. Did we have anything to declare? No. Fortunately that was accepted and we tried to move on again but were waylaid this time by the security people. Our luggage had to go through the X-ray scanner. Then we were faced with a gate at which we showed our passports. Finally we had to trundle our complaining luggage along the road until, with one last check of our passports, we felt we were properly in Turkey.

Fending off various barrow boys we rolled our luggage into the nearby town of Nusaybin. We were a sight of great amusement to the locals sitting by the roadside. Occasionally barrow boys would pedal their cycle barrows alongside offering to help. They found us very strange in choosing to pull our own luggage. It was warmer than Damascus so it was a relief to reach the top of the hill. In the centre of Nusaybin I saw a microbus with Midyat on its destination board. This was our bus. The conductor helpfully stowed our luggage and we got two comfortable seats in the modern vehicle. The conductor then collected the fare and we were off – we could not have timed it better!

Once clear of the town limits the bus took the road to Midyat. Almost immediately we were driving into some beautiful countryside. Green valleys with woodland surrounded by steep limestone cliffs, which were sometimes surmounted by villages. Local people were playing in rivers, or sitting alongside their cars in these beauty spots. Gradually the bus climbed higher and was once stopped at a security check point. This and the fact that some of the villages looked abandoned were stark reminders that this was not a settled area. The Turkish army was showing its presence heavily as this was part of the area claimed by some Kurds as Kurdistan. Having reached a plateau the bus then gradually descended towards the town of Midyat. A town at a crossroads, the outer limits sign declared the population to be 61,600. I wondered what it might have been but for the ethnic cleansing that had been going on.

Getting out of the bus we were swarmed over once more by barrow boys. I shooed them away as we were not going anywhere on foot. I called a taxi over and negotiated a fare to take us to the monastery of Mor Gabriel. This was a drive of about twenty minutes, along a remote winding road with pleasant, if unspectacular, vistas. A tourist sign for Mor Gabriel took us a couple of kilometres up a minor road and we arrived at the hilltop location that is the monastery. Set in its extensive grounds, a large wall was being built to contain its boundaries. Coming to a stop on the gravel pathway a young man rushed forward and carried my heavy suitcase up the steps into the monastery. I carried Carol's case, and she carried the hand luggage.

We arrived on an open air balcony on which a group of men was sitting. They were drinking tea. One of them, dressed in red, was undoubtedly the Bishop of Tur Abdin and Abbot of Mor Gabriel Monastery, Timotheos Samuel Aktas. I introduced myself and he looked unmoved.

'You were due last week,' he said, not looking up from inspecting his hands.

I apologised for any confusion but said that I had understood that Stephen Griffith had arranged everything. He shrugged his shoulders. That was the end of that topic. 'Sit down,' he ordered. 'Why have you come?' I realised he was playing games because Stephen had told me that the arrangements had been agreed and confirmed. I reminded him of this and he motioned us to sit down.

The bishop cut an impressive figure, with a large greying beard. He wore a red cassock and, like the people around him, was sitting on a white plastic patio chair. Around him the men sat in silence. Occasionally one would speak to him in English. He was a Belgian telephone engineer, in the area to install mobile phone antennae. There was a kind of unwritten rule. You speak when addressed but not otherwise. We sat in silence whilst other people were drawn into the conversation at the invitation of Bishop Timotheos. He would sometimes laugh, sometimes respond in short measured tones. Within his own domain the bishop was like a tribal chief. He was considered by his people as being endowed with wisdom; his word was final. Yet all the time he fidgeted with his hands. He was a man who was anxious.

The language used in the area by the Syriac Christians was Turoyo – a dialect of Aramaic. It seemed as if few people could speak English. But one who could was a young man, Isa. He had a smiling face although sometimes lines of sadness betrayed that he knew suffering. A local boy, he had managed to pursue education and eventually went to university in London, followed by post graduate studies in Oxford. Unlike most of his compatriots he had returned to Tur Abdin. The trend – one might call it an avalanche – has been that anyone who can gets out of this area because of the problems and persecutions suffered continually by the Christian community. But Isa was different. He felt a call to serve his church and people in the cradle of their culture, even though this was a real sacrifice.

Just then the bishop beckoned us to go through a doorway where we found a meal had been provided. This was rice wrapped in vine leaves. It was a welcome booster for our flagging energy levels. Isa came and talked to us. He explained that the monastery had been exceptionally busy the previous day and that they were now unwinding. Stephen had warned us that it would be likely that our accommodation would be in separate buildings. He expected Carol to be sent to the convent whilst I would be with the monks. Isa astonished us when he said that they had accommodation set aside for us. It turned out to be a perfectly adequate en suite double guest room. Subsequent conversations have raised the query as to whether Carol was the first woman to sleep in the monastery since it was constructed one and a half millennia previously!

Isa told us about what had been happening to the local Christians. Until a couple of years earlier it had been particularly dangerous in the area around the monastery owing to the activities of the Kurdish revolutionary force, the PKK. Christians were squeezed by both the Kurdish separatists and the Turkish troops. As the area was under martial law things happened for which there seemed no redress. Whole villages would be evicted without either notice or compensation. People would be killed and no one would be brought to trial. Rebels in particular were prepared to kidnap and torture people who they thought might inform on them. The monasteries in the area were officially prevented from doing any maintenance or from receiving guests. The clergy were not allowed to wear clerical dress whilst outside churches or monasteries. It all added up to a fairly gloomy picture. The oppression along with the massive rush to leave meant that the Christian population in the area was down to a couple of thousand souls.

We had a rest after the meal and emerged in time for the service of Vespers. The bell on the church was ringing as we made our way inside the ancient church. Carol had to wear a headscarf and sit on the right whilst I sat with the men on the left. In a tradition with which I had become familiar, two groups of people gathered around two lecterns to sing the service antiphonally. I learned that each of the three daily non-eucharistic services at Mor Gabriel was a combination of three services. The chanting was eager, even raucous at times. Boys as young as 12 were involved and their voices brought the pitch much higher than I had experienced it at Seidnaya for example. The boys were from local villages but lived in the monastery in order to learn Syriac and the services. Because the Turkish Government did not permit Christians to have their own schools they had to be sent daily by bus to the state school in Midyat. The education they received was poor as most teachers were those who were unable to get a posting elsewhere.

At the end of the service a man approached me. In his fifties with a greying beard, he did not look like a Syriac Christian. Wearing an academic gown, a skullcap and a clerical collar he introduced himself to me as Father Dale Johnson. This American United Methodist minister who had trained in an Episcopal Seminary had been taken up with the cause of Syriac Christians in Turkey for a number of years. Eventually the Syriac Orthodox patriarch in the

USA had made him a Syriac priest. He had come to Mor Gabriel only a few months earlier but was finding great blessing in having done so. He had sold all his possessions in the USA and emptied his bank account in favour of his two adult children and elderly mother. He said he felt liberated by having to depend utterly on God. He offered to escort us around the church. Founded by the saints Simeon and Samuel in 397AD it had recently been renovated. Of particular interest was the jewelled mosaic ceiling over the altar. The Persians had stolen most of the jewels during periodic raids but there were still several kilos of gold in the ceiling.

We were also shown the cell in which Mor Gabriel himself used to hole himself up in prayer. The tradition of ascetic monks used to be very strong amongst the Syriac Christians but the last one had died in the 1960s. Dale was very keen on the idea of these 'spiritual athletes'. In many ways they were completely eccentric but in another they were competitive and single minded. They used their spirituality very publicly and many people would come to see them. Perhaps the most famous of all was St Simon Stylites in what is now Syria. The idea was to be famous so that pilgrims would come and this way be influenced by the church. Mor Gabriel used to be in a dark cell for weeks on end, praying. Another monk near to him spent days standing up. Jesus died upright so why should he sit down?

The whole idea of spiritual asceticism both repelled and attracted me. I thought of people in the West who might have a biblical text or Christian symbol on their car. It might evoke a question which then might lead on to discussion and entry into faith – or not. The high profile ascetic would draw pilgrims from all over. That way he would influence them to faith. But it was all a bit bizarre!

Life in a monastery is one of regular rhythm. When the alarm clock sounded at ten minutes to five it seemed like a real intrusion. Nevertheless we quickly slipped down in the cold night air for the first service of the new day and found the staff and pupils were already arriving. Silently they formed into two antiphonal groups and began to chant even as some stragglers were still struggling in. Clearly it was not only the Western visitors who found it difficult to get up. The service seemed to be similar in form to that of the previous evening and as more men arrived the sound became richer and mellower. The sub-deacon stoked up the incense and shook it vigorously all around the church. When he reached the north side of the church a shaft of light from the sun shot through the only window on the east side of the church. It came through no more than a slit but was very dramatic. As the smoke of the incense caught the ray of light it gave it an ethereal feel. To me it brought back memories of Marple Regent cinema when I was a boy. In those days cinemas were full of smokers and I used to love to watch the smoke rise into the projector beam.

After a light breakfast, Dale took us for a walk. We enjoyed his kindness towards us and clearly he enjoyed both the opportunity to speak English and also the chance to interpret what we encountered. In some ways this was much appreciated but in other ways we soon realised that everything we experienced was being filtered through Dale. Visiting the gardens we were able to see the nuns busy on their hands and knees looking after the growing vegetables. A great deal of the food in Mor Gabriel came from homegrown resources. It was good to be self-sufficient, we were told. That way, during times of tension, the monastery would not run out of food.

The boys set off in the school minibus as we inspected various gardens by walking along the ample walls. However nothing was as substantial as the walls the bishop was having constructed around the outer limits of the monastery grounds. I was told the reasons were two-fold. Firstly there had been no land registration in the area so no one had title to land. By building the 'Great Wall of

China' it was likely that any confiscation of land might be better resisted. Secondly the bishop believed that if in the future a security problem occurred as it had done in the past, then villagers could gather in the monastery lands. Touring the gardens gave an opportunity to observe the monastery's situation more clearly. It was situated at the highest point in an area of gradually rising upland. No other habitation could be seen other than the Turkish military observation post on the opposite hill. Away to the east were the Ararat Mountains, supposed resting place of Noah's Ark. The Judy Mountains also to the east marked the way into Iraq about sixty kilometres away. It was clear that this was going to be a militarily sensitive region even without the ethnic and religious complications. During the first Gulf War the monastery had been a distribution point for United Nations aid to Syriac Christian and Kurdish refugees in Northern Iraq. At that time Father Dale had been driving medical aid into the stricken area on a daily basis. It had, of course, been distributed on the grounds of need rather than tribe, race or religion.

Later that morning we met up with Dale once more and he took us around more of the hidden recesses in the monastery. In recent years a number of large vaulted rooms had been discovered at lower levels under the monastery. These dated from the early years and had been sealed up at some point, perhaps in times of decline. It was possible that they had originally housed large numbers of monks. As the requirement for accommodation reduced they might have been sealed up. One large vaulted room had a number of modern murals of the life of Jesus. They painted by Iraqi Christian refugees during the first Gulf War. The crucifixion scene showed a very Iraqi-looking Jesus suffering on the cross.

It was Dale's dream to make Mor Gabriel a centre for Syriac culture, spirituality and learning. Some of these rooms could be developed as a museum and library. Various ancient artefacts and manuscripts were scattered around various churches in the area but were vulnerable to desecration or theft. To house them in a humidity-controlled atmosphere in the historic setting of Mor Gabriel could help to gain world recognition for the monastery. This might also bring a further form of protection in case the Government might at some time return to its more oppressive policy.

The noon prayers were very different in atmosphere to the morning prayers. Although they followed the same format, the absence of the boys at school meant that all available male voices were required to help with the chanting. Even the bishop came out from the sanctuary to get things going. As ever the nuns were at the back, silently involved in the worship. There was no suggestion that they might assist in the liturgical side of the worship. Their lives seemed to be filled with producing food, cleaning, and attending services. In contrast the monks seemed to me to be involved in receiving guests and offering hospitality. I know which I prefer.

After lunch I asked Dale what he felt the Syriac church could offer Christians of other traditions. I touched a rich seam. 'Oh, it's in the area of spirituality and monasticism,' he began. He explained that, regardless of the dismissive view I might have of the monks at Mor Gabriel, they were largely there 'just' for prayer. This prayer life was seen by Dale as the pivot of everything. 'If we don't believe in the power of prayer we might as well give up. Churches in the West are being run as imitation businesses but here they are run on prayer.' Dale made an extreme point to illustrate his case.

I could see his argument but was the Syriac model a valid one? It seemed to me to be mainly concerned with its culture and language in a fairly inaccessible part of Turkey. How would it retain second and third generation Syriacs in the West? The idea of evangelism of non-Syriacs was surely a million miles from this and yet would it not be the only chance of long-term survival? Dale told me that in the United States the Syriacs were attracting converts through their English language Liturgy and because of their monastic spirituality.

The evening prayers were at six o'clock but we crept in late. The boys had returned from school and were adding volume to the singing. I also noticed an old man in his seventies standing with them. Dressed impeccably in a suit he cut a distinctive if diminutive figure. This, I was to learn after the service, was Malfono ('Teacher') Abrohom Nuro. After the service there was great excitement as people crowded around the Malfono. Dale explained that the Malfono was visiting from Aleppo in Syria and was one of the world's greatest authorities on modern Syriac. The author of several books on grammar he had also worked out a way of evolving new words. I had noticed how languages like Arabic had imported words of a technical nature wholesale from English. Such words, like 'Computer', usually stood out like a sore thumb in the smooth flow of the host language. This was being avoided in modern Syriac thanks to the work of people like the Malfono. He was a delight to meet, and over the next twenty-four hours we were to enjoy his company very much. It began with supper.

We were making to go to the dining room after the bell had been rung but were told by the bishop to stay on his terrace. He was chatting to some members of the Syriac diaspora just returned to visit after many years of life in Sweden. They chatted loudly and the bishop clearly enjoyed their company. Suddenly he stood up and asked us to join them in his dining room. We sat next to the bishop. The conversation was loud, and in Syriac. Occasionally the Malfono would try to change it to English and draw us in. Whilst we felt socially excluded by language, it was clear that these visitors were raising the bishop's spirits. And that was good. We felt honoured to be invited and, of course, enjoyed the meal of chicken and vegetables. At one point the bishop turned to me and asked about our plans for the next day. I asked if it might be possible to visit villages and meet Christians. Unlikely, he thought, and then continued to chat with the Swedes.

Dale could not wait to find out whether we had sorted out arrangements for the next day. He had joined us on the terrace and said that now the bishop knew of our requirements something would emerge. This was all part of the ritual. I could not ask to do something but, by ascertaining what I would like to do, the bishop could then suggest it. Over coffee the bishop advised us that a vehicle had been arranged for the following morning.

After breakfast the next day we were summoned to the gate. The bishop was sitting on a chair under a tree chatting with some men. A Ford Transit minibus was parked nearby but there was little sign of an imminent departure. After about twenty minutes the Swedish families and the Malfono turned up. We then got in the vehicle and the bishop waved us away.

A few kilometres out of Midyat we turned along a narrow lane. As we surmounted a low ridge we saw a village strung along the opposite side of the valley. This was Salah. Between it and us was a series of old stone buildings surrounding a courtyard. Resembling a farm with enclosed courtyard, it turned out that this was the monastery of Mor Yakub. The entrance was through an arched gateway. Monasteries like this were built as much for protection as the glory of God. The sixth century church and monastery were in the process of renovation. Like a number of sites we were to see that day, the opportunity of an unofficial relaxation in the strict anti-restoration legislation by the Government was being used to repair a number of properties. Funding came from the Syriac diaspora in the West.

Mor Yakub monastery had three monks, one of whom was away on military service when we called. We were greeted warmly by Father Yakub and shown around the church. His brother monk came down from the roof where he was assisting some Kurdish workmen in restoration work. This was a much younger man, Father Daniel. Clearly the monks here had a different role to the silent men at Mor Gabriel. They were active, hands-on, men who were pleased to stop and chat with visitors. During conversation it was explained that under Turkish law priests and monks were called up for military service just as any other young men. There was no concession to their beliefs and it was particularly difficult to maintain their rhythm of devotion and prayer. They were expected to use guns in their training although Christians in general were distrusted. Often they would be given chores that were degrading.

We also met one of the two nuns resident in the monastery. Nuns maintained the domestic side of life. She explained to us that Salah had until comparatively recently been a Christian village. The fear instilled into the resident Christians by Kurdish separatists and Government oppression had resulted in their fleeing. Their homes and farms had been taken over by Kurds. In the absence of any property titles squatters had as much right to live in a particular property as its long-term residents.

Driving on we arrived at the village of Irnis. The bus drew up alongside some flat rocks on which a group of Kurdish women were hammering on goat skins, watched by a number of small ragged children. Johannes, one of the Swedes, went over and spoke to them, saying that we wanted access to the village church. The church here was locked but abandoned. The Kurds held a key and, after some time, this was produced. We were followed into the building by some of barefoot children. This caused Johannes to shout at them to go away. He treated the Kurds like vermin and I shuddered. He clearly felt that this was his heritage and that the Kurds were usurpers. But who had left? We climbed over fallen masonry that once had been a wall to the churchyard. A goat bleated and rushed out of our way. Then turning the key in the lock we entered a strange unreal world. It was as if the congregation had just left. Even the electric lights worked. Books were produced and Malfono poured over them with the glee of a child at Christmas. I wandered around and then returned to the sunshine. A Kurdish child was peeping over the wall. Clearly she was afraid of these big well-fed strangers. I was sorry that Johannes had been so gruff with them because once we had left who would be there to look after the church? It would have been better to be nice to the Kurds.

Driving through the hilltop village of Achlah, we were told that there was only one Christian left in this village. The church had been converted into a mosque. This was so painful to some of the group that we did not stop. We would enjoy the next village, we were told. The church at Kfarze was built on a knoll commanding a fine view across the valley along which we were approaching. Like so many Christian buildings in the area it had been built with half an eye on security. This eighth century church, dedicated to St Izozoel, stood out conspicuously with its ornate twentieth century bell tower. It served thirteen Christian families from the village and seemed in a good state of repair. It was unusual in having the benefit of a resident priest.

From Kfarze we drove on to one of the real gems of Tur Abdin, the monastery church at Hah. At one time Hah was an important city, and local tradition has it that the Three Kings visited it. They were reputed to have built the church of Yoldath Aloho (Mother of God), although this one was actually constructed in the seventh century. The monastery and church were happily undergoing major restoration work.

Walking up the hill, along rocky footpaths, we entered the ancient Christian village of Hah. A maze of narrow alleyways, it looked as if it had not changed in hundreds of years. At the highest point of the village we were welcomed into a courtyard by Habib, the local mayor. He escorted us up some stone steps and into his home. This unassuming man in his late thirties was apologetic that his wife was out but he showed us into his gracious lounge. It was carpeted, but there were no chairs. We sat on cushions on the floor around the four walls. Animated Syriac conversation between the Swedish Syriacs went on whilst a gruesome Turkish soap opera was on the television in the corner. Habib offered us water and then tea. We gleaned that the village had seventeen families living there. Tensions remained high but there had been no 'incidents' recently, Habib assured us.

Overlooking the village was a tall watchtower of the Turkish Army, a little reminder that this was an area under military occupation. As we walked back to the Mother of God Church two military helicopters were passing overhead giving a further reminder, if one were needed, of this. There were no monks here but a great deal of restoration work was in progress. Funded by Syriacs living in the West, it seemed incongruous to restore this beautiful church yet have no monks, nuns or priests to seve it.

After lunch we drove up to the barracks and, having surrendered our passports or identification cards, were allowed to proceed beyond the security barrier to the village of Bekusyone. Pausing briefly on top of the hill overlooking the village we learned that Bekusyone, home to about fifteen Christian families, was the original home of Bishop Timotheos of Mor Gabriel. It was the scene of ethnic genocide in 1915 and it was years before it was resettled. We visited the church of Mor Eliyo with its ancient oak tree in the courtyard. Then we headed back to the military checkpoint where we had our passports returned.

The afternoon was far advanced by the time we reached the village of Inwardo. This was the most spectacular of all the villages we visited. Situated on top of a steep hill and with a church built as a fortress it became a natural rallying place for Christians from surrounding villages in times of trouble. Thick walls surrounded the church of Mor Had Bshabo and it was possible to see shrapnel damage from earlier years. However it never fell during the massacres of 1915. Nevertheless the constant attrition suffered by Christians in the twentieth century resulted in depopulation so that by the time of our visit only seven Christian families remained in Inwardo. They still had a resident priest to serve them.

On the way back, on the outskirts of Midyat, we called at the monastery of Mor Abraham. Founded in the fifth century as a daughter house of Mor Gabriel it was founded by two monks, Abrohom and Hobel. However much of it was destroyed over the years and the present buildings had been constructed since 1900. Its graveyard served the Christian people of Midyat. The grave of the only Christian doctor in Midyat was pointed out to us. He had been assassinated in 1994 but no one ever was arrested for his murder. Cumulatively this was taken, along with other acts of repression, to have been sanctioned by the local Government forces to inspire fear into the Christians. The monastery was not used at the time of our visit but was being restored in concert with what was being done with other monasteries. Technically illegal, the church authorities were making up for lost time whilst the authorities seemed to be in benevolent mode. Nevertheless, with declining numbers of Syriacs it seemed a desperate act to restore churches that might one day be museum pieces administered by the Tourist Authority.

CHAPTER NINETEEN

ARRIVAL IN BYZANTIUM

I woke at five o'clock. I suppose that Mor Gabriel had got me into that habit. We were rolling across the Turkish countryside at a sedate speed and I realised that all night we had been listening to the clickety-clack of the tracks. This was the Ankara to Istanbul sleeper express. I went back to sleep until the attendant walked along the corridor at half past six tinkling a little bell. Arrival at Haydarpasha station in Istanbul was almost an anticlimax. The train became slower in its progress and then limped around a bend past lines of carriages before easing to a stop. The attendant walked along the corridor at that moment calling out that this was the terminus.

Slowly we lowered our baggage to the platform and then walked the length of the train. Haydarpasha station building was an imposing French chateau-style edifice with grand waiting rooms and booking halls. The smell of the sea, the cries of the gulls, and the wind in our faces were experiences that were alien to all we had got used to. Heaving the suitcases up a rickety gangplank, we settled down on the ferryboat to Karakoy. What a wonderful way to enter the ancient capital of Byzantium. With a weak sun filtering through the morning haze, the boat picked its way across the choppy waters of the Bosphorus, one of the world's busiest shipping lanes, taking us from Asia to

Europe. The glimpses of old Byzantium, symbolised by the massive pile of Hagia Sophia, were tremendous. Then the boat turned up the Golden Horn, beneath the Galata Bridge, and landed at Eminonu. We had arrived at the former hub of the empire that had stretched the full distance of my travels: Byzantium.

Our journey nearly over, it was a relief to find Christ Church, the Anglican Crimean Memorial Chapel. It was situated in the middle of an area of densely packed houses, along a narrow lane that slithered its way down the side of the hill that forms the suburb of Galata. I rang the bell on the gate. There was no response. I rang the other two bells. After a few minutes two Sri Lankans came and opened the old cast iron gate. We were informed that Ian Sherwood, the Chaplain, was in the church. To reach it we had to descend a steep flight of stone steps pushing aside overhanging bushes. Our cases were definitely a disadvantage once more.

Deliciously out of context in Istanbul, this fine example of English Gothic church architecture seemed to envelope us as we entered. A small congregation in the chancel was singing, 'Alleluia, Sing to Jesus.' It was the end of Matins. The priest said the final prayers and, accompanied by his spaniel, walked down the aisle to the church door, welcoming us as he passed by. When he returned from changing out of his robes he introduced himself, and invited us into his home. There we were installed into a gracious guest room before joining him in the kitchen for coffee.

Ian explained about the work of the chaplaincy. He was involved not only with Christ Church but also with the chapel in the British Embassy and another church on the Asian side of the Bosphorous. It was apparent that he had a rare gift of attracting able people to take responsibility for a wide variety of opportunities. This ranged from running a refugee hostel in the church garden to helping students from a wide variety of backgrounds discuss issues through literature, thus exposing them to Christian values.

After coffee we went for a walk to Taksim to help us orientate ourselves in this huge city. Walking along Istiklal Cadesi, the pedestrianised street that formed the spine of Galata, it was with a sense of culture shock that I felt almost unable to cope with what I was experiencing. The area was so western with its fashion chains and swish modern shopping facilities, symbolised by McDonald's, that there was something disappointing about it all. We took lunch in a restaurant, a novelty after Tur Abdin. As we ate I commented that clouds were scudding across the sky. After weeks of sunshine this seemed quite novel. Leaving the restaurant, a few spots of rain were falling and an hour later we could hardly believe our eyes. Rain was pouring down, bouncing off the leaves.

Whilst in Istanbul I wanted to visit the Phanar, the Oecumenical Patriarchate of the Eastern Orthodox Church. Ian Sherwood had suggested that we ought to visit the Chora Museum en route. This was a former church, later converted into a mosque. However it was now a museum in view of the incredible mosaics on the walls and roof. When this Byzantine church had been converted into a mosque all the beautiful Christian mosaics had been covered over. It was only in comparatively recent years that they were rediscovered and they now form a real jewel of Christian culture from those far off days. Paintings and mosaics illustrating Biblical scenes were ways of telling the Christian story in days when many people were illiterate. Of particular interest was a series depicting scenes from the non-canonical Gospel of Barnabas.

Getting from the Chora Museum to the Phanar was not easy. By a system of trial and error we found the Phanar by walking. Taxi drivers were most unwilling to take us there and we concluded that this was part of the anti-Christian attitudes that Turkey had propagated for many decades.

The Patriarchate was surrounded by a high wall and was overlooked by a sentry box on both sides of the street. I went to the gate and found an electronic security arch like one encounters at airports. I enquired whether this was the Patriarchate and was delighted to discover that it was. Ian Sherwood had put us in contact with Father Tarasios, the Grand Archdeacon, and so we asked to see him. He was out, we were told. It was his day off. It was no use arguing, especially as the security men had about one percent English and I had less than one percent Greek, the language used in the Patriarchate.

We negotiated to see the church, however. It was beautiful, sumptuous even. The pews were like uphol-stered dining room chairs. There were some beautiful icons and pictures, none more so than a picture contain-ing scenes from the life of Elijah. The detail with which every scene had been painted showed not only the craft of the painter but also the deep understanding of Scripture. With some difficulty we made ourselves understood in enquiring about the evening service. There would be vespers at five o'clock and we would be welcome.

When we returned with five minutes to spare two priests, one short and one tall, were busying themselves in front of the decorated screen. At exactly five o'clock they began their antiphonal chanting. But where was the con-gregation? We were the congregation! The tall priest did most of the long prayers whilst the short one walked around the church with the incense. The whole service took about half an hour and then it was over. We hung around a little in the hope of chatting to one of the priests but they never came to the narthex. Instead one of the security men switched off the lights and made it abun-dantly clear that our time was over. We left and the door was locked behind us. Out in the street again, the clouds had regrouped and rain was sweeping in along the Golden Horn. I was missing the hospitality of the monastery at Mor Gabriel.

Since the fall of Constantinople in 1453 life in the city had been difficult for Christians. The old city had been taken as a result of incompetence and a lax attitude on behalf of the Byzantines, cunning and military brilliance on behalf of the Ottomans, and political expediency on the part of the Venetians who lived in Galata. Christians were 'encouraged' to become Muslims. Part of the 'deal' for Christians was that they had to agree not to evangelise Muslim people. They were taxed extra for remaining outside Islam and were officially treated as second-class citizens. That situation has gripped the Orthodox Christians across the region, none more so than those in Istanbul. Secrecy and security have become part of the culture of Christians living under fear.

That night I managed to contact the elusive Father Tarasios by telephone and he invited us to come round the following morning. It took some time to negotiate with a taxi driver but eventually I convinced one that the Phanar was a real place and he delivered us to the security gate. The doorman looked blankly as I asked for Father Tarasios. He then shook his head glumly and appeared to want to dismiss us. 'No English,' he muttered. I wondered whether he was referring to his lack of a linguistic skill or his view about our suitability to enter. I tried offering my business card. It had worked with Israeli Security in Jerusalem so why not here? The man stared at it blankly. He repeatedly turned it over and inspected it as if he were looking at counterfeit money. Then he called his colleague from a back room and they conversed in subdued tones. His friend then vanished with my card into a large house inside the compound.

After no more than a couple of minutes a man with a beaming face appeared from the house. He looked eager as he approached us and gave us a warm welcome, shaking our hands vigorously. 'Please come with me,' he motioned. 'This is the Patriarchate.' We were taken upstairs to a comfortable waiting room and offered coffee and biscuits. He spoke limited English but was most concerned that we had to wait. 'Only ten minutes', he apologised.

In less than that time a short priest with balding black hair and plain black cassock swept in. 'Good morning,' he said in an American accent. 'I am Father Tarasios.' What a relief to meet the elusive man. Ian Sherwood had said that the Greek Orthodox were normally excellent on intention but poor on organisation! This had been my experience so far.

Father Tarasios took us into his comfortable office and motioned us to sit down. He then sat behind a large polished desk. The room had some beautiful icons and pictures on the walls but, otherwise, might have passed for a top executive's office in America.

'I'm sorry not to have been in yesterday,' he began. 'However, I do want to help you. I wonder in what ways I can?' I explained the purpose of my trip and he wanted to know how I had found the Orthodox Church in the different countries I had visited. This was the Oecumenical Patriarchate after all, and this man had a wider view than just Turkey. I explained that much of my experience had been with the Oriental Orthodox rather than the Byzantine branch. I told him of the encouraging work I had seen in southern Syria but, not wishing to be rude, had heard lots of complaints in Palestine. He was thoroughly aware of these difficulties and expressed his personal exasperation about the Greek hierarchy in Jerusalem.

He was eager to hear what we had found in Tur Abdin. Of course the Syriac Christians in that place had a problem shared with the Oecumenical Patriarchate – that of the Turkish state. This triggered something within Father Tarasios. 'Let me help you understand a little of the position of the Patriarchate in Istanbul', he offered. The situation had been difficult over a number of years.

When the current Patriarch had been enthroned in 1991 there was little coverage in the press and there was sometimes open hostility, such as spitting, when he appeared in public.

Tarasios leaned forward across the vast expanse of desk, wringing his hands as he talked. 'You should understand that the church in Turkey is Turkish, and that the Patriarch is Turkish. Of course the church is also Greek in culture and language, but its people are Turkish nationals. At times of international tension or whenever the Greek Church did something against Greek Muslims, there was a rebound effect in Turkey.'

He stopped to see if we understood this. 'People ask us why we don't leave. Why should we? We are the custodians of the ancient church going back to the days of the Romans. There was a time, say in the 1970s, when things were very bad. But it is not like that now. Maybe it's that relations with Greece are better now. Remember the help when we had the earthquakes? Maybe Turkey wants a slice of religious tourism? Or maybe it's because Turkey wants to join the European Union? Whatever it is, we are finding that things are better every day.'

He leaned back, looking pleased. 'Recently I went with the Patriarch to Cappadocia. Just to be allowed to go there was a miracle compared with a few years ago. But we were able to have a Liturgy in the valley overlooked by the ruined cave churches. When we went through the town we had crowds cheering and waving. Civic dignitaries escorted us. It was like a homecoming. He was their Patriarch – even though they were Muslims! Unbelievable.'

I asked what life was like for the Greek Orthodox community itself. Father Tarasios rolled back in his chair then gesticulated with his hands. 'It's very difficult still, especially for the young. They now speak Turkish as their first language. Our community is still shrinking by the death of old people and by emigration. We still have many closed churches going to ruin. Young people do not want to be associated with a cultural burden that is too heavy'.

Whilst I could understand that young people might be attracted to a living faith rather than maintenance of heritage structures and buildings, I wondered whether there was anything more. There was. 'Another problem is marriage to Muslims. Of course I try and advise against it. But when you're young and in love…I would never try and prevent it. We have to work with the situation. But it's not just a matter of two people. It's not like relationships in the West where it's a personal decision. Here, a marriage involves two families, two communities. And that's where problems can erupt.'

I wondered what Father Tarasios saw in the immediate future. Given a stable political climate, might the church grow? He was circumspect. 'We have lost our ability to engage in mission. For centuries we have been in preservation mode. If we were given the liberty to be evangelistic then we would need to be guided. I think that some Protestants could help. Last week people from Billy Graham's organisation came to talk to the Patriarch. Maybe that could be a way forward for us?'

The idea of Billy Graham amongst the Orthodox in Turkey was revolutionary. Father Tarasios explained that of all Protestant groups this organisation had the best track record of working with the local churches regardless of denomination. They were not into proselytism.

I mentioned that I had understood that the Greek Orthodox Church was evangelistic in many parts of Africa. Perhaps they could help? He became very excited at this and showed me a new book he had just received from the USA about Orthodox mission in Africa. 'It is possible,' he said. 'But we need to move carefully. At the moment we are heavily restricted. We have five archdioceses in Turkey, but some of their Patriarchs have never been allowed to visit them. 'Our theological seminary on the island of Heybeliada is something we need to reopen. At the moment we can only have priests who are Turkish citizens, but we can't train any ourselves. They go to Greece or America. Some stay there. Others come back, but with a Greek perspective. We want to train our own priests here in Turkey.'

I enquired as to whether I understood this correctly. After all Father Tarasios himself was an American. How was he acceptable to the Turkish Government? 'I'm here on a Tourist Visa.' He seemed to detect my mental gasp. 'They know what I'm doing. They seem prepared to turn a blind eye at the moment, but I'm on thin ice. If the regulations were changed it would make for less tension'.

'Could international pressure be brought on the Government?' I asked.

'It could, but it might not be helpful,' was his response. 'We want to demonstrate that we are good Turks and that the Government can count on the Christian community for support. If then they can see that their restrictive legislation is counter productive then they will decide to remove it. That way honour is preserved.'

It was a long-term view. They were in for the long haul. But then they always have. But I was really encouraged to find a senior churchman who is hopeful that things are getting better. Maybe it was because he was American? After all if things got too warm he could always go back to America. But I think not. He was totally committed to the church in Turkey and his view gave great cause for hope. Father Tarasios had given us two hours. I had occasionally made noises about taking up his valuable time but he kept motioning us to remain seated and plied us with cups of herbal tea. 'No, don't go,' he would say. 'I'm really enjoying this!'

We were eventually shown out through the grand hallway and then out into a courtyard. Taking one more look at the icon of Elijah in the narthex of the church we then headed back into the city. There still remained one outstanding piece of business. I had promised Sevak, my Armenian friend in Jerusalem, that I would visit his friend, Varashak, in Istanbul. Only possessing the most rudimentary address, I flagged down a taxi to take us to Kumkapi, the area in which the Armenian Patriarchate was situated. We wandered along Capariz Sokak, a street of fish restaurants, and wondered about taking a late lunch. Having selected the Kalamar Restaurant I suddenly began to feel that we ought to 'do' the Armenian Patriarchate first, then we would enjoy our meal better. I explained this to the restaurateur who immediately deputed one of his waiters to guide us through the maze of narrow streets to the Patriarchate.

It was just as well that he did. The narrow streets were clearly down on their fortunes. Beautiful buildings in what was once a Christian quarter were now in distress. Kurds or Turks occupied many, often with many families in each house. Some, perhaps those owned by Christians who had fled the violence in the 1970s, were in a state of advanced dereliction. There were some with collapsed ceilings, with roofing dangerously suspended over the street, boarded up at ground level. A Greek Orthodox Church was derelict behind locked metal gates. Wooden scaffolding leaning against the adjacent house propped one of its twin bell towers up.

Eventually we reached our goal. On the left behind a security gate was the cathedral church. On the right, the Patriarchate. We went to the security gate and, as the guards spoke no English, I asked to speak to Deacon Varashak Serovbian. They pointed across the road to the Patriarchate. Entering the gate to this fine wooden mansion we were hailed from a window on the first floor. This was the Reception and was reached by climbing steps to the front door. It appeared that the ground floor was actually ten feet above the ground! A security guard and female receptionist spoke to us in what might have been either Turkish or Armenian but which was probably the latter. I looked blank and called out the name Varashak. The girl shrugged her shoulders. I kept saying his name and pointed to my bit of paper. Eventually they let us in to read the name. I also gave them my visiting card – it had worked wonders on other occasions.

Yes they knew him but were unable to tell us how to contact him. Meanwhile tea was brought and various calls were made on the phone. Everyone seemed unavailable. Well, it was Saturday afternoon. The receptionist motioned us to wait and, after about five minutes, a fair-haired girl who spoke English appeared. Communication could now be simplified. She was a Pole who spoke English and Turkish. Varashak, it transpired, was out at that time but would be back by six o'clock. It was now nearly three. There was a service in the church at five if we wished to attend. Now we had decisions to make. Deciding to look around the church, go and have the meal we had postponed, we would then return for Vespers and, hopefully, meet Varashak.

It was such a contrast to the churches we had experienced of late. The main impression on entering was of white woodwork and gold painted ornamentation. The whole ambience was bright and clean. The pews were of polished wood and rather more austere than the ambience of the church would suggest. Our Polish friend whispered in surprise that it was more like a Catholic Church back home. And so it was. After the Syriac Orthodox, then the Greeks, with their fine but ornate trappings, the stark clean but ornamented interior of this church owed more to Western tradition than that of the East. But then the Armenian Church is an ancient church…maybe the West has borrowed their styles and traditions?

Leaving the church, we found our way back through the narrow streets to the Kalamar Restaurant. The proprietor was delighted, and probably relieved, to see us return. He wanted us to sit outside at a table by the pavement but, by now, the wind had increased and the clouds were making it dull. Frankly it was too cold to sit out. And this was Istanbul in June!

We ordered soup, followed by mezze (basically anchovies and beans). Then we had the restaurant's own delicacy of squid, followed by sea bass. Free beer, water and 'raqi' were also supplied. As we were the only customers the restaurateur seemed desperate to keep us at table as a sort of advert to other passers-by. He chatted periodically. The restaurant had belonged to an Armenian but he had finally retired and sold the business. Our host was a Kurd but was sick of the war in the East of Turkey. Everyone really wants peace, he assured us.

After we had settled the bill, we headed back to the Armenian Cathedral. Initially we were the only people in the congregation but gradually a handful of people arrived. The service was conducted antiphonally. On the left hand side the Chancellor led a group of deacons whilst on the right two men led a couple of girls aged about eight or nine. It was a delight to hear the rich Armenian male voices raising the roof and 'interesting' to hear the little girls. However, it was not a performance for my entertainment. It was worship and it was good to see the active involvement of children so young.

After the service we were crossing the road when a tall bearded young man in a black cassock came in the opposite direction. 'Are you Varashak?' I asked. He was. 'I have a letter from your friend Sevak in Jerusalem', I explained. All this time we were standing in the middle of the road. 'Come this way,' he suggested, motioning us back towards the church. 'Perhaps we can meet tomorrow? I have a morning service at the hospital.' My heart sank. After some deliberation I explained that I really only wanted to deliver the letter and to meet Varashak. I regretted that we couldn't come back. He then took us inside the church where we were introduced to the Chancellor, Father Gregor. He spoke good English.

'Why not chat now?' he suggested. We went into a comfortable meeting room alongside the church. Strangely it was also a mausoleum for an Armenian benefactor of the nineteenth century. All around the walls were pictures of Armenian Patriarchs looking both dignified and mysterious with their peaked black hoods. We sat on four upright chairs and I gave Father Gregor my visiting card. He became the spokesman and Varashak fell silent. I explained the purpose of my journey, and how I wanted to discuss the situation facing Christians today.

'Oh, political!' moaned Father Gregor. He seemed to write me off in a stroke. I tried to save the meeting. 'I realise that there are things that you cannot talk about freely here. They told me that in Jerusalem. I won't ask you for your thoughts about the massacres of eighty five years ago but I would like to know how things are now.'

'Things are fine today,' Father Gregor said, in a rapid fire retort that signalled the end of the topic. Varashak shifted a little uneasily on his upright chair.

I tried to restart the conversation. 'But on our way here we have passed ruined houses and an abandoned church, just down the street.'

'That's a Greek Church. Not one of ours,' he countered defensively.

I realised that we were not going to have quality time with Varashak, and that we would only get the standard party line from Father Gregor. It was time to cut our losses. Explaining that I appreciated the time they had given and that I hoped that Varashak enjoyed having a letter from Sevak, we made a slow departure. As soon as we were out of the gate I noticed Father Gregor dashing off somewhere. Clearly we had interrupted his busy schedule and he had graciously given us time. When compared with the time with Father Tarasios earlier in the day it was disappointing. I felt a bit flat. This was the last interview of a very long journey and it had failed.

CHAPTER TWENTY

JOURNEY'S END

After eleven weeks on the road, it seemed as if the end was rushing towards me like the ground to someone in free fall. I needed to discover the ripcord. The disappointment of our time in the Armenian Patriarchate, seemed to drip the odour of failure over the whole journey. How I had wanted a triumphant end to the trip!

The same evening Ian Sherwood had invited us to meet him, and a group of friends, for an evening out. Late, and in the dark, we missed him. Then just as we were about to give up I saw the back of Ian's unmistakable cream jacket leaning on the upper balcony of a restaurant near the Hagia Sophia. It was a chance meeting as he was nowhere near where we had expected him.

We were meeting up in order to go to a performance of highlights from Faure's *Requiem* and other pieces in Hagia Eirene, a church in the first court of the Topkapi Palace. One of the oldest surviving Christian Churches in Istanbul, it was enlarged by Justinian. It was never turned into a mosque following the Islamic Conquest as it was used as an arsenal for the Sultan. Normally closed to the public it was a rare treat to be allowed to go in for this concert. The City of Lyons Orchestra accompanied the Istanbul European Choir.

We joined a lively crowd in an unlit section of the palace gardens. The sense of anticipation was building up when the large doors swung open and we seemed to be catapulted down a brick lined corridor into the auditorium. Quickly all the seats were filled and I realised that most of the audience were Europeans. On either side of the stage, at the point where the Byzantine screen would have been, two illuminated signs reminded us that this free concert was sponsored by Renault. High above the east windows was a large black cross painted on the curved roof of the apse. It had survived for five centuries since the building had ceased to be a church. As the warm tones of the Requiem got under way I realised how much I had missed classical music during my eleven-week journey. Now here I was at the end of my journey being bathed in it. A *real* Turkish Bath! My mind drifted back over the journey to the wrecked churches and to the struggling Christian communities. I thought of the violent religious wars that the area has experienced. Yet here we were on the tip of Europe, in a church built in the days of the Roman Empire, listening to music glorifying God through Jesus Christ. The light had not gone out.

The experience had moved me deeply, and it was with a certain reluctance that I accepted the end of the concert. It was only highlights after all, and it seemed too short. Along with throngs of concert-goers we made our way out of the park. The night was warm and balmy, very pleasant after the chill and rain of the last few days. Along the tree-lined street illumination was provided by large bowls of flaming tallow on pedestals. The flames kept licking at unwary passers by but we saw no one catch fire. At last, somewhere near the Hagia Sophia we hailed a couple of taxis to take us back to Galata. We met up at McDonald's, shining out as a temple to western globalism on Istiklal Caddesi. Already those who had ridden in the first cab were tucking into French Fries and Big Macs, but something emotional within me was in revolt. I found that I could not bring myself to join in. I was still musing about the moving experience in the concert and it seemed like an intrusion to break the spell. Stretched out across the Levant were my friends struggling with life against the assaults of Islam and western economic imperialism. To join in seemed like dining with the enemy. By now it was getting on for midnight and the proprietor was trying to lock the doors of McDonald's. It had been a long day

The following morning dawned bright. It was the last day before returning home and we wanted to fill it. After attending a very high church service at Christ Church, Carol and I took the underground cable tram down to the Galata Bridge. Being Sunday it seemed as if half the population was on the bridge, either walking or fishing. The fishermen were so cramped that they were wedged in by one another. Incessant excitement was in the air as, one after another, they would reel tiny flashing fish up from the swirling waters of the Golden Horn beneath. Every now and again they would cast out, sometimes nearly catching an unwary pedestrian in the process. And what was the prize? Each fisherman had a pot or a bucket in which small fish (were they sprats?) were gradually accumulating. It seemed a gargantuan effort for such a minuscule reward. Still it kept them out of the house!

Our aim was to catch one of the ferry boats to the Princes' Islands situated out in the Sea of Marmara. As we had nearly an hour to wait before departure, Carol went off to find some food whilst I found two seats on the deck. The sun came out and I realised that, once under way, this would be very pleasant. I was quietly musing, minding my own business, when I realised that my sandal was being removed. Looking down a man was by my feet with shoe cleaning equipment. In alarm I tried to stop him, trying to point out that my sandals were brushed suede. No problem, the cleaner gesticulated, he had the right cleaning agent. But how much? He suddenly went dumb and vigorously started the cleaning process. I repeated the question and shouted 'Lire?' but still he played dumb. Once he finished he demanded an exorbitant sum. I remonstrated. My dignity had been affronted and I was not in control of the situation. By gesticulation I inferred that I had not asked him to clean them and this amount was outrageous. He then halved the sum demanded. It still seemed to be way out of line so I offered him a fifth of that, thinking we would bargain upwards from there. He suddenly looked uncomfortable and walked quickly away diving out of sight into the main part of the ship. Perhaps he was allowed as long as he didn't aggravate the passengers. Perhaps he was not allowed to work on the boat, and a controversy with me might draw the attention of the ferry operators. I felt very sorry that we had not reached an agreement, but that was that. Inadvertently I had humiliated a poor man trying to make a living, and there was no way I could make amends. Just then Carol returned with two corns on the cob. They had been roasted on a charcoal fire and were delicious, if cold, by the time she had walked back to the ship with them.

Soon the ferry was ready for departure and swung around, heading out into the Bosphorus before going south to the Sea of Marmara. Sailing with the Topkapi Palace to the right of the boat and the industrial areas on the Asian side to the left it seemed wonderful to be in fresh air with the sun shining. After about half an hour we arrived at the first of the islands, Kinali. A smart sea front and beach led on to the ferry jetty where a number of trippers disembarked. Then we moved on to Burgaz where more got off. Heybeli was the location of the Greek Orthodox Seminary. This was the one we had been told was unable to train priests owing to the restrictive policy of the Turkish Government. Finally we pulled into Buyak Ada, the largest and most popular of the islands. We had heard that the Monastery of St George was to be found by heading uphill from the jetty so we decided that was to be our destination. Horse-drawn phaetons, and donkeys serve the islands, motor transport being illegal except for certain tasks such as the emergency services. The atmosphere upon leaving the ship was very strange for here was a town centre that, apart from the occasional clattering of hooves, was largely silent.

We walked quickly away from the phaeton drivers who were eager to obtain our trade and struck out upwards along very pleasant tree-lined streets. The houses were fine wooden-framed structures and clearly represented a great deal of wealth. Greek Orthodox or Armenians had built most of these but now many were in the hands of Turkish Muslims. Occasionally a boarded up derelict house that was standing as a rebuke marred the opulence. Presumably it belonged to a family that had fled Turkey during one of the purges on Christians. Such houses looked like bad teeth in an otherwise good set of molars.

At the top of the hill, after a number of stops for breath, just past the Monastery of Christ, was a huge wooden building. It was several storeys high but in a state of near collapse. In the grounds a watchman and his family had their home but the whole building looked as if it could fall down like a pack of cards. We walked around the perimeter fence and wondered what this magnificent wreck had once been. Later we discovered that it had been a Greek Orthodox Orphanage. It seemed to epitomise the state of Christianity in so many places we had been. The fabric was there but if push came to shove, then it would not survive.

The monastery of St George was on the neighbouring, higher hill. Trees all the way up the long and tiring hill had ribbons tied to their twigs. If ribbons were not available, shredded plastic bags seemed to have sufficed. Even unravelled cassette tapes had been used. We never discovered the reason for this but presumed it to be some kind of prayer request to St George. It was with relief that we reached the summit. Entering the monastery precincts a notice informed us that 'inappropriate' dress such as shorts or mini-skirts were not permitted in the church. We were both in shorts! Nevertheless we were permitted to look through the doorway and I went over to the priest guarding it to apologise for not having the correct attire. A quick mention of Father Tarasios with whom we had spent part of the previous day resulted in a miraculous change in the demeanour of the priest. No longer were we merely tourists. He offered to lend a skirt and some trousers and we gratefully accepted.

Inside the church were some beautiful and ornate icons, some depicting St George. But the prized treasure was in the reliquary. Here was a finger of the saint preserved in a silver casket in a display cabinet. After spending some time in the church we thanked the priest and returned the clothes. He wanted to chat about the time he had spent as a young man at an Orthodox monastery in Essex. At last, however, we managed to extricate ourselves as it was drawing near to the time for our return ferry.

On returning to the ferry it seemed as if there were thousands of people on the jetty. To complicate matters there were two queues. One was for Istanbul, the other for the Asian coast. But it was difficult to ascertain which was which. We fought our way to the front of a queue piling on to a ship moored alongside the jetty only to be told that it was the wrong one! After a few minutes our ship hove into sight and quickly docked. Pushing and shoving, everyone heaved aboard.

All around us were good-natured young people. Clearly it had been a good day out for many. The singing, the joking and laughter, all made for a very pleasant journey. But in addition there were the seagulls. Someone threw some bread for a seagull and within minutes we were being followed by flocks of the birds. Displaying incredible powers of flight, sometimes seemingly able to hover in the air, these graceful birds would suddenly swoop down on pieces of bread. Occasionally they would even snatch bread from the hand of a brave soul. However there were far more people trying to entice seagulls in this way than were likely to be successful. Even cigarette buts were offered to the birds that would excitedly swoop and fight over what must have ended up a bitter disappointment.

At each island we collected more passengers than we deposited so that when we pulled out of Kinali the ship was very heavily laden. All the way the seagulls kept trailing us. The man selling bread cakes was doing a roaring trade. As we approached Istanbul the sun was setting and casting a trail of molten gold across the choppy waters of the channel on our left. We seemed to be in a race to reach the Bosphorus with a container ship of the Athenian Line. We won and then passed in front of the path of the red and white Leviathan as it cut its way through the darkening sea. On the left the sun was almost scorching the roof-tops of ancient Byzantium. The Blue Mosque and then Hagia Sophia in turn were silhouetted against the sunset. As we rounded the headland by the Topkapi Palace it was going dark so that as we left the ship on the quayside the light had gone.

It seemed inconceivable after such an epic trip to be walking off the Air France flight from Paris at Manchester Airport. By now it was cold, dark and raining. Waiting for those suitcases to come off the carousel we began to think that they had finally beaten us when, with a lurch, they burst through the rubber flaps long after most other luggage had been collected. But it was good to be back. Soon we were enveloped in the warmth of the train as it ate up the miles across the Pennines to York.

York! The significance of that city to my entire trip only hit me later as I was passing York Minster. This great edifice, the largest medieval gothic cathedral north of the Alps, dwarfs any other building nearby. Outside the Minster is a statue of the Roman Emperor Constantine. He is seated and looks rather imperiously at the tourists flocking to the South Transept entrance. Constantine was a commander of the Roman army based in York when news came that he was to be the new emperor. When he converted to Christianity the whole ethos of the empire changed. And so did that of the church. From being a persecuted minority that was fervently evangelistic, the church tasted patronage from its previous tormentor, the state.

Seventeen centuries later, modern Western popular culture has increasingly rejected an authoritarian and dogmatic stance. This means that a church that tries to define its beliefs and practices is perceived as anachronistic. As a result the Church in Western Europe has become outmoded for many. They perceive it as being allied with the command and rule attitudes of imperialism. Yet how far that is from the simple message of Jesus! In recent years the huge rise of spiritual searching that is devoid of 'church' culture is a sign of this outright rejection of organised Christianity. Ironically, in a world of confusion, the Christian faith ought to be able to provide a clarion call. Yet the waters are muddied by the way the church in the West has often presented itself as the handmaiden of the state, or the status quo, rather than being at the prophetic edge of life.

In contrast, the Christians I met on my travels were able to give a helpful and refreshing pointer. After years of persecution and living as a minority, they remain buoyant. I had seen plenty that could cause cynicism, or outright rejection of the claims of Christ. But overall, the Christians were displaying an increased level of confidence both in their faith and their ability to survive. I had felt this in almost tangible form in Egypt and Turkey. Even the idea of evangelising both Jews and Muslims has begun to emerge as an authentic activity for the indigenous Christians, after decades of seeing most evangelistic activity being contained within the Christian community.

The sign of the cross is a strong metaphor particularly for believers in the Orthodox tradition. For them it is a continual reminder that Jesus died. Amongst a predominant Islamic culture that accepts much of Jesus, but not the death on a cross, this has become a point of particular poignancy. Each time the cross is seen it seems to declare the death and resurrection of Jesus. The cross also symbolises suffering, and reminds them that God, far from sprinkling the world with glittering Disney dust, is fully identified with humankind, and knows what it is like to be at the bottom of the heap. To see the cross as a symbol throughout my journey was a constant reminder that Jesus calls people to live as disciples rather than interested onlookers. That is gritty. It is powerful. The evidence of its efficacy is all around.

Right across the region, I had met Christians who took their faith seriously at a deep level. They were prepared to stand up and be counted as Christians. I thought of Nader in Jordan, Jihad in Syria, and Isa in Turkey. Whilst, inevitably, the sense of being besieged in an Islamic or Jewish context would make people herd together, I was struck by the deep devotion to Christ that came out in ordinary ways. They have a faith that has answers and meaning for the whole of life. In contrast, the reality of the supernatural, the importance of the Bible, and the historic continuity of the Liturgy are things that many Christians in the West have largely put aside. It is easier to accept the prevalent two-dimensional secularist worldview than to stand out and be different.

Looking at Constantine's statue I felt as if I were being sucked back into materialism, into a way of life that can easily rely on the things we can see rather than the deeper mysteries of God. It was as if its enigmatic smile, directed at me, seemed to scorn what might be seen as spiritual. But as I turned away into the narrow streets of York, I thought of my new friends and of their faith, hewn in the quarry of suffering. I thought of a loving God who sent His only Son to die for our sins. At that point I realised that I would always have to be conscious of the need to retain a sense of the majesty of God, or else succumb to the temptation of reducing my faith to the mundane. Authentic Christianity can confidently square up to any situation in the world of today but it is never the easy option. As I had learned on my travels, it can sometimes be the way of suffering and always the way of the cross.